THE DIAMOND NEEDLE

TREATISE ON DOCTRINAL DISTINCTIONS
OF THE HUAYAN ONE VEHICLE

THE KEY TO THE SECRET
OF THE HEART SUTRA

BDK English Tripiṭaka Series

THE DIAMOND NEEDLE

(Taishō Volume 32, Number 1642)

Translated by Yuto Kawamura
and Jinghao Bai

TREATISE ON DOCTRINAL DISTINCTIONS OF THE HUAYAN ONE VEHICLE

(Taishō Volume 45, Number 1866)

Translated by Taitetsu Unno, Mark Unno,
and Monica E. McLellan

THE KEY TO THE SECRET OF THE HEART SUTRA

(Taishō Volume 57, Number 2203A)

Translated by Matthew D. McMullen

BDK America, Inc.
2023

First Printing, 2023
ISBN: 978-1-886439-91-7
Library of Congress Control Number: 2023934846

Published by
BDK America, Inc.
1675 School Street
Moraga, California 94556

Printed in the United States of America

A Message on the Publication of the English Tripiṭaka

The Buddhist canon is said to contain eighty-four thousand different teachings. I believe that this is because the Buddha's basic approach was to prescribe a different treatment for every spiritual ailment, much as a doctor prescribes a different medicine for every medical ailment. Thus his teachings were always appropriate for the particular suffering individual and for the time at which the teaching was given, and over the ages not one of his prescriptions has failed to relieve the suffering to which it was addressed.

Ever since the Buddha's Great Demise over twenty-five hundred years ago, his message of wisdom and compassion has spread throughout the world. Yet no one has ever attempted to translate the entire Buddhist canon into English throughout the history of Japan. It is my greatest wish to see this done and to make the translations available to the many English-speaking people who have never had the opportunity to learn about the Buddha's teachings.

Of course, it would be impossible to translate all of the Buddha's eighty-four thousand teachings in a few years. I have, therefore, had one hundred thirty-nine of the scriptural texts in the prodigious Taishō edition of the Chinese Buddhist canon selected for inclusion in the First Series of this translation project.

It is in the nature of this undertaking that the results are bound to be criticized. Nonetheless, I am convinced that unless someone takes it upon himself or herself to initiate this project, it will never be done. At the same time, I hope that an improved, revised edition will appear in the future.

It is most gratifying that, thanks to the efforts of more than a hundred Buddhist scholars from the East and the West, this monumental project has finally gotten off the ground. May the rays of the Wisdom of the Compassionate One reach each and every person in the world.

NUMATA Yehan
Founder of the English
Tripiṭaka Project

August 7, 1991

Editorial Foreword

In the long history of Buddhist transmission throughout East Asia, translations of Buddhist texts were often carried out as national projects supported and funded by emperors and political leaders. The BDK English Tripiṭaka project, on the other hand, began as a result of the dream and commitment of one man. In January 1982 Dr. NUMATA Yehan, founder of Bukkyō Dendō Kyōkai (Society for the Promotion of Buddhism), initiated the monumental task of translating the complete Taishō shinshū daizōkyō edition of the Chinese Tripiṭaka (Buddhist canon) into the English language. Under his leadership, a special preparatory committee was organized in April 1982. By July of the same year the Translation Committee of the English Tripiṭaka was officially convened.

The initial Committee included the following members: (late) HANAYAMA Shōyū (Chairperson), (late) BANDŌ Shōjun, (late) ISHIGAMI Zennō, (late) KAMATA Shigeo, (late) KANAOKA Shūyū, MAYEDA Sengaku, (late) NARA Yasuaki, (late) SAYEKI Shinkō, (late) SHIOIRI Ryōtatsu, (late) TAMARU Noriyoshi, (late) TAMURA Kwansei, (late) URYŪZU Ryūshin, and (late) YUYAMA Akira. Assistant members of the Committee were as follows: KANAZAWA Atsushi, WATANABE Shōgo, Rolf Giebel of New Zealand, and Rudy Smet of Belgium.

After holding planning meetings on a monthly basis, the Committee selected one hundred and thirty-nine texts for the First Series of the project, estimated to be one hundred printed volumes in all. The texts selected were not limited to those originally written in India but also included works composed in China and Japan. While the publication of the First Series proceeds, the texts for the Second Series will be selected from among the remaining works; this process will continue until all the texts, in Japanese as well as in Chinese, have been published. Given the huge scope of this project, accomplishing the English translations of all the Chinese and Japanese texts in the Taishō canon may take as long as one hundred years or more. Nevertheless, as Dr. NUMATA wished, it is the sincere hope of the Committee that this project will continue until completion, even after all the present members have passed away.

Dr. NUMATA passed away on May 5, 1994, at the age of ninety-seven. He entrusted his son, Mr. NUMATA Toshihide with the continuation and completion of the English Tripiṭaka project. Mr. Numata served for twenty-three years, leading the project forward with enormous progress before his sudden passing on February 16, 2017, at the age of eighty-four. The Committee previously lost its able and devoted first Chairperson, Professor HANAYAMA Shōyū, on June 16, 1995, at the age of sixty-three. In October 1995 the Committee elected Professor MAYEDA Sengaku (then Vice President of Musashino Women's College) as Chairperson, and upon the retirement of Professor Mayeda in July 2016, the torch was passed to me to serve as the third Chairperson. Despite these losses and changes we, the Editorial Committee members, have renewed our determination to carry out the noble ideals set by Dr. NUMATA. Present members of the Committee are Kenneth K. Tanaka (Chairperson), MAYEDA Sengaku, ICHISHIMA Shōshin, KATSURA Shōryū, MINOWA Kenryō, SAITŌ Akira, SHIMODA Masahiro, WATANABE Shōgo, and YONEZAWA Yoshiyasu.

The Numata Center for Buddhist Translation and Research was established in November 1984, in Berkeley, California, U.S.A., to assist in the publication of the translated texts. The Publication Committee was organized at the Numata Center in December 1991. In 2010, the Numata Center's operations were merged with Bukkyō Dendō Kyōkai America, Inc. (BDK America), and BDK America continues to oversee the publication side of the English Tripiṭaka project in close cooperation with the Editorial Committee in Tokyo.

At the time of this writing, in July 2017, the project has completed about sixty-five percent of the seven thousand one hundred and eighty-five Taishō pages of texts selected for the First Series. Much work still lies ahead of us but we are committed to the completion of the remaining texts in order to realize the grand vision of Dr. Numata, shared by Mr. Numata and Professor Hanayama, to make the Buddhist canon more readily accessible to the English-speaking world.

Kenneth K. Tanaka
Chairperson
Editorial Committee of
the BDK English Tripiṭaka

Publisher's Foreword

On behalf of the members of the Publication Committee, I am happy to present this volume as the latest contribution to the BDK English Tripiṭaka Series. The Publication Committee members have worked to ensure that this volume, as all other volumes in the series, has gone through a rigorous process of editorial efforts.

The initial translation and editing of the Buddhist scriptures found in this and other BDK English Tripiṭaka volumes are performed under the direction of the Editorial Committee in Tokyo, Japan. Both the Editorial Committee in Tokyo and the Publication Committee, headquartered in Moraga, California, are dedicated to the production of accurate and readable English translations of the Buddhist canon. In doing so, the members of both committees and associated staff work to honor the deep faith, spirit, and concern of the late Reverend Dr. Yehan Numata, who founded the BDK English Tripiṭaka Series in order to disseminate the Buddhist teachings throughout the world.

The long-term goal of our project is the translation and publication of the texts in the one hundred-volume Taishō edition of the Chinese Buddhist canon, along with a number of influential extracanonical Japanese Buddhist texts. The list of texts selected for the First Series of this translation project may be found at the end of each volume in the series.

As Chair of the Publication Committee, I am deeply honored to serve as the fifth person in a post previously held by leading figures in the field of Buddhist studies, most recently by my predecessor, John R. McRae.

In conclusion, I wish to thank the members of the Publication Committee for their dedicated and expert work undertaken in the course of preparing this volume for publication: Managing Editor Marianne Dresser, Dr. Hudaya Kandahjaya, Dr. Carl Bielefeldt, Dr. Robert Sharf, and Rev. Brian Kensho Nagata, Director of the BDK America English Tripiṭaka Project.

A. Charles Muller
Chairperson
Publication Committee

Contents

THE DIAMOND NEEDLE

Translators' Introduction

Yuto Kawamura and Jinghao Bai

The *Diamond Needle* (*Jingang zhen lun*) is known as a work that critiques the Varṇa system, in which the class of brahmans has the highest status. The author regularly proceeds by citing classical texts accepted as authoritative by brahmans to undermine their position and lampoon their claims. This work was translated into Chinese by Fatian (法天, ?–1001 C.E.) in the latter half of the tenth century, during the Song dynasty (960–1279 C.E.), and is included in the Taishō canon (volume 32, no. 1642). The Sanskrit text of *The Diamond Needle* (*Vajrasūcī*) contains a verse that declares its author to be Aśvaghoṣa (ca. first–second centuries C.E.), a well-known Buddhist poet. Nevertheless, the aforementioned Chinese translation ascribes the work to Dharmakīrti (ca. seventh century C.E.), another well-known Buddhist philosopher. Whether the work was composed by the former or the latter remains in dispute. The most detailed survey of the scholarship on this work can be found on a website set up by Professor Kiyoshi Okano (see Bibliography), to which interested readers are directed for further information. Since this translation is generally designed for English readers, the bibliography also lists major English-language publications on *The Diamond Needle* that the website may not include, as well as some Japanese works that do not appear on the website.

Fatian's Chinese translation of *The Diamond Needle* is not faithful to the Sanskrit original in our possession; the translation does not correspond to the Sanskrit text in multiple places. The version Fatian used for his translation might be from a different recension than the Sanskrit original. Fatian's translation is entirely in prose, with a fairly standard four-character prosodic pattern. The Sanskrit original is a mixture of prose and verse. Both in the Sanskrit original and the Chinese translation, the target of severe criticism is the class of brahmans among the four classes that constitute the Varṇa system, brahman (priest class), *kṣatriya* (ruling/warrior class), *vaiśya* (merchant class), and *śūdra* (servant class). Colorful arguments are deployed to challenge and defy the authority of the brahmans.

In the following translation, interpolations of the basic components of a sentence (e.g., subject, object, complement, and verb) that are easily understood from the context are not marked by square brackets to avoid distraction.

Acknowledgement

We would like to thank the two anonymous reviewers for their valuable comments on an earlier draft.

The Diamond Needle

169b

By Dharmakīrti Bodhisattva

Having received an imperial edict, I, Fatian from the western direction (India), a translator of Buddhist texts, Tripiṭaka Master, Junior Fifth-and-under Ranking Official, Senior Vice Minister for Foreign Affairs, a great teacher who spreads the doctrine, translated this work.

As the brahmans have said, of all the scriptures, the four Vedas are a valid [means of knowledge]. And among them (the four Vedas), what has been memorized is viewed as a valid [means of knowledge]. And among them (what has been memorized), what interprets (speech), and what is interpreted (meaning) are valid [means of knowledge]. And of these two, what interprets is viewed as a valid [means of knowledge]. This (speech) alone is supreme and there exists nothing better than it. How do individuals of the world spend their lives without this (speech)? Using this interpreter (speech), affection or hatred is born from it. Just as the brahmans are the best among all the classes, so is this speech in question, which is the interpreter.

This perspective is illogical. Shall I give reasons? What type of birth does a brahman have? What type of living [body] does a brahman have? What type of knowledge does a brahman have? What types of customs and work does a brahman have? How does a brahman come to obtain the title brahman? Additionally, how do you declare those Vedas to be a valid [means of knowledge]?

How does Indra become an animal while having Indra[hood] for his primary cause? How is an animal born as the moon god while having animal[ity] for its primary cause? Additionally, the sun god, which has the sun god[hood] as its primary cause, is born as an animal; the wind god, the fire god, and the water god, having the wind god[hood], the fire god[hood], and the water god[hood], respectively, as their primary causes, are reborn [as animals] after having died again and again. How can this phenomenon be possible?

Additionally, the brahmans mistakenly insist on the following belief: a god, after having died among the gods, is reborn among them; a human, after having died among humans, is reborn among them; and the same is true of animals. Regarding the four Vedas, [however,] such a claim is not valid. What is this soul? On what basis do you call it a "soul"? The same question is posed regarding concepts such as brahman.

Furthermore, you non-Buddhist brahmans state the following; [that is to say,] the following is stated in their scripture: Mount Bhārate[1] gives birth to the seven types of beasts; the country of Daśārṇa feeds the other group of deer; there is Mount Kālañjara and all the animals (e.g., parrots, herons, swans, and deer) on that mountain were born among humans in Kurukṣetra (i.e., a place of blessedness). After having died there, they are born among brahmans and can elucidate the teachings of the four Vedas.

These beasts—deer, swans, and mandarin ducks—were born among humans. Their souls are simultaneously brahman and not brahman. The reason [for this dichotomy] is that if their soul is a brahman, they do not become animals. [On the other hand,] if their soul is not a brahman, how are they born as brahmans? The aforementioned quote ("a god, after having died among the gods, is reborn among them; a human, after having died among humans, is reborn among them; and the same is true of animals") is not valid;
169c however, the brahmans adhere to this belief.

[For the brahmans,] the four Vedas are the source of all the teachings; they are called truth. Although brahmans are not permitted to receive food from the other classes, they receive benefits repeatedly from *śūdra*s; this practice is against their foundational teachings. Why are they called practitioners of noble deeds? On the basis of this information, my proposal is that they are not true brahmans.

Moreover, the teachings of the brahmans, which are the four Vedas, mistakenly insist on a soul that serves to make the brahmans superior. However, the brahman class [advocated] in the correct teachings (the four Vedas) has no logical support. Why then do you call the four Vedas the correct teachings?

Why do you refer to the brahmans as the best when different classes are mixed within [the brahman class]? There is no need to explain my point. The brahmans are not the best; [different] classes are mixed there. What does this mean?

Now, for example, a father is named Narakṣa,[2] but his son is a sage called Piṅgala.

Additionally for example, a father is named Agasti and his son also is called Agasti.

Additionally, for example, a father is named Puṣyasa,[3] but his son is called Kauśika.

Additionally, for example, a father is named Kuśa,[4] but his son is called Sambhava.[5]

Additionally, for example, a father is named Kapilā,[6] but his son is also called Kapilā.

Additionally, for example, a father is named Śaragulma,[7] but his son is called Gautama.

Additionally, for example, a father is named Kalaśa,[8] but his son is called Droṇācārya.

Additionally, for example, a father is named Tittirī,[9] but his son is called Tittirī-suta.

Additionally, for example, a father is named Rāma,[10] but his son is called "[Antelope-]horned Sage."

Additionally, for example, a mother is named "Wild Deer" and she is a fisherwoman. She gave birth to a son and he is called Vyāsa; she gave birth to another son and he is called Kuśika.

A father belongs to the *śūdra* class, but his son is called Viśvāmitra.

A mother is an untouchable, but her son is called Vasiṣṭha.

A mother is named Urvaśī, and because she was born among the gods she is not a brahman.[11]

This being the case, on what basis can you absolutely insist on and present the view that the brahmans are the best of humans?

Additionally, according to [the teachings to which the brahmans] adhere, the Vedic scriptures are the valid [means of knowledge]; however, this claim is also not reasonable. Therefore, the reasoning in any teaching of the brahmans is faulty.

Furthermore, according to the teachings of the brahmans to which they adhere, the *śūdra*s are allowed to receive items such as fresh meat, purple ore (red dye), and salt. [On the other hand,] it is not proper for you the brahmans to do so. Why do you not follow this rule?

Moreover, brahmans, flying across the sky, fall if they sell milk while measuring its amount, and they lose the state of being brahmans. Likewise, if they eat meat, they fall from the sky [and lose the state of being brahmans]. Although such conduct (selling milk and eating meat) is not according to the rules, you are doing this.

Thus, the following is to be known: buying and selling milk or meat is taught as being improper for brahmans, but proper for *śūdra*s. For this reason,
170a the following is to be known: Do individuals who do not eat, buy, or sell milk or meat earn the appellation brahman?

Therefore, the following is to be known: brahmans, when selling milk or meat measuring their amount, lose the state of being brahmans; [nevertheless,] they mistakenly insist on the incorrect teaching [that their state of being brahmans is guaranteed by their birth, and hence, that status is not lost even if they engage in the aforementioned activities.]

Furthermore, the brahmans mistakenly insist that the brahman class is the best among all the classes in the world. Such a view also is not valid. [For] all the classes would be called the brahman class if *kṣatriya*s, *vaiśya*s, and *śūdra*s respectively insisted that their class is the best.

Additionally, the brahmans insist that the body experiencing suffering is called a brahman.[12] [If so, however,] anyone whose body experiences suffering would be called a brahman.

Additionally, they mistakenly insist that killing brahmans is a great sin. However, the same is true of killing the relatives of the brahmans.

Additionally, the brahmans mistakenly insist on the following view. They were born from the mouth of a god in heaven, the *kṣatriya*s were born from the arms of the god, and the *vaiśya*s and *śūdra*s were born from the thighs and the feet [of the god]. Killing brahmans is tantamount to killing the god; a great sin is committed. This view to which they adhere is not valid. Shall I explain why? The brahmans neither think that they do not commit a sin even if they kill those of the non-brahman class, nor assume a sin even if they kill the relatives of those who belong to the non-brahman class. This view mistakenly insisted on is not valid.[13]

Moreover, they insist that if an individual obstructs their activities, namely giving and receiving gifts, and harms their knowledge or bodies, then that individual has committed a great sin. [However,] this is not the case. Shall I explain why? Is an individual called a brahman on the basis of either an individual's body or knowledge? [The answer is negative.] For all individuals, such as *śūdra*s, have bodies and knowledge. Should it be the case that they are all called brahmans?

Furthermore, they mistakenly insist that individuals who understand the four Vedas and the treatises on Mīmāṃsā, Sāṅkhya, and Vaiśeṣika, and who are familiar with all the treatises are called brahmans. This reasoning is also wrong. Should it be the case that if *śūdra*s and others also understand those treatises and comprehend their meanings, all of them are to be called brahmans?

If the brahmans call those who perform asceticism brahmans, *śūdra*s also can perform it. Are they called brahmans as well?

If the brahmans call those who know skills brahmans, are fishermen and musicians also called brahmans when they know different skills?

Thus, the following is to be understood. Religious austerities are not equivalent to brahman[hood]. Activities are not equivalent to brahman[hood]. Giving and receiving gifts are not equivalent to brahman[hood]. *Kṣatriya*s, *vaiśya*s, and *śūdra*s are also able to perform these [actions]. Should it be the case that they are all called brahmans?

Hence, the following is to be known: It is not based on their birth, activity, asceticism, soul, or merit that living beings are called brahmans.

On what basis is the name [brahman] established? It is said that an individual 170b
is called a true brahman when the following conditions are fulfilled. Like a *kuṇḍa* flower, or like a white moon, individuals who are free of all impurity, cultivate good conduct very well, do not lack [good] behavior, and follow the rules; individuals who control their senses very well and abandon and renounce worldly desires; individuals who do not cling to the ideas of self and other, to attachment, to affection, to hatred, and to delusion. Moreover, an individual is called a brahman if they avoid sexual desires, do not have affection and attachment even if reborn as an animal, and cultivate pure conduct.

Thus, the following is known, as taught by the great sage Śukra:

> This brahman[hood] is not by birth, activities, merit, asceticism, and craft. Is a *caṇḍāla* called a brahman when he is familiar with the four Vedas, craft, and art, accumulates merit, and practices asceticism?

Hence, the following is to be known: It is not based on their soul, birth, knowledge, body, activity, and asceticism that living beings are called brahmans.

Additionally, for example, a *śūdra,* after having practiced asceticism and studied and understood the four Vedas, attains the state of a sage with the five supernormal abilities. Why do you brahmans serve one who is from the low class?

Moreover, individuals from any four classes can attain such sagehood. Thus, why are the members of the other classes not called the best?

Furthermore, for instance, Indra practiced good deeds in the past and succeeded in being born to that heavenly state. He was originally from the low class. In the main body of the brahmans' scripture it is taught that the Bhagavan and Indra were originally from the low class. Thus, we can attack you in the aforementioned way.[14]

Additionally, you brahmans teach that the god Indra, the other various deities, and this shared sensory world are born from the mouths of Maheśvara and his divine wife, and that Maheśvara and his divine wife are not born from the world. The root produces the branch; the branch does not produce the root. Thus, this teaching of yours is against your "correct" claim [that the brahman class is the best and that the *śūdra* is a low class].[15] They (Maheśvara and his wife) were originally from the low class. Why do you mistakenly insist that we were born from them? Thus, we know that your claim is not valid.

Additionally, for example, after dying, a *śūdra* was reborn as that Maheśvara. Why are you brahmans serving one who is from the low class?

Furthermore, according to the brahman's teaching that you impart, individuals are called brahman when they perform a special breathing exercise, drink a magical elixir, perform asceticism, and fast. [However,] *śūdra*s can do such things as well. Are they also called brahmans?

Moreover, brahmans adhere to the following view. If a brahman receives food from the hands of a *śūdra* in his residence for one month, in this very life his body changes into that of a *śūdra*. Thereafter, in the next world, where the result of an individual's action is supposed to occur, the brahman becomes a dog without exception. Additionally, if a brahman marries a *śūdra* woman,
170c his parents and the deity of his house leave him. After death, the brahman goes to hell.

These mistaken viewpoints are invalid. [For] what difference is there between the brahman class and that *śūdra* class?[16]

For example, the great sage Kapila, born from a female deer, became a sage after having practiced asceticism and acquired knowledge. Was this sage born from a female brahman?

For example, the great sage Vyāsa was originally born from a fisherwoman; after having practiced asceticism and acquired knowledge, he became a sage. Did this sage belong to the brahman class? Therefore, this mistaken viewpoint [that brahmanhood is based on birth] is not legitimate.

Moreover, for example, the great sage Vasiṣṭha, born from the divine female Urvaśī, became a sage after having practiced asceticism and acquired knowledge. Did this sage belong to the brahman class?

Furthermore, for example, the great sage Ṛṣyaśṛṅga, born from the womb of a female deer, became a sage after having practiced asceticism and acquired knowledge and skills. Did this sage belong to the brahman class?

Additionally, for example, the great sage Viśvāmitra was born from a woman of a *caṇḍāla*'s family. Did this sage belong to the brahman class?

On the basis of the aforementioned information, the following is to be known. An individual is called a true brahman when they control the senses, do not distinguish between self and other, diligently observe celibacy, stay far away from poluting desires, and have forever laid all delusion to rest. On the other hand, it is not the case that brahmanhood was founded based on a family line. Why do you mistakenly insist that the brahman class is the best class in the world and the purest in terms of following rules and practicing asceticism, without any admixture from other classes? Following this mistaken viewpoint, you consider who is not the best to be the best.

Hence, the following is to be known. It is not based on one's class, soul, family line, asceticism, activity, or birth that an individual is called a brahman.

Moreover, many individuals can be born in heaven if they follow the rules and accumulate merit, even if they originally belonged to the lower classes. Were they born in heaven by virtue of their family line?

Furthermore, for example, great sages such as Kapila, Vyāsa, Vasiṣṭha, Ṛṣyaśṛṅga, Viśva, Mitra, and Nārada are mentioned in your statements. These great sages were born to the lower classes. They became sages after having practiced asceticism and accumulated [good] seeds. Why do you mistakenly insist that your class is unmixed and is the best in the world? Thus, this is a false statement not to be believed and accepted.

Moreover, [brahmans] adhere to the following view: the brahman class was born from the mouth of the god Brahmā, the *kṣatriya* class was born from the arms of the god Brahmā, the *vaiśya* class was born from the thighs
171a of the god Brahmā, and the *śūdra* class was born from the feet of the god Brahmā. This view is faulty. The brahmans frequently adhere to this view.

Furthermore, [brahmans] insist that if individuals, while performing asceticism, are firm in sticking to their purpose, they are called brahmans. [However,] does it then follow that if a fisherman, a dyer, a leather craftsman, or a *śūdra* and the like also practice asceticism while firmly sticking to their purpose, they are called a brahman?

Additionally, [brahmans] adhere to their appearance. They think that those who bind their hair up in a topknot, wear a cord around their waists, carry a wooden staff in their hands, dress in white, and have a restricted diet are called brahmans. [Yet] other individuals, for example, *śūdra*s, can also adopt these types of form. Should it be the case that these individuals are all called brahmans?

Moreover, [brahmans] insist that all the four classes are born from the god Brahmā. [If this were the case, however,] why are the classes of children different when their father is one and the same [god]? [If it is the case that these classes of children are different when their father is one and the same god, then] the same would be true of [fathers belonging to] the *śūdra* class and the other classes. That the classes of children born from the same father differ is not valid. Why do they adhere to such a view?

Furthermore, the brahman class was born from the mouth of one and the same god, Brahmā. Globally, incest between brothers and sisters is blamed and hated. [Yet] you frequently engage in this. Why are you [considered] pure? Hence, you mistakenly insist as follows, considering individuals who are not pure to be pure.

For instance, suppose the same father and mother gave birth to four babies. It is not the case that their classes differ respectively. Why do you mistakenly insist on this view: "This baby is a brahman, this baby is a *kṣatriya,* this baby is a *vaiśya,* and this baby is a *śūdra.*" Why do the classes of children born from the same father differ? Thus, you mistakenly insist that the four classes are differentiated.

It is unlike the footprints of elephants, horses, cows, sheep, camels, deer, lions, tigers, and wolves, which all differ and can be distinguished from each other, such that one can say, "This is a cow's footprint . . . this is an elephant's footprint." Unlike this, the four classes cannot be distinguished.

Furthermore, for example, flowers and fruits produced from the same tree cannot be distinguished. [On the other hand,] flowers and grasses produced from different trees are different. Because they have were not produced from the same [tree], they cannot be regarded as the same.[17]

The same logic applies to the current four classes you claim. Because brahmans, *kṣatriya*s . . . and *śūdra*s are all born from the same father (the god Brahmā), why do you mistakenly insist that the four classes are distinguished?

Moreover, there was a god-king called Yudhiṣṭhira. After having approached the sage Vaiśampāyana with his palms joined, faithfully and reverently, and having paid homage by bowing his head to the sage's feet, he asked the sage, "What are the so-called brahmans' qualities? Moreover, what are the so-called brahmans' characteristics? Furthermore, how many distinguished characteristics are there? Please explain them to me now. Please make me understand them."

Subsequently, the sage Vaiśampāyana said to the king, "Endurance, effort, meditation, and wisdom are called the brahmans' qualities. Avoiding greed, anger, and killing any living being—this is called the first characteristic of brahmans. Any property belonging to others are not to be coveted with a greedy mind—this is called the second characteristic of brahmans. If one avoids violence and hatred, is mild in nature and behavior, does not distinguish
between self and other, and gets rid of entanglements and polluting desires— 171b
this is called the third characteristic of brahmans. Always avoiding attachment to human and divine females and even [female] animals—this is called the fourth characteristic of brahmans. Furthermore, if one matures all living beings, is always compassionate, controls their senses, and becomes a pure and excellent person—this is called the fifth characteristic of brahmans. Thus, if one is fully equipped with these five characteristics, one is called a brahman. If one makes a distinction between others and themselves and is not equipped with the five characteristics, one is called a *śūdra*."

Then, the sage said to Yudhiṣṭhira, "It is not on the basis of one's family line, birth, or [practice of] austerity that one becomes a brahman. *Caṇḍāla*s and others who possess these five characteristics could also be called true brahmans. In the same vein, it is also possible to say that brahman is called a *śūdra* and a *śūdra* is called a true brahman."

Yudhiṣṭhira said to the sage, "A brahman attains a pure result by not killing any creatures. Thanks to this [instruction], I know somehow that such a person is called a brahman."

Additionally, the sage said to Yudhiṣṭhira, "The distinction of these four classes is due to deeds and conditions accumulated in the past. Moreover, for example, all living beings in the world, who are born from their mother's body, are those born through a dirty organ. Then what type of distinction is there [between living beings?] Therefore, one is called a brahman if one practices asceticism following the monastic rules and does meritorious deeds. Even a *śūdra,* if they cultivate meritorious conduct, becomes a brahman. If a brahman does not practice meritorious deeds, they also obtain the name of 'lower *śūdra*.' Furthermore, one should always control the five senses since they lead one to bad deeds. They (the five senses) are like an ocean in which living beings drown, so one should seek to save them and bring them to the far shore."

Then, King Yudhiṣṭhira, after having heard this from the sage, understood what has been said and thinks with a joyful heart, "I will teach the limitless living beings what I have just heard and make them all understand. This is neither for my own sake nor out of greed for my own life. From today on, night and day, I will cultivate endurance, avoid retinue and envy, not be greedy for anything desirable, go forward to seek salvation, and always cultivate pure conduct."

Furthermore, the sage said to Yudhiṣṭhira, "Not killing living beings, avoiding greed and anger, and matchless purity—these are called the conduct of brahmans. Controlling the senses, giving gifts, cultivating endurance, truly practicing asceticism, being compassionate toward all living beings, loving and protecting them, and accumulating knowledge—these are called the conduct of brahmans. Avoidance of improper asceticism and offering help to living beings according to their abilities and numerous sufferings—these are called the conduct of brahmans. Moreover, it is taught in the *Gāyatrī*[18] of the

brahmans that one can only be called a true brahman after they have spent a thousand *kalpa*s performing asceticism without holding on to anything, controlling their senses, giving gifts four times a day, thinking lovingly of 171c
living beings, getting rid of sleepiness, and always cultivating pure conduct."

Additionally, the sage said to Yudhiṣṭhira, "If one understands the teachings of the four Vedas, one is called a brahman and the best among the classes. Why then are the other individuals like *śūdra*s also not the best when they also can understand the teachings of the Vedas?"

For example, individuals from the four classes wander through a sacred place. All of their footprints cannot be distinguished in such a way that it could be said that this footprint is from this person, not from that person. This phenomenon is true of [footprints made by individuals within] either one class or the four classes. The division of the four classes is due to linguistic convention. Originally, there was no such division.

Moreover, for example, although in this world the forms of cows, horses, and other animals differ, they belong to the same category since they have male or female sexual organs. When the brahmans examine individuals from one class, such as *kṣatriya*s, *vaiśya*s, and *śūdra*s, or individuals from the four classes, they (the brahmans) understand in the same manner.

Furthermore, for example, blood, flesh, excreta, limbs, and the senses of one person and those of many persons belong to the same category and hence are not different.

Additionally, for example, the shapes and colors of a lotus, a flower of the *tilaka* tree,[19] and a moonlike conch are distinguishable. On the other hand, there is no distinction between the shapes and colors of individuals from the four classes. Why are they distinguished?

Moreover, for example, cows, horses, elephants, and deer act out of their polluting desires, but they do not have a sexual intercourse with each other and they are distinguished. Now, brahmans have [sexual intercourse] with *kṣatriya*s, *vaiśya*s, and *śūdra*s and act from their polluting desires. They all are born from a mother's body. What type of distinction is there between them?

Furthermore, for example, why does a woman born from a brahman have sexual intercourse with an individual of the same class who is close to her in relation, that is, with her relatives?[20] Even *śūdra*s do not do such a thing in this world.

For example, although several flowers, fruits, branches, and leaves are grown in the *udumbara* tree in this world, the root and the trunk of this tree are not distinguished. There is no distinction such that this is the flower from this tree and this is the flower of that tree. This fact is also said of you brahmans. You should not have sexual intercourse with individuals of the same class who are close to you in relation. This [kind of act] is blameworthy and despised in the world. You must not do this.

Moreover, for example, individuals are called brahman if they avoid evil acts in word and deed and always cultivate pure conduct. *Vaiśya*s, and the like, also do this and can become a great sage, now called Vasiṣṭha.

Furthermore, for example, fire in this world can burn brushwood and firewood and all of [these kinds of fuel] are not distinguished [when they are being consumed by fire.] Now, when the brahmans interact with individuals from the other classes, there is no distinction between them all.

172a Additionally, for example, the great sage Vyāsa was originally born from a fisherman. Therefore, he also was not born from a brahman.

Moreover, for example, the five Pāṇḍava brothers of the royal family were born from the same mother but they have different fathers. It is the result of the deeds performed by them in the past and not because of their class that they have the same mother but different fathers. However, you mistakenly insist on the distinction [between their classes].

Furthermore, for example, in this world salt dissolves in water. In this case, the shape of the salt disappears yet its taste still remains. The results of deeds performed in the past come to us. The disappearance and appearance of these results are the same [as salt dissolved in water].

Wise individuals should know the details of the aforementioned mistaken viewpoints, which cannot be relied upon or believed.

Notes

1 Poluodishan 婆囉帝山, "Bhārate mountain," seems to be a translation of *bhārate,* which in the Sanskrit text originally means "in the [*Mahā*]*bhārata.*"

2 Naluoqicha 那洛乞叉 is probably a transliteration of "Narakṣa" (?), but this is not found in the Sanskrit original. The origin of *naluoqicha* is uncertain. The word *ulūkī,* "female owl," appears in the corresponding part of the Sanskrit text.

3 Bushayezuo 布沙野左 is probably a transliteration of "Puṣyasa," but this word is not found in the Sanskrit original. It is likely that the transliteration *bushayezuo* is rooted in *puṣpāc ca,* "and from a flower," in the Sanskrit text.

4 "Kuśa" is the name of a type of grass.

5 Sengsaduoe 僧薩多誐 (for the name "Sambhava") is probably a transliteration of *saṃsataḥ,* but this word is not found in the Sanskrit original. *Sengsaduoe* probably originates from *-sambhavaḥ,* "birth," in the Sanskrit text.

6 "Kapilā" means a brown cow.

7 "Śaragulma" means a clump of *śara,* a sort of reed or grass.

8 "Kalaśa" means a water pot.

9 "Tittirī" means a female partridge.

10 Naluoman 捺囉鋡 (for the name "Rāma") is probably a transliteration of *drāmam,* which comprises *d* and *rāmam.* The corresponding part of the Sanskrit text reads: *reṇukājanayad rāmam ṛṣyaśṛṅgamuniṃ mṛgī.* It is likely that the former *d* is the last letter of the finite verb *ajanayad,* and that the latter *rāmam* is an accusative form of the word *rāma.* It is very probable that the conjunct consonant *drā* generated by the adjacency of the two words was not resolved correctly and this error was reflected in the Chinese translation.

11 The Chinese translation in this passage is difficult because (1) the classes of the parents and their children can differ, but (2) the children are customarily classified into the same brahman class; thus, (3) there exist various classes within the brahman classes; consequently, (4) it is unreasonable to claim that the brahman class is superior to the other classes, because such a claim presupposes a clear distinction between the classes.

12 What is meant is that an individual is called a brahman when they torment themselves through asceticism.

13 There is no difference between the brahmans and the other groups of people (*kṣatriya*s, *vaiśya*s, *śūdra*s) because it is true that they all were born from parts of the god. Whomever you kill, you will have committed a great sin.

[14] Since they can attack the brahmans, the question is why do the brahmans serve a god that originated from the low class?

[15] The gist is as follows: the brahmans admit that Śiva is originally from the *śūdra* class and that Śiva and his wife created the other deities and the world. Hence, Śiva is deemed to be superior to the other deities and the world, because only someone/something superior can produce someone/something inferior. Thus, the brahmans accept that those belonging to the *śūdra* class can attain the state of one who is superior to anyone/anything. This fact contradicts their claim that the brahman class is the best and the *śūdra* class is low, a claim that should be abandoned.

[16] The point is that any idea that presupposes the distinction of the brahman and *śūdra* classes is invalid because there is no such distinction.

[17] On the other hand, according to the view the brahmans accept, all four classes were born from the same god, Brahmā. If this is the case, there can be no difference between them.

[18] *Eyedalijingzhou* 誐野怛哩經呪.

[19] We take *chadalihua* 刹怛哩花 as the translation of *chattrapuṣpaka,* "*tilaka* tree," which is not found in the Sanskrit original.

[20] *Zimei* · *xiongdi* · *fuqi* 姊妹・兄弟・夫妻 is presumably used in the sense of "relatives" in this case.

Bibliography

Bharadwaj, Ramesh. *Vajrasūcī of Aśvaghoṣa and the Concept of Varṇa-Jāti through the Ages.* Delhi: Vidyanidhi Prakashan, 2007.

Byōdō Tsūsyō 平等 通昭. "'Kongōshinron'「金剛針論」," in *Kokuyaku Issaikyō ronshūbu* 6 『國譯一切經論集部 六』, pp. 3–27. Tokyo: Daitō shuppansha, 1931.

Hodgson, Brian H. "A Disputation Respecting Caste by a Buddhist, in the Form of a Series of Propositions Supposed to Be Put by a Saiva and Refuted by the Disputant," *Transactions of the Royal Asiatic Society of Great Britain and Ireland* 3/1 (1831): 160–169.

Kanazawa Atsushi 金沢篤. "'Bonbun *Kongōshinron*' o yomu: Bongo gakushūsha no tameni 梵文『金剛針論』を読む―梵語学習者のために―," *Komazawa daigaku bukkyōgakubu ronshū* 駒澤大學佛教學部論集 41 (2010): 344–374.

Morton, William. *Vajra Suchi the Needle of Adamant; Or the Original Divine Institution of Caste.* Jaffna: The Jaffna Religious Tract Society, 1851.

Mukhopadhyaya, Sujitkumar. *The Vajrasūcī of Aśvaghoṣa: A Study of the Sanskrit Text and Chinese Version with Introduction, English Translation, and Notes.* Santiniketan: Visvabharati, 1960, second ed.

Okano Kiyoshi 岡野潔. "4. Vajrasuucii Kongō no hari 金剛の針." Main text: http://gdgdgd.g.dgdg.jp/vajrasuci.html; notes: http://gdgdgd.g.dgdg.jp/vajrasuci-note.html. Accessed August 19, 2020.

Shastri, Losang Norbu, and Lobsang Dorjee (Rabling). *Ācārya Aśvaghoṣa's Vajrasūcī.* Sarnath: Central Institute of Higher Tibetan Studies, 2006.

Wilkinson, Lancelot, and Sūbajī Bāpū. *The Wujra Soochi or Refutation of the Arguments upon Which the Brahmanical Institution of Caste is Founded, by the Learned Booddhist Ashwa Ghoshu. Also the Tunku by Soobajee Bapoo: Being a Reply to the Wujra Soochi.* Bombay: Nabu Press, 1839.

TREATISE ON DOCTRINAL DISTINCTIONS OF THE HUAYAN ONE VEHICLE

Translators' Introduction

Taitetsu Unno, Mark Unno,
and Monica E. McLellan

The *Treatise on Doctrinal Distinctions of the Huayan One Vehicle* (*Huayan yisheng jiaoyi fenqi zhang,* T. 1866) is a seminal text in East Asian Mahayana Buddhism, and a foundational text of Huayan (Kor. Hwaeom, Jp. Kegon, Viet. Hoa Nghiêm) Buddhism in particular. It promotes the universal vision of the *Avataṃsaka-sūtra*—in this translation, the *Flower Garland Sutra*—as the ultimate realization of the Buddhist teachings, in which all interpretive contradictions are reconciled. But this reconciliation is only one facet of the larger vision of Huayan, in which there are no real contradictions at all, for each and every phenomenon is affirmed as a necessary participant in the ultimate wholeness of the Dharma realm of Vairocana Buddha.

Fazang (643–712) composed the *Treatise* in the early Tang dynasty, during a time when the canon of texts available to Buddhism in China was expanding rapidly and somewhat unsystematically through the importation of texts and efforts to translate them. It no doubt seemed to scholarly Chinese Buddhists of the time (as indeed it may to readers of the still incomplete English version of the Buddhist canon today) that these proliferating Buddhist texts contained contradictory or irreconcilable teachings. According to Fazang, these seeming discrepancies are merely superficial; they are expedient means to prepare beings for the ultimate truth of One Vehicle Buddhism, which is only fully realized in Huayan. The *Treatise* can be best understood as an argument for the organic coherence of Buddhist philosophy as seen from the perspective of the Huayan One Vehicle, the vehicle that encompasses all vehicles.

Fazang's ancestors came from Sogdiana, but he was born and raised in the Chinese imperial capital of Chang'an. He is considered the systematizer and third patriarch of Huayan, after Dushun and Zhiyan. Fazang composed other important works including a commentary on *The Awakening of Faith* and the original *Treatise on the Golden Lion.* He was also a translator and lecturer, as well as a miracle-worker, showman, and habitué of the imperial court. The patronage of Empress Wu Zetian helped Huayan Buddhism gain recognition and prestige early in its development. Fazang's influence within and beyond Huayan was considerable. Fazang corresponded closely with his Korean Dharma-brother Uisang (625–702), who founded the Korean branch of Huayan (Hwaeom); and taught Simsang (d. 742), the Korean monk who went on to teach Ryōben, the founder of the Japanese branch of Huayan (Kegon). Through the Huayan fifth patriarch, Zongmi (780–841), Fazang's teachings also had a significant impact on Chan (Zen) Buddhism.

The Huayan Buddhism of the *Treatise* is based on the *Flower Garland Sutra*'s vision of universal buddhahood and nonobstruction. The most important concept for understanding the *Treatise* is the Huayan vision of causation, which differs significantly from older understandings of dependent origination. This is expressed in the *Treatise* in several ways, including in the traditional metaphor of organic growth from seed to fruit, but the unique contribution of Huayan is best illustrated in the teaching of principal and attendants. This could also be translated as "master and servants" or "lord and retinue." One may imagine a very worldly scene that would have been familiar to Fazang's original audience: the lord of an estate and his retinue of servants, advisors, and bodyguards. Without his retinue, the lord could not manage and secure his estate, and so would not be the lord. Without the lord, the retainers would be retained by no one and would not be a retinue. Yet when the lord of the estate goes to the capital, he is but one of many courtiers, a retainer of sorts, in the court of the king; and when an individual of the lord's retinue goes to his quarters for dinner, he is the lord of his home. So lord and retinue are both essentially interdependent and entirely devoid of essential self-identity.

In Huayan, the "principal" is any particular phenomenon and the "attendants" are everything else—all of the other phenomena in all possible universes. The one particular phenomenon attended to is principal from this perspective, but is one of the attendants from any other perspective. Thus, the distinctive characteristic of causation in Huayan is that it is not linear or discreet; rather, it is omnidirectional and omnipresent. In this vision, every being's karma is profoundly interfused with that of every other being, which means that buddhahood is truly universal. All other versions of Buddhism, according to Fazang, did not quite reach the point of understanding the total pervasiveness of interdependence, nor of true buddhahood. The structure of principal and attendants is both a description of the Huayan cosmos and also the organizational framework of the *Treatise.* In Fazang's exposition, all Buddhist teachings may be principal or attendant, depending on perspective.

The *Treatise* is organized in ten chapters or "gates." We have chosen to translate the term rather literally, as it sometimes refers to a chapter or section or a particular thread of discourse, but can also mean a perspective on a topic, a point of entry; generally, the "gates" in this text are ways of accessing the ideas under discussion. The first two gates lay out the scriptural and conceptual basis for the systematization of Buddhist teachings into various vehicles, and the third provides an account of historical developments leading up to Fazang's own systematization from the One Vehicle perspective. The fourth gate identifies five phases of the teachings that most essentially articulate the development and realization of Buddhism according to Huayan. The sixth through eighth gates consider the different phases in terms of their interpretations of various fundamental doctrines and the degree to which they express the universality of Huayan. The ninth and tenth gates are where Fazang expounds the unique contributions of Huayan in detail. In the ninth gate, Fazang demonstrates how Huayan is a philosophical advancement over Yogācāra, with technical discussions on topics including the levels of consciousness, seed-natures, and the severing of afflictions. In the tenth gate, Fazang elaborates on the philosophical contributions of his immediate predecessors, especially his teacher Zhiyan, and provides concrete illustrations of Huayan doctrine in the well-known analogies of counting coins and building a house.

Within the ten gates the argument is strictly organized, but it is so complex as to be potentially disorienting. Each gate is separated into numbered sections, with further division into many layers of subsections; some subsections are many pages long. The main topic of each section and subsection is often implicit after the initial exposition, or may be indicated only by a number that was assigned to it at some earlier point in the argument. Meanwhile, there are frequent digressions in dialogue form, as if some students are ocassionally interrupting the teacher's carefully structured lecture to ask for immediate clarification. This parallel discourse is set off from the overall organization by its question-and-answer format. To help the reader navigate the text, we have made Fazang's outline explicit by adding headings, and we have included these headings in the Outline of Contents, below. In addition, we have explicitated the numbering system of subsections and lists in some places where it is implicit in the text, while in other places we have rendered some of the more repetitive numbering schemes with non-numerical wording for clarity.

Regarding the text itself, we have followed the standard Taishō edition, T. 1866, which is based on a version of the *Treatise* brought to Japan during the Song dynasty. This text is based primarily on a Qing dynasty printing (c. 1663), with variants included from print and manuscript editions dating from 1290 to 1706. We have incorporated some textual variants included in the Taishō edition when they seemed much more logically appropriate. In a few instances, when it seemed clearly to produce better coherence than not, we have interpreted words in terms of graphically or aurally similar words. These variations are infrequent and relatively minor, and we believe the interpretation conveyed in this translation is well within the range of graphic instability inherent to the centuries of manuscript culture that preceded the Taishō text.

Fazang refers to a great many sutras and other texts in the *Treatise,* and often directs the reader to consult these texts for a more thorough discussion of the topic at hand. The texts that may be most helpful to the reader for understanding the more technical parts of the *Treatise* are the *Flower Garland Sutra,* the *Lotus Sutra, The Awakening of Faith,* the *Treatise on the Ten Stages,* the *Treatise on Yogācāra Stages,* the *Summary of the Great Vehicle,* and the *Treatise on the Larger Prajñāpāramitā Sutra.* Some of the texts or passages to which he refers are no longer extant, or the specific version of a text is difficult to identify; sometimes he mentions a primary text when the language or idea he cites actually comes from a commentary on that text. To assist the reader who would like to explore further, we have compiled a list of the texts cited, complete to the best of our ability, and included it in the Bibliography of this volume, after the Glossary. The list is organized by the English titles we have used, and also gives the Chinese titles used in the text and full or alternate titles.

Comments by Monica E. McLellan

I must express my deep gratitude to Taitetsu Unno, whose drafts are the basis of this work, and within whose formidable shadow it was completed. I have done my best to complete what he began. My qualifications in no way measure up to the beginning he provided, and any errors that are to be found in this published version are my own. I would like to thank Mark Unno for providing so many opportunities for spiritual, intellectual, and career growth as I have navigated the challenges of the past many years, including inviting and supporting my involvement in translating this work. I am grateful to the patient editorial staff at Bukkyō Dendō Kyōkai; the reviewers, who provided careful criticism of early drafts; and to the library staff at the University of Oregon, who found ways to assist even during prolonged building closures. Finally, thank you to my blood and chosen families, without whom I could not have completed this work.

I would like to conclude this introduction with a reflection on relevance. When I wrote this, in September 2020, ash was drifting down from an opaque orange sky from wildfires burning all across the state of Oregon, where I live. Fires were burning across the entire west of North America, and also in the Amazon basin. Even before these fires, the world was struggling with a global pandemic that brought about millions of deaths. At such a time, the *Treatise on Doctrinal Distinctions of the Huayan One Vehicle* may seem too concerned with precious abstractions, such as Indra's infinite net of jewels, to be considered relevant at all. What could such a deeply scholastic text teach us at this seemingly apocalyptic juncture? But the text begins with a discussion of the parable of a burning house in the *Lotus Sutra,* and ends with Fazang's original exposition on the building of a house. Although it begins with a house—our world—on fire, as a whole it is a profoundly affirmative project. The simple message is, first, that the proliferating mass of the Buddhist Dharma, as well as the massive conflagration of phenomenal dharmas that we inhabit, is, ultimately, whole; and second, that all of these finite teachings and experiences and things are, as a consequence of their essential participation in the whole, themselves whole. It affirms the world we live in, even as it burns. It affirms every mote of ash: each is the realm of its unique buddha; each is the mirror of every other buddha realm. I believe the house that is built at the end of this book refers, for us, to making a home for all beings: a refuge that is both phenomenal and real, where all beings can awaken true compassion.

Outline of Contents

- X. Distinctions in Doctrinal Principles
  - A. Similarities and Differences in the Three Natures
    - 1. Specification
      - i. Direct Explanation of Natures and their Aspects
      - ii. Determination of Correct Understanding
        - a. Maintaining Attachments
        - b. Showing the Errors of Attachment
          - b1. Fully Perfected Nature
          - b2. Other-dependent Nature
          - b3. Imagined Nature
        - c. Demonstration of Significance
    - 2. General Explanation
  - B. The Six Significances of the Causal Aspect of Interdependent Arising
    - 1. Exposition of Characteristics
    - 2. Establishment of the Doctrine
    - 3. Enumeration of Logical Possibilities
    - 4. Analysis and Synthesis
    - 5. Fusion and Inclusion
    - 6. Perspectives of the Teachings
  - C. The Ten Mysterious Dharma Gates of Unobstructed Interdependent Arising
    - 1. Verification of the Ultimate Result
    - 2. Discernment in the Causal State
      - i. The Analogy of Counting Coins
        - a. Differentiated Essence
        - b. Common Essence
      - ii. Discernment from the Perspective of Dharma
        - a. Simultaneous Repletion and Mutual Correspondence
        - b. Mutual Accommodation of Difference
        - c. Autonomous Mutual Identification
        - d. The Realm of Indra's Net
        - e. Mutual Accommodation of Subtle Particulars
        - f. Esoteric Concurrent Formation
        - g. Endowment with all Pure and Mixed Virtues
        - h. Unique Formations of the Ten Temporal Worlds

Treatise on Doctrinal Distinctions of the Huayan One Vehicle

Composed by Fazang, *Śramaṇa* of Dajianfu Temple,
Tang Dynasty[1]

Now I will expound the One Vehicle doctrine of the ocean-seal *samādhi* of the Tathāgata,[2] in summary, through these ten gates. 477a

I. Establishing the One Vehicle
II. The Benefits of the Doctrines
III. Classification of the Teachings, Ancient and Recent
IV. Divisions of the Teachings and Analysis of the Tenets
V. Analysis and Synthesis of Vehicles and Teachings
VI. The Sequence of the Emergence of the Teachings
VII. Determining the Reasons for the Sequence of the Teachings
VIII. Comparison of their Formulations
IX. Differences in their Explanations
X. Distinctions in Doctrinal Principles

I. Establishing the One Vehicle

First I will clearly establish the One Vehicle. I will divide the doctrinal distinctions of this One Vehicle into two gates: first, the Distinct Teaching and second, the Common Teaching.[3]

A. Distinct Teaching

Within the first, there are two aspects.

1. Resultant State

First is the resultant state of the ocean of original nature (i.e., buddhahood). This is inexpressible. Why so? Because it cannot be accommodated by teachings. It is the realm of the ten buddhas themselves. This is stated in the *Treatise* on the "Bodhisattva Stages" chapter of the *Flower Garland Sutra:* "The causal state is expressible, but the resultant state is inexpressible."

2. Causal State

Second is the causal state of interdependent arising;[4] that is, the realm of

Samantabhadra. These two are nondual and totally pervade each other, like a wave and the water. Consider this and you shall see.

In the realm of Samantabhadra there are again two gates. First is the gate of differentiation. Second is the gate of inclusivity.

i. Differentiation of One and Three Vehicles

As to differentiation, this is the Distinct Teaching of One Vehicle; it is distinct from the three vehicles. In the *Lotus Sutra,* the three carts beyond the gate (goat, deer, and ox carts), pointed out from within the burning house to entice the children to exit, are the teachings of the three vehicles. The great white ox carts given to them on open ground, beyond the triple world, are the teaching of the One Vehicle. Thus, the One Vehicle and the three vehicles are distinct. The sacred teachings give, in sum, ten explanations for this.

First is the distinction between the provisional and the ultimately real. Since among the three the ox cart is like the goat and deer carts—a provisional way to entice the children to leave—then it is clear that all three of the carts by the gate are actually skillful means. The great white ox carts were given to them at the crossroads instead to show the true and real.

If the ox cart among the three were the ultimately real [ox cart/teaching], then when the father pointed it out to entice the children from inside the house, they should have been able to see it immediately upon exiting the
477b gate. Why did they come out to where the carts had been indicated to be, and yet, not finding them, search for them? It is incorrect to say that only those of the two vehicles continue searching for carts beyond the triple world. The sutra does not say that those people searching for the ox cart found that ox cart upon exiting the gate. It also does not say that those who sought the carts formerly promised were only those of the two vehicles. The sutra states that all of the children, having exited the house and reached the open ground, said to their father, "The wonderful toys you promised us earlier—goat cart, deer cart, and ox cart—please give them to us now." By this we know that all three carts were equally sought. The three carts are taught from the standpoint of the results sought by those of the three vehicles. They are proposed according to their original aspirations.

Question: The two vehicles each attain some lesser results (e.g., arhatship). Why do they continue searching beyond the gate?

Reply: Those who rely on the Lesser Vehicle would say that they have the teachings and they have practice-results. Now, those who rely on the Great Vehicle would say that those Lesser Vehicle practitioners of ancient times had only the verbal teachings and no real practice-results. So it is said that all three carts are empty. If you take the point of view of the tenets of the respective teachings themselves, then each attains their result. If their goals were not attained, how could they have exited the triple world? The statement that none of them attain their goal is from the point of view of the One Vehicle. For this reason, when the ultimately real illuminates that which is provisional, the forms of expediency disappear completely: none has attained the goal. What is desired is to convert the people of those three vehicles to the One Vehicle, and so those of the Great Vehicle must also be converted. If it was not so, then those who sought the ox cart would be different from ordinary beings as soon as they exited the triple world. Not seeking the goat and deer carts, they are different from those of the two vehicles; not yet attaining the great white ox carts on open ground, they are different from those of the One Vehicle. If, among the three [kinds of people represented by the children], they are not of the Great Vehicle, then what kind of people could they be? Because all have arrived at the farthest point they intended, later they all will advance into the Distinct Teaching of One Vehicle.

Question: Are the three carts by the gate real or unreal?

Reply: They are both real and unreal. Why so? Because they are skillful means. Since as skillful means they do entice the children to exit, they are not unreal; since they entice them as skillful means, they are not truly real. These two are nondual, simply a single form.

Second is the difference between the teaching and its significance. The ox cart by the gate, as well as the goat and deer carts, exists in name only. From the point of view of the One Vehicle you see that they are all teachings [but without ultimate significance]. Thus, the sutra states, "Through the gate of the Buddha's teachings, the suffering of the triple world is overcome." Moreover, one cannot say that the words "the Buddha's teachings" only refer to the two vehicles, because the sutra does not make such a specification. Those people who seek the ox cart search for the teachings' ultimate significance, and so are the same as those of the two vehicles: none of them attain it.

Third is the distinction in what they expected. Since the One Vehicle is different from the three carts promised earlier within the triple world, when it was given to the children at the crossroads, they all exclaimed that it was not what they had originally wanted. Thus, the sutra states, "At this time all
477c of the children clambered onto the great carts, and obtained something unprecedented, not what they had originally wanted." Now, it is incorrect to say that the words "not what they had originally wanted" refers only to the two vehicles, because the sutra does not make such a distinction. The sacred words never err. Clearly, none of the objects promised within the house were obtained, and the ox carts on the open ground were not the ones they had each desired. Thus, what they have now obtained is called "not what they had originally wanted."

Fourth is the distinction in the extent of their qualities. When the father in the house points outside, he simply says, "ox cart" without describing any of its qualities. But what are given at the crossroads are seven-jeweled magnificent carts, adorned with a countless variety of jewels, including jeweled tassels, jeweled bells, and so forth. Such are their innate qualities. Now, the father simply said "ox" and did not say anything about its characteristics. However, the sutra describes white oxen that are robust, extremely strong, swift as the wind, and so on. These are the surpassing excellences of their function. It also describes many attendants who guard the ox carts, symbolizing the retinue of religious practitioners. These extraordinary characteristics all clarify their distinction from the perspective of the Common Teaching of One Vehicle.

Furthermore, among the three carts there is only one ox cart. That is to demonstrate that their tenets are uniform as skillful means and lack the [infinitely adaptable] teaching of the interdependent arising of principal and attendants. But these ox carts are not like that. Only when the teaching of principal and attendants is complete can [a cart/vehicle] encompass innumerable virtues. Thus, the sutra states, "I have magnificent seven-jeweled carts like this; they are countless in number." Countless jeweled carts cannot mean only one. This presents the infinite doctrine of the One Vehicle. Its significance is extensively explained in the *Flower Garland Sutra.* This clarifies its distinction from the perspective of the Distinct Teaching of One Vehicle.

Fifth is the distinction in ranks attained. The *Sutra on Basic Activities,* the *Sutra for Benevolent Kings,* the *Treatise on the Ten Stages,* the Liang

dynasty translation of the *Summary of the Great Vehicle,* and so on all put the first, second, and third bodhisattva stages in the mundane world. They put the fourth stage to the seventh stage in the supramundane world. The eighth stage and above they put in the supra-supramundane world. Of the supramundane world, they equate the fourth stage and fifth stages with the Dharma of the *śrāvaka*s. The sixth stage they equate with the Dharma of the *pratyekabuddha*s. The seventh stage is equated with the bodhisattva Dharma. The eighth stage and above they equate with the One Vehicle Dharma. If the Great Vehicle (i.e., the bodhisattva Dharma) were actually the One Vehicle, then the seventh stage would actually be in the supra-supramundane, and the One Vehicle should not be put in the eighth stage. Because of this, we can understand the people of the three vehicles in the *Lotus Sutra.* They all go out beyond the gate in search of the three carts, so all three vehicles are of
the supramundane; for each it is the final goal. That is, among these stages, 478a
the fourth stage through the seventh stage are the supramundane. The great white ox carts are given separately at the crossroads, at a place above and beyond the supramundane, and are therefore the One Vehicle Dharma of the supra-supramundane. Thus, among the stages, the eighth stage and above are the One Vehicle Dharma.

Question: If so, why does the Liang translation of the *Summary of the Great Vehicle* state, "The good virtue of the two vehicles is called 'supramundane'; from the eighth stage and above up to the stage of buddhahood is called the 'supra-supramundane'"? It does not say that the three vehicles are of the supramundane. How is your interpretation possible?

Reply: Both the fourth and fifth stages are for the *śrāvaka*s, and the sixth stage is for the *pratyekabuddha*s. The eighth stage and above are of the supra-supramundane. Those of the seventh stage—which beings are they? [They are the bodhisattvas.] Thus, you should understand that the statement, "the good virtue of the two vehicles is called the supramundane" is precisely the "great" and "lesser" two vehicles, of which the *śrāvaka*s and *pratyekabuddha*s are both called "lesser" [and of which the bodhisattvas are called "great"]. The name "two vehicles" is used in this way, as explained completely below.

Sixth is the distinction in the entrusting of the teachings according to practitioner's capacities. As the *Lotus Sutra* states:

> If in the future eras there be good men and good women who believe in the wisdom of the Tathāgata, then you should recite this *Lotus Sutra* so that they may hear and understand it, in order to make others obtain the wisdom of the Buddha. If among living beings there are any who do not believe in it, then from the Tathāgata's other profound Dharma you should show them the teachings that bring them profit and joy. If you are able to do like this, then you will have repaid the Buddha's blessings.

Interpretation: The "other profound Dharma" is, precisely, the Great Vehicle. Because it is not the One Vehicle it is called "other," and because it is not the Lesser Vehicle it is called "profound." Surely, one cannot explain the Lesser Vehicle as the other profound Dharma; the *Lotus Sutra* directly refutes the Lesser Vehicle, so how could it possibly praise its profundity? Thus, you should know that the *Lotus Sutra* has a distinct significance: it is truly of the One Vehicle. This is the reason for entrusting the teachings to practitioners this way.

Seventh is the distinction in the spiritual predispositions of practitioners. As the chapter on unconditioned arising in the *Flower Garland Sutra* states:

> Buddha disciples! Bodhisattvas and *mahāsattva*s who for innumerable billions of trillions of *kalpa*s practice the six perfections, cultivate the factors for enlightenment, and establish roots of good practice, but haven't heard this sutra; or, although they have heard it, they do not have faith in it, uphold it, and obey it—these are known as "provisional bodhisattvas."

Interpretation: This clarifies that the roots of spiritual practice of the bodhisattvas of the three vehicles are not yet mature. Although they may have practiced in this way for so many *kalpa*s, those who do not believe or do not hear this One Vehicle sutra are these people. You should know that these are those previously mentioned in the *Lotus Sutra* who take profit and joy in being shown the "other profound Dharma." From the point of view of the ultimate Dharma of the One Vehicle, they are described by comparison as "provisional bodhisattvas." But from the point of view of their own respective tenets, they are true bodhisattvas. This passage clarifies that the *Flower Garland Sutra* is the Distinct Teaching of One Vehicle, and is not the same as the scriptures of the other vehicles.

Eighth is the distinction between difficult faith and easy faith. As [the bodhisattva Queen Bhadraśrī says] in the "Chief in Worthiness" chapter of the same [*Flower Garland*] *Sutra:* 478b

> Among the multitudes of living beings in all the worlds, only a few have the desire to seek the vehicle of the *śrāvaka*s, and those who seek the vehicle of the *pratyekabuddha*s are far fewer. Seekers of the Great Vehicle are extremely rare. And yet, to seek the Great Vehicle is easy; to be able to have faith in this Dharma is extremely difficult.

Interpretation: Since this chapter clarifies that the final state of mind (i.e., the last of the ten ranks of faith) encompasses all ranks even up to the achievement of buddhahood, so it transcends the three vehicles. It may be difficult to believe and accept this, so the three vehicles are juxtaposed with it and the matter is settled by comparison.

Ninth is the distinction in basic principles from the perspective of different spiritual capacities. As the opening verse[5] in the section on the ninth bodhisattva stage of this [*Flower Garland*] *Sutra* states:

> If among living beings there are those who are degraded, their hearts wearied and dejected, then show them the path of the *śrāvaka* so they may escape the many kinds of suffering. If among sentient beings there are those whose faculties are a little keener, who take pleasure in the Dharma of causes and conditions, for them explain the way of the *pratyekabuddha*s. If there are those beings whose faculties are keen, their hearts filled with great compassion, who desire to benefit all beings, for those explain the way of the bodhisattva. If there are those of unexcelled mind, determined to take pleasure in the Great Matter [of universal awakening]—for those, manifest the buddha body and explain the infinite Buddha-Dharma.

Interpretation: This clarifies that in the One Vehicle Dharma gate the teaching of the interdependent arising of principal and attendants is complete, so it is called "the infinite Buddha-Dharma." It is not the same as the three vehicles' teachings of one mark, one quiescence, and so on. It is in this latter stage that one becomes a great Dharma master and clarifies the proper manner of teaching the Dharma. This elucidates the scriptural distinction between the three vehicles and the One Vehicle.

Tenth is the distinction made in the analysis and synthesis of the root and ramifications of the teachings. As the *Sutra on the Common Nature of the Great Vehicle* states:

> All of the *śrāvaka* teachings, the *pratyekabuddha* teachings, the bodhisattva teachings, and the teachings of all the buddhas—all such dharmas flow completely into the great ocean of the matrix[6] of Vairocana Buddha's wisdom.

This passage makes distinctions from the perspective of root and ramifications, and furthermore unifies the ramifications by returning them to the root; it clearly reveals the distinction between the One Vehicle and the three vehicles.

The ten proofs above are as decisive as turtle shells and mirrors.[7] The characteristic practices, ranks, theories of cause and effect, and so on of the Distinct Teaching of One Vehicle are completely dissimilar from those doctrinal distinctions postulated in the three vehicles. This fact is to be found extensively throughout the scriptures, as summarily discussed below. And even if the teachings offered no such proofs, still, as there are differences in their significances, it is clear that the tenets must also be divided. How much more so when the [nourishing] clouds of the sacred teachings have split open so that [the sun/the true Dharma] brilliantly floods the eyes!

ii. Inclusivity of Three Vehicles within One

Second [counterpart to the gate of differentiation] is the gate of inclusivity. All the teachings of the three vehicles and the rest are originally nothing but the Dharma of the One Vehicle. Why so? From the point of view of the One Vehicle, the three vehicles have two gates [within this gate of inclusivity]. These are known as "not different" and "not one."

a. Not Different

First, as to not being different, there are also two parts. One, because the three are one, they are not different. Two, because the one is three, they are not different.

Question: If we were to try to base a conclusion on the first point, that the three are one, we still don't know if the three are to be maintained or refuted. If they are maintained, how could there be only one? If they are refuted, then upon what Dharma will those with the spiritual capacity for the three vehicles
478c rely to advance in spiritual practice?

Reply: There are four logical possibilities.[8] (1) Because they are one, it is not necessary to refute them. (2) Because they are one, there is no obstruction to maintaining them. (3) Because they are one, none of them is not refuted. (4) Because they are one, none of them can be maintained. By the former two principles the practitioners of the three vehicles obtain something upon which they can rely. By the latter two principles, the practitioners of the three vehicles obtain entry into the One Vehicle. Since these four logical possibilities are all inseparable as one, therefore there is only the One Vehicle and nothing else.

Second, as to clarifying that they are not different in terms of the One Vehicle being three, there are the four logical possibilities regarding how this is concealed and revealed; review the above and consider it accordingly. For these reasons, there are only the three vehicles, and not One. This is addressed below in the discussion of the Common Teaching.

b. Not the Same

Second is "not one." These three, having been identified as one, and the above one, having been identified as three, are not one gate. This does not refute their non-oneness, but clarifies their nondifference. Moreover, the non-oneness described here is the same as the gate of differentiation above. The nondifference described here is this gate of inclusivity.

B. Common Teaching

Second is the Common Teaching, within which there are two parts. First are the divisions into various vehicles; next is the fusing of root and ramifications.

1. Divisions into Various Vehicles

Within the first part, there are six kinds of divisions.

i. One Vehicle

The first section clarifies that there is but one vehicle, and includes seven perspectives. One, the One Vehicle is clarified from the perspective of the coincidence of characteristics of the various teachings. For example, the three vehicles do have teachings on Indra's net and the simultaneous accommodation of subtle particulars and such matters, but they are incomplete in regard to the interdependent arising of principal and attendants. Or, although they have teachings on the lotus flower treasury world, they do not teach about all ten such worlds. The characteristics of teachings of the three vehicles are also found in the One Vehicle; for example, the five eyes of wisdom [of the three vehicles] are of course found among the ten eyes of wisdom [of the One Vehicle], and the six cognitive powers [of the three vehicles] are of course found among the ten cognitive powers [of the One Vehicle], and so on. And yet, their doctrinal principles are completely different. This is the One Vehicle carrying the three vehicles, and the three vehicles partaking of the One Vehicle. This is the two traditions meeting and joining, guiding the establishment of spiritual roots, aspiration, and inclination, so that beings enter the Distinct Teaching of One Vehicle.

Second is clarification from the perspective that encompasses skillful means. The teachings of the three vehicles are all considered to be the skillful means of the One Vehicle, so they are all called One Vehicle. This is in the scriptures in statements such as "all the activities performed are for the one Great Matter."

Third is discernment from the perspective of the flowing streams of truth. It is said that the three vehicles all flow out from the One Vehicle. Thus the [*Lotus*] *Sutra* states, "All of the practices you undertake are the bodhisattva
479a way," and so on. Another scripture states, "The Vinaya is nothing but the Great Vehicle."

Fourth is from the perspective of special excellence. If among the three the Great Vehicle is considered to be the One Vehicle, then from the point of view of the Distinct Teaching, even though [the great and the distinct] are different in terms of representing provisional and ultimate reality, they are the same as the vehicles of the bodhisattvas. Thus, the [*Lotus*] *Sutra* states, "Only this one matter is ultimately real. The other two are not true." It also states, "For the sake of those who pursue the way of cessation (i.e., *śrāvaka*s and *pratyekabuddha*s), I explain it as being two." These passages have two meanings. One, from the point of view of the Distinct Teaching as explained above, "the other two" are the two vehicles great and lesser. Although the *śrāvaka*s and *pratyekabuddha*s differ in the keenness of their capacities, still they are the same in expecting the lesser result (i.e., individual liberation); while the One is unfolded and differentiated as two (great and distinct). Two, from the point of view of the Common Teaching, then the *śrāvaka*s and the *pratyekabuddha*s are the two; the Great is fused with the One.

Fifth is from the perspective of the depth and subtlety of the teachings. As the [*Lotus*] *Sutra* states, "I abide eternally on sacred Vulture Peak," and so on.

Sixth is from the perspective of the purport of the eight significances [of the Buddha's ways of converting beings to the One Vehicle]. This is based on the *Summary of the Great Vehicle,* and as in the discussion in the *Fifty Essentials of Huayan by Question and Answer.*[9]

Seventh is from the perspective of the skillful means [aspect of the One Vehicle] in the ten significances, as explained in the *Essays on the Contents of the Flower Garland Sutra.*

Based on the reasons above, the three vehicles can all be called the One Vehicle. This has been determined in accordance with their basic tenets. But because they do not have the teaching of interdependent arising of principal and attendants, they are the Common Teaching, not the Distinct Teaching.

ii. Division into Two Vehicles

The second section clarifies that there are two vehicles; there are three kinds [of this view]. The first is that the One Vehicle and the three vehicles, respectively, are called the two vehicles. That is, in the scripture, the carts given at the crossroads and the three carts by the gate. Within this, those ignorant of [Mahayana] Dharma and those subject to conversion are unified and both identified as the one Lesser Vehicle, so [together with the One Vehicle] there are two. The second [view] is that the Great Vehicle and the Lesser Vehicle are the two. Within this, the One is unified and identified with the Three; those ignorant of Dharma and those subject to conversion are differentiated and distinct. The third [view] is that the *śrāvaka*s and *pratyekabuddha*s are the two. This includes those ignorant of Dharma and those subject to conversion. In other words, the first [view] is from the perspective of the One Vehicle, the second is from the perspective of the three vehicles, and the last is from the perspective of the Lesser Vehicle. You should understand this accordingly.

iii. Division into Three Vehicles

The third clarifies that there are three vehicles, of which there are also three kinds [of this view]. First: The One Vehicle, the three vehicles, and the Lesser Vehicle are the three. This is in order to show the root and ramifications [of the development of the teachings]. The One Vehicle is revealed to upper-level practitioners and the ignorant teaching is revealed to lower-level practitioners; thus, there are three. Because in the scripture the beings of the two vehicles of the ignorant teaching are among the children enticed to exit, we understand that in addition to the three vehicles, there is also the Lesser Vehicle. Because the three carts entice all the children, we understand that in addition to the Lesser Vehicle, there are also the three vehicles. When all three kinds of beings have left the burning house and arrived on open ground, they then receive the great white ox carts. Thus, we understand that in addition to the three vehicles there is also the One Vehicle.

Question: How do we know that those beings of the two vehicles of the ignorant teaching are among the children enticed to exit?

Reply: From the perspective of the Final Teaching of the Great Vehicle and above, those ignorant of Dharma cannot be said to have finally exited the triple world. Why is that? Because they are attached to afflictions and have not yet permanently severed them; they are only able to suppress them. Thus, the *Treatise on the Sutra of the Questions of Maitreya* states:

> All of the *śrāvaka*s and *pratyekabuddha*s are unable to truly practice the
> 479b four immeasurable minds, so they are unable to finally sever all afflictions; they can only suppress all of their afflictions.

Another sutra, [the *Lotus,*] states, "The nirvana that you have attained is not true extinction and crossing over." That sutra also states, "For one to not believe in this Dharma and yet attain the result of arhatship—that would be impossible." And the *Larger Prajñāpāramitā Sutra* states, "If you wish to attain the result of arhatship, you must master *prajñāpāramitā.*" By this you must understand that the true significance of arhatship is to be found in the Great Vehicle.

Thus, the Great Vehicle necessarily contains the three. The *Sutra on Mañjuśrī's Transcendental Samādhi* states:

> In this way the Great Vehicle contains within it the three vehicles. They are the three treasuries: the *śrāvaka*s' treasury, the *pratyekabuddha*s' treasury, and the bodhisattvas' treasury. Only the Great Vehicle includes all three treasuries; the other two vehicles do not have this.

The *Treatise on Entering the Great Vehicle* is in agreement with this statement. You should understand that the three carts outside the gate have nothing in common with the ignorant teachings, because the *Lotus Sutra* is not of the Lesser Vehicle. The differences between such treatises as the part of the "Decision" section on *śrāvaka*s in the *Treatise on Yogācāra Stages* and the [*Treatise on the*] *Collected Abhidharma* [on the one hand], and the *Abhidharma-mahāvibhāṣā-śāstra* and *Abhidharmakośa-bhāṣya* [on the other hand], in the distinctions they discern among the teachings, practices, ranks, results, and ways of severing delusions of the *śrāvaka*s and so on, attest to this fact. For these reasons, you should know that the doctrinal distinctions of the One Vehicle, the three vehicles, and the Lesser Vehicle are separate.

Due to this significance, the *Treatise on the Larger Prajñāpāramitā Sutra* states, "There are two kinds of *prajñāpāramitā:* one is shared; the other is not shared." As to "shared," it refers to this Mahayana sutra, as well as other *vaipulya* sutras, that share teachings with all those collected by the *śrāvaka*s. What is not shared is, for example, the "inconceivable scripture": its teaching is not shared with the *śrāvaka*s.

Interpretation: The inconceivable scripture is the *Flower Garland,* as the treatise itself points out. Because it only expounds the Distinct Teaching of One Vehicle, it is called "not shared." Understand it accordingly. Scriptures such as the *Four Āgamas Sutras* are also called "not shared," because they only expound the ignorant two vehicles teachings. Scriptures such as the *Larger Prajñāpāramitā Sutra* gather together the assemblies of the three vehicles and thoroughly expound the Dharmas of the three vehicles so that they completely gain the benefits of the three vehicles. Thus, they are called "shared."

Within this view, the lesser teachings that are found within the Great Vehicle are not the ignorant teaching; the greater teachings that are found within the Lesser Vehicle are not the One Vehicle. Based on these three doctrines (ignorant, three/Great, and One) the Liang *Summary of the Great Vehicle* states:

> There are three kinds of the proper establishment of the Dharma: One, the Lesser Vehicle. Two, the three vehicles. Three, the One Vehicle. The third is the highest. It is most truly called "the proper establishment."

If there is anyone who says that at the time of teaching such scriptures as the *Larger Prajñāpāramitā Sutra* the One Voice was differently understood, producing lesser results, and so there are three vehicles—then, at the time of teaching the *Flower Garland,* why was it not differently understood to produce the lesser results? And at the time of the *Incremental Āgama Sutra* and so on, why was it not differently understood, producing a greater result? Thus, you should know that each of the three tenets is distinct. The principle of this is not to be doubted.

The second [view on the division into three vehicles][10] is that the Great Vehicle, the Middle Vehicle, and the Lesser Vehicle are the three vehicles.
479c This has three significances. One is that the One Vehicle is fused together with the Great Vehicle, [and added to the Middle and Lesser to make three]. [Two is that the] ignorant teaching is unified with the Lesser Vehicle [and added to the Great and the One], and so there are only three. This can be understood from the principles of their teachings. This is as distinguished from the perspective of the One Vehicle. Three is that within the Great Vehicle itself there are three vehicles, as explained above.

The third [view] is that within the Lesser Vehicle there are also three; as in the commentaries on the Lesser [Vehicle scriptures] which have the *śrāvaka* Dharma, the *pratyekabuddha* Dharma, and the Buddha-Dharma. Among these, the Buddha-Dharma only differs from the other two vehicles in the practices of compassion, altruism, and so on.

iv. Division into Four Vehicles

The fourth section clarifies that there may also be four vehicles; in this there are also three kinds of significance. The first maintains that the One Vehicle and the three vehicles are the four. This separates the One to differentiate it from the three, and unites the two kinds of *śrāvaka*s. The second maintains that the One Vehicle, the three vehicles, the Lesser Vehicle, and the human and heavenly vehicles are four. This is meant to be a comprehensive analysis. The third maintains that the three vehicles and the human and heavenly vehicles are the four. This can be understood according to the above.

v. Division into Five Vehicles

The fifth section clarifies that there may also be five vehicles; there are also three kinds [of this view]. The first maintains that the One Vehicle, the three vehicles, and the Lesser Vehicle are the five. The second maintains that the three vehicles, the human vehicle, and the heavenly vehicle are the five. The third maintains that the buddha vehicle and the two vehicles, along with the heavenly and Brahmā vehicles, are the five. You can understand them all according to my explanation.

vi. Division into Innumerable Vehicles

The sixth maintains that there may also be innumerable vehicles. This refers to the all-inclusive Dharma gate. Thus, the [*Flower Garland*] *Sutra* states, "Within one world, those who hear the teachings of One Vehicle may understand there to be two, three, four, five, or even innumerable vehicles." It is referring to this. Here I conclude the above discussion of the divisions of the vehicles.

2. Fusing of Root and Ramifications (Unity of Vehicles)

The second section is the fusing of root and ramifications. This is the Common Teaching that all vehicles interfuse without duality, as a singular Dharma universe. In this there are two gates. One is the gate of submerging the provisional and returning to the ultimately real. This is the One Vehicle teaching. The other is the gate of seizing the ultimate while establishing the provisional; that is, the teachings of the three vehicles. The former does not destroy the provisional teachings, but only submerges them. That the three vehicles are identified with the One Vehicle does not obstruct the three. The latter does not differentiate the ultimately real from the provisional, but identifies it with the provisional. That the One Vehicle is in fact the three does not obstruct the One. For these reasons the One and three interfuse and encompass one another, and their essence is without duality.

Question: If that is so, then the two gates would be completely equal. How can you continue to teach the existence of both the provisional and the ultimately real?

Reply: Because the doctrinal gates are different, the provisional and the ultimately real are preserved forever. Because the true principle is universally pervasive, they are entirely nondual. The reason is that the provisional must necessarily arise in total dependence upon the ultimately real. Thus, although you seize the ultimate, the ultimately real is not diminished. However, the manifestation of the ultimately real does not necessarily totally depend on the provisional. So, when you eliminate the provisional, the provisional is not established. Therefore, the three vehicles are in fact One; although they are both preserved and destroyed, finally they must be exhausted. The One Vehicle is in fact three; although it is both hidden and manifest, in the end it is eternally inexhaustible.

From this melding and fusion, we can extrapolate four logical possibilities. (1) It may be that there is only One Vehicle, as maintained by the Distinct Teaching. (2) It may be that there are only three vehicles, as in the teachings of the three vehicles, because they do not know of the One. (3) Or, it may be that there are both the One and the three, as in the Common Teaching. (4) It
480a may be that there is neither One nor three, as in the above-described ocean of result (i.e., buddhahood). Among these four logical possibilities, to follow through any one gate is to completely receive the totality of the Dharma. Therefore, the many vehicles may or may not exist, and they do not obstruct one another. Reflect on this accordingly and you will understand. Other interpretations of the vehicles, their names, and their essence will be explained separately. This concludes the foregoing section on the establishment of the One Vehicle.

II. The Benefits of the Doctrines

Second gate: The benefits of the doctrines.[11] This gate has two parts. First I expound the distinctions among the doctrines; then I clarify the distinctions among the benefits.

A. Distinctions Among the Doctrines

Within the former, there are also two parts. First I will show the characteristics they display; then I will analyze and synthesize them.

1. Characteristics Displayed

Within the first there are three significances. One is that the great white ox carts on the open ground have a doctrine of their own. That is, the teaching of the interdependent arising of principal and attendants in its manifold infinitude is completely expressed, as in the *Flower Garland Sutra.* This corresponds to the Distinct Teaching of One Vehicle. Two is that each of the three carts by the gate has a doctrine (i.e., teaching and significance) of its own. That is, what it shows within the mundane world is its teaching, and how it causes beings to leave the mundane is its significance. However, the doctrine is in fact undivided. This corresponds to the three vehicles teachings, as in the *Sutra on the Explication of Underlying Meaning* and the explanations of the Yogācārins. Three takes the three carts by the gate to be the opening of teaching by skillful means, while the great white ox carts given separately beyond the triple world are a means to show the true and ultimate significance. This corresponds to the Common Teaching of One Vehicle, as in the *Lotus Sutra.*

2. Analysis and Synthesis

The second part, analysis and synthesis, has two parts: first specification, then integration.

i. Specification

Within specification, the One Vehicle and the three vehicles each have three logical possibilities. As to the three possibilities of the three vehicles, either (1) both teaching and significance exist—the perspective of the three vehicles according to their own tenets; (2) only the teaching exists, not the significance—the perspective of the Common Teaching of One Vehicle; or (3) neither teaching nor significance exist—the perspective of the Distinct Teaching of One Vehicle, as it (i.e., the Distinct Teaching) is what they truly intend.

As to the three possibilities of the One Vehicle, either (1) both teaching and significance exist—the perspective of the One Vehicle itself; (2) only the significance exists, not the teaching—the perspective of the Common Teaching; or (3) neither teaching nor significance exist—the perspective of the three vehicles, as for them the [One Vehicle's] infinite doctrine is concealed.

ii. Integration

Next is integration. Either teaching and significance are both seen as just teaching, which is the case when the three vehicles are seen from the point of view of the One Vehicle; or teaching and significance are both seen as just significance, which is the case when the One Vehicle is seen from the point of view of the three vehicles; or both of these possibilities exist—the perspective of the Common Teaching; or all include both teaching and significance, each according to the differences in their own tenets.

B. Distinctions among the Benefits

The second part clarifies the distinctions among the benefits offered; within it there are three parts. First, it may be that the only benefit offered is that the beings within the mundane world are made to attain the supramundane; this they take to be the ultimate achievement. This is the perspective of the tenets of the three vehicles, and as in the Yogācārin arguments.

Second, it may be that the benefit offered is that the beings beyond the triple world are made to attain the supra-supramundane, as a means to the ultimate goal. Here there are two kinds. If they first attain their exit by means of the three vehicles, and later by skillful means attain the One Vehicle, this is taught as the fusion of the three vehicles and the One Vehicle. This is included in the benefits of the Common Teaching. It is also called "the teaching
480b of converting the three into the One." This is as taught in the *Lotus Sutra.* Or, if they first complete understanding and practice in the One Vehicle, and later verify that Dharma in supramundane lifetimes, this is included in the Distinct Teaching of One Vehicle. This is as taught in the "Lesser Characteristics" chapter of the *Flower Garland Sutra.*

Third, it may be that the two benefits—supramundane and supra-supramundane—are extended to both kinds of beings—those within and beyond the triple world. This also has two kinds. If they first are enticed to exit by the three vehicles and later are made to attain the One Vehicle, this is three and One harmonized to encompass the two kinds of beings and the two benefits. This belongs to the Common Teaching, as the *Lotus Sutra* explains. If they see and hear the teachings within the mundane world, attain the Dharma in the supramundane, and fully realize it in the supra-supramundane; or if they both see and hear, and understand and practice the teachings within the world, only understand and practice in the supramundane, and only realize entry into the buddha realm in the supra-supramundane—these belong to the Distinct Teaching of One Vehicle. This is as taught in the *Flower Garland Sutra.*

III. Classification of the Teachings, Ancient and Recent

Third gate: I will narrate the establishment of the classifications of the teachings, ancient and recent. As the gates of teaching established by all the worthy teachers of ancient and recent times are diverse and different from each other, I will summarize by presenting ten masters[12] to serve as our turtle shells and mirrors.

A. Bodhiruci

Bodhiruci established the teaching of One Voice relying on such scriptures as the *Vimalakīrti-sūtra.* He said that all of the sacred teachings are one voice, one taste, one rainfall, and so on. But the capacities and practices of the multitude of living beings are not the same, so beings understand the Dharma differently, resulting in many kinds. If we focus on their origin, there is only the teaching of the one perfect voice of the Tathāgata. As the [*Vimalakīrti-*]*sūtra* states, "Buddha expounds the Dharma with one voice. Living beings attain understanding according to their kind."

B. Hu, et al.

Dharma Master Hu and others established the two teachings of Gradual and Sudden, relying on such scriptures as the *Laṅkāvatāra-sūtra.* They said that because first the Lesser Vehicle was studied and later the Great Vehicle arose, the Great Vehicle arose out of the Lesser, so it is called "gradual." But also, the Great and Lesser Vehicles are both set forth simultaneously, as in the teaching of the *Nirvana Sutra* and others. In the case of the directly advancing bodhisattvas, the Great Vehicle does not come out of the Lesser, and so it is called "sudden." Or, it may be called "sudden" because there is no Lesser Vehicle, as in the *Flower Garland Sutra.* Dharma Master Yuan and many other venerables of later times agree with this explanation.

C. Guangtong

Vinaya Master Guangtong (also known as Huiguang) established three kinds of teachings: Gradual, Sudden, and Perfect. The meanings of Master Guangtong's formulation are as follows.

One: For those of immature capacity, first [the Buddha] explained impermanence, and later explained permanence; first he explained emptiness, and later the profound and subtle significance of nonemptiness; he taught in this way by gradual progression, so it is named "Gradual Teaching."

Two: For those of mature capacities, the entire Buddha-Dharma is expounded completely in one Dharma gate; permanence and impermanence, emptiness and nonemptiness all are taught at the same time without gradual progression, so it is named the "Sudden Teaching."

Three: For those most accomplished practitioners who have nearly ascended to the buddha realm, he explains the unimpeded liberation of the Tathāgata, the absolute perfection of the ultimate ocean of result, the esoteric Dharma gate of complete autonomy; so, it is named "Perfect." It refers to this very sutra [the *Flower Garland*]. Later, Guangtong's disciples, including such venerables as Master Zuntong (also known as Tanzun), all received his tenets and were in agreement with this teaching.

D. Dayan, et al.

480c The Dharma Master of Dayan Temple (also known as Tanyin) and other venerables of his age established the teaching of the Four Tenets, thereby gathering together all the sacred teachings of the Buddha's time. One is the tenet of causes and conditions, as in the Sarvāstivāda and other branches of the Lesser Vehicle. Two is the tenet of name-only, as in the Satyasiddhi and Sautrāntika schools. Three is the tenet of nonreality, as taught in all the branches of the Perfection of Wisdom schools; that is, the principle of emptiness illuminates the nonreality of all dharmas, and so on. Four is the tenet of true reality; the *Nirvana* and *Flower Garland* sutras illuminate the true principles of buddha-nature and the Dharma realm.

E. Hushen

The Dharma Master of Hushen Temple (also known as Zigui) established five kinds of teachings. Three kinds are the same as Master Dayan's, discussed above. The fourth is called "the tenet of the true." As in the *Nirvana* and other sutras, it illuminates the true principle of buddha-nature and so on. The fifth is called "the tenet of the Dharma realm." As in the *Flower Garland,* it illuminates the Dharma realm as the Dharma gate of unimpeded autonomy, and so on.

F. Qishe

Dharma Master Qishe (also known as Anlin) established six tenets. The first two are the same as Master Dayan's. The third is called "the tenet of nonreality." It clarifies that all Great Vehicle doctrines teach in common that all dharmas are illusory transformations. Fourth is called "the tenet of the true," and it illuminates the principle of the emptiness of all dharmas. Fifth is "the tenet of permanence." It clarifies that the merits of the true principle, which are as numerous as the grains of sand of the Ganges River, are eternal,[13] and other such significances. Sixth is called "the tenet of perfection," and it illuminates the freedom of the Dharma realm, the unimpededness of interdependent arising, and the perfect provision of meritorious functioning. These are the Dharma gates of Huayan.

G. Si of Nanyue and Zhizhe of Tiantai

Meditation Masters Si (also known as Huisi) of Nanyue and Zhizhe (also known as Zhiyi) of Tiantai established four kinds of teachings to encompass all the sacred teachings of the Buddha's time that have flowed to the east [from India].

One is called the "Three Treasuries of Teachings" (i.e., the Tripiṭaka); this refers to the Lesser Vehicle. They quoted from the *Lotus Sutra,* which states, "Do not become close with the Lesser Vehicle scholars of the three treasuries." Also, in the *Treatise on the Larger Prajñāpāramitā Sutra* it is taught that the Lesser Vehicle is the teachings of the three treasuries, while the Great Vehicle is the teachings of the Mahayana treasuries.

Two is called the "Shared Teachings." That is, in many of the Great Vehicle scriptures, it is taught that the benefits of the Dharma are shared by the beings of all three vehicles; and as in the *Larger Prajñāpāramitā Sutra,* the stage of philosophical reasoning and the rest of the ten bodhisattva stages are shared with those of both Great and Lesser Vehicles.

Three is called the "Distinct Teaching"; namely, those principles found in the Great Vehicle scriptures that are not shared with the Lesser Vehicle. 481a

Four is called the "Perfect Teaching"; that is, the absolute freedom of the Dharma realm, complete with every inexhaustible Dharma gate, where one is everything and everything is one, and so on. This is the teaching of the *Flower Garland Sutra.*

H. Min of Jiangnan

Dharma Master Min (also known as Famin) of Jiangnan established two teachings. One is the scriptures of Śākyamuni. They are called the "inflected (i.e., indirect) teachings," because they accord with the spiritual abilities of practitioners to strategically destroy their attachment. These are scriptures such as the *Nirvana Sutra.* Two is the scriptures of Vairocana. These are called the "level (i.e., direct) teachings," because they accord with the nature of Dharma, teaching with absolute autonomy. This is Huayan.

I. Yun of Guangzhai Temple

Dharma Master Yun (also known as Fayun) of Guangzhai Temple of the Liang dynasty established the teaching of four vehicles; namely, the three carts by the gate are the three vehicles, and the great white ox carts given at the crossroads are the fourth. This is because the ox cart by the gate, like the goat and deer carts, is not obtained; the further significance of this is the same as in the discussion above. Meditation Master Xinxing, based on these tenets, established two teachings: One Vehicle and three vehicles. As to the three vehicles, they have distinct understandings and distinct practices, as well as the differences among the three vehicles; and its practitioners are those who first study the Lesser Vehicle and later turn to the Great Vehicle. As to the One Vehicle, it refers to the comprehensive understanding and comprehensive practice that is found only in this One Vehicle; it is indeed the Dharma gate of Huayan, and its practitioners are the directly advancing bodhisattvas.

J. Xuanzang

The Dharma Master of the Three Treasuries, Xuanzang of the Tang dynasty, relied on the *Sutra on the Explication of Underlying Meaning,* the *Sutra of Golden Light,* and the *Treatise on the Yogācāra Stages* to establish three kinds of teachings. These are the three aspects of the wheel of the Dharma. One is called "the turning of the Dharma wheel"; that is, the first period, when Śākyamuni Buddha turned the Dharma wheel of the four noble truths in Deer Park. This is the Dharma of the Lesser Vehicle. Second is called "the illumination of the Dharma wheel"; that is, the middle period, when the concealed profundities, such as the emptiness of all dharmas, emerged within the Great Vehicle. Third is called "the confirmation of the Dharma wheel"; that is, the latter period, when the completely elucidated intentions of the Great Vehicle, such as the principles of three natures[14] and the nonemptiness of thusness are taught. These three aspects of the Dharma wheel only include the Lesser Vehicle and, of the three vehicles, the Early Teaching and the Final Teaching. It does not include the Distinct Teaching of One Vehicle. Why is that? Because the *Flower Garland Sutra* was taught during the first period, but it is not of the Lesser Vehicle; "the confirmation of the Dharma wheel" is taught during the latter period, but it is not Huayan. Thus, Xuanzang's classification does not include the Dharma gate of Huayan.

K. Summary Explanation

The venerable ones who founded the above ten schools of thought were all heroically awakened leaders of the Dharma, peerless in their own times, history's shining examples of practitioners who attained incalculable rank. Only those such as Meditation Masters Huisi and Zhizhe were of the miraculous spiritual sensibility to ascend to high rank; their memory of hearing the Dharma at Vulture Peak remains today. Various other spiritual communications are extensively recounted in the *Biographies of Monks.* As to Dharma Master Yun, when he founded his tradition and lectured on the *Lotus Sutra,* flowers rained down from heaven in response. Such miracles are recorded in the *Biographies of Monks.* The practices and understandings of the rest of these Dharma masters likewise surpassed their contemporaries. These are also found in the *Biographies of Monks.*

It is not the case that all these venerable masters enjoyed creating differ- 481b
ences; rather, by completely and thoroughly investigating the three treasuries, they saw that the differences were numerous and couldn't do otherwise than analyze them. Following each of the teachings upon which they respectively relied, they founded traditions that endeavored to preserve and integrate the different teachings. They made firm doubts and large blockages become as clear as ice melted into flowing water. The differences in the sacred teachings each fit together perfectly [to form a single whole].

IV. Divisions of the Teachings and Analysis of the Tenets

Fourth gate: The divisions of the teachings and analysis of the various tenets. Within this there are two parts. First, the teachings are divided according to their Dharmas; there are five kinds of teachings. Then the tenets are analyzed according to their principles; there are ten tenets.

A. Teachings Divided according to their Dharmas

Of the innumerable differences to be found in the sacred teachings, only five are most essential: the teaching of the Lesser Vehicle; the Early Teaching of the Great Vehicle; the Final Teaching; the Sudden Teaching; and the Perfect Teaching. The first [Lesser Vehicle] is the two vehicles of the ignorant teaching; the last is the Distinct Teaching of One Vehicle. The name of the latter comes from a passage in the last chapter of the [*Flower Garland*] *Sutra,* in which the teaching expounded to the prince named Good Discipline is called "the sutra of perfect fulfillment."

The three teachings in the middle [Early, Final, and Sudden] have their own three significances. First, they may be combined as one, since they are all of the three vehicles teaching. Considered this way, they all serve the three kinds of practitioners to attain their respective goals, as in the passages explained above.

Second, they may be divided into two, which are called Gradual and Sudden. Because in the Early and Final Teachings, the understandings and practices they have are within the verbal teachings, their ranks are attained in order, cause and result develop sequentially, and there is a progression from subtle to obvious; so Early and Final can both be called "gradual." The *Laṅkāvatāra-sūtra,* in reference to this, states, "Gradual is like the *amalā* fruit, ripening gradually, not suddenly." As to the Sudden Teaching, in it verbal teachings are suddenly severed, original nature is suddenly manifest, and understanding and practice are suddenly accomplished. Not one thought is produced: just this is to be equal to Buddha. In reference to this, the *Laṅkāvatāra-sūtra* states, "Sudden is like the image in a mirror, appearing suddenly and not gradually." This is because all dharmas are originally true of themselves, and depend neither on verbal teachings nor on contemplative wisdom. This is Vimalakīrti manifesting nonduality by remaining silent. Also, in the treatise on the *Accumulation of Jewels Sutra* there is a mention of a *Sutra of the Sudden Teaching;* its name was established according to this.

Third, they may be divided into three, when the Early and Final teachings are separated out from within the Gradual, as they are in the above discussion of [Xuanzang's interpretation of] the *Sutra on the Explication of Underlying Meaning* and other texts: [Early and Final] are the latter two aspects of the three aspects of the wheel of Dharma. According with the significance of this, the *Dharma Drum Sutra* maintains that the gate of emptiness is the Early Teaching and the gate of nonemptiness is the Final Teaching. Thus, that sutra states:

> Kāśyapa addressed the Buddha, saying, "All the Mahayana scriptures offer abundant teachings on the significance of emptiness." The Buddha told Kāśyapa, "All the scriptures on emptiness are teachings with remainder. Only this sutra is the unexcelled teaching, for it is not a teaching with

remainder. Indeed, Kāśyapa, it is like King Prasenajit, who in the eleventh month of the year always prepares a great alms feast for all, first feeding the hungry ghosts, orphans, and beggars, then offering to the *śramaṇa*s and brahmans. There are delicious foods of various flavors to accord with 481c
their varied desires. The buddhas, the world-honored ones, are also like this. In accord with the diverse desires of various living beings, they expound diverse teachings of the scriptures. If there are various living beings who are idle and inattentive, who transgress the precepts of moral conduct, who do not strive in practice, who abandon the marvelous canon (i.e., the Mahayana) of the eternally abiding *tathāgatagarbha*—they will still take pleasure in cultivating and studying the diverse scriptures' teachings on emptiness," and so forth.

Interpretation: The perspective that maintains the principle of emptiness with remainder is called the Early Teaching, and the perspective that maintains the marvelous canon of the eternally abiding *tathāgatagarbha* is called the Final Teaching. In the *Treatise on the Awakening of Faith in the Great Vehicle,* the perspective from the gate of the Sudden Teaching is shown as the thusness that severs language, while the perspective from the gate of the Gradual Teaching is explained as the true thusness that relies on language. Reliance on language includes the perspectives of both the Early and Final teachings, which respectively teach the thusness of emptiness and the thusness of nonemptiness.

This concludes the division of teachings according to their Dharmas. As to the significances attributed to their Dharmas, it is discussed separately below.

B. Analysis of Tenets according to True Principles

Second, the tenets are analyzed by means of true principles. There are ten tenets.

1. Existence of Self and Dharmas

The first is the tenet that self and dharmas both exist. There are two versions of this teaching. One is the human and heavenly vehicles. The other is the Vātsīputrīya school and others of the Lesser Vehicle. They established three groupings of dharmas: created dharmas, uncreated dharmas, and dharmas that are neither created nor uncreated. The first two groupings are [objective] dharmas and the latter grouping is self. [Thus, they maintain the tenet that self and dharmas both exist.] They also established the five treasuries of dharmas: past, future, present, the uncreated, and the inexpressible. This latter one is precisely self, because self cannot be expressed in terms of created or uncreated.

2. Existence of Dharmas but Nonexistence of Self

Second is the tenet that dharmas exist but self does not exist, as in the Sarvāstivāda and others like it. They teach that all dharmas are included within two kinds (i.e., modes of existence): name and form. Or, they are all included in four: the three times—past, present, and future—and the uncreated. Or, in five: mind, mental functioning, form, factors that don't correspond to the preceding three, and the uncreated. Thus, all dharmas without exception really exist.

3. Dharmas are Devoid of Past and Future

Third is the tenet that dharmas have neither past nor future existence, as in the Mahāsāṃghika and the like. They teach the existence of only present and uncreated dharmas, because in the past and future essence and function do not exist.

4. Both Nominal and Real in the Present

Fourth is the tenet that the present has both nominal and real dharmas, as in the Prajñaptivāda and others. They teach that there is no past and future, and that all the dharmas of the present time are real insofar as they are aggregates, but are merely nominal in terms of cognition and sensation. Whether dharmas are nominal or real is not fixed, but accords with the situation. The *Treatise on the True Attainment* and other texts, and certain masters of Sautrāntika, are also of this category.

5. Mundane as False but True as Real

Fifith is the tenet that the mundane world is false and the truth [of enlightenment] is real, as in the Lokottaravāda and the like. All the dharmas of the
482a mundane world are nominal, because they are delusions. The dharmas of the supramundane are real, because they are not delusions.

6. Nominal Existence of all Dharmas

Sixth is the tenet that all dharmas exist in name only, as in the Ekavyāvahārika and the like. Self and dharmas, everything, only exist as provisional names, and all are without essence. You should understand that this view is found throughout the early phase of the initial teaching.

7. Emptiness of all Dharmas

Seventh is the tenet that everything is empty, as in the Early Teaching of the Great Vehicle. It teaches that all dharmas are truly empty. This is beyond deluded sentience, where there is no false discrimination. This is in the Prajñāpāramitā teachings.

8. True Quality of Nonemptiness

Eighth is the tenet that the true essence of all things is not empty, as in the Final Teaching. Various scriptures teach that all dharmas do have this true thusness, the real virtue of the *tathāgatagarbha.* They have their own essence, and are completely endowed with the virtue of true nature.

9. Severance of Both Subject and Object

Ninth is the tenet that characteristics (i.e., of objects of perception, dharmas) and perception [of characteristics] (i.e., a perceiving self) are both severed, as in the Sudden Teaching. It manifests the principle that severs language—like what is manifested in the silence of Vimalakīrti, and so on. Understand this accordingly.

10. Perfect Illumination Endowed with Virtues

Tenth is the tenet of perfect illumination endowed with all virtues, as in the Distinct Teaching of One Vehicle, the Dharma gate that manifests the infinite freedom of the interdependent arising of principal and attendants in full.

V. Analysis and Synthesis of Vehicles and Teachings

Fifth gate: Analysis and synthesis of the relationships among the vehicles and teachings. There are three parts within this. First, analysis and synthesis from the perspective of teachings. Second, encompassing the vehicles within the teachings. Third, all the teachings mutually include each other.

A. Analysis and Synthesis from the Perspective of Teachings

As to the perspectives of the teachings: although these five kinds of teachings mutually interfuse and pervade each other, still, my analysis yields five distinct significances.

One, they may be combined as one. That is, the root teaching and its ramifications are fused into a single great teaching of skillful means.

Two, they may be divided into two: the root teaching, that is, the Distinct Teaching of One Vehicle, which is the root of all teachings; and the ramified teachings, that is, the three vehicles and Lesser Vehicle, which spread out [from the root teaching]. These two are also called the ultimate and the expedient, because from the point of view of the One Vehicle, it's clear that the three vehicles and the Lesser Vehicle are all skillful means.

Three, they may be divided into three: the teachings of the One Vehicle, the three vehicles, and the Lesser Vehicle. Within the expedient teachings, the two vehicles of the ignorant teaching are separated out.

Four, they may be divided into four: the Lesser Vehicle, the Gradual, the Sudden, and the Perfect. They can be divided in this way because the Early and Final teachings are both within the verbal teachings.

Five, they may be separated into five, as explained above.

B. Encompassing the Vehicles within the Teachings

As to using the teachings to encompass the vehicles, there are two aspects. First, the One Vehicle accords with the teachings in five ways. One is as the Distinct Teaching of One Vehicle, and so forth. Two is as the Common Teaching of One Vehicle, and so forth. Three is as the One Vehicle that severs conceptualization, as in the *Laṅkāvatāra-sūtra;* this is the Sudden Teaching. Four takes the universality of buddha-nature to be the One Vehicle; this is the perspective of the Final Teaching, and so forth. Five is as the One Vehicle of esoteric intention, as in the eight implicit intentions of the teachings; this is the perspective of the Early Teaching, and so forth.

Second, in clarifying how the three vehicles accord with the teachings, there are also five ways. One, the three are within the Lesser Vehicle; that is, the beginnings are different, but the ends are the same, because they all reach the stage of arhat. Two, the three are within the Early and Final teachings; the beginnings and ends are both different, because they enter into their respective quiescences. Three, the three are within the Final Teaching; the beginnings and ends are the same, and all become buddhas. Four, the three
482b are within the Sudden Teaching; beginnings and ends are abolished, and so forth. Five, the three are within the Common Teaching; the beginnings and ends are all the same. "Your practices are the bodhisattva way," [as stated in the *Lotus Sutra*] and so on, and so forth.

C. The Various Teachings Mutually Include Each Other

As to the ways in which the various teachings mutually include each other, there are two gates: the gate of the root containing the ramifications, and the gate of returning to the root by way of its ramifications.

As to the former gate, within the Perfect Teaching there may be only the one Perfect Teaching, because all the characteristics of the others are exhausted; or there may be all five teachings, because the Perfect Teaching encompasses them all as skillful means. In the Sudden Teaching, there may be only the one Sudden Teaching, also because the characteristics of the others are exhausted; or it may contain four teachings, because it too encompasses skillful means. In the mature teaching, there may be one or three. In the initial teaching, there may be one or two. In the Lesser Vehicle there is only one. You should understand all of this according to the above.

The latter gate is that of returning to the root by way of its ramifications. Within the Lesser Vehicle, there may be one, because it is based on its own tenets; or there may be five, as it is considered to be skillful means within the four later teachings. In the initial teaching there may be one, as by its own tenets, or four, as the three later teachings all have it serve as skillful means. In the mature teaching there may be one or three. In the Sudden Teaching there may be one or two. In the Perfect Teaching there is only one. You should understand this accordingly.

Such are the distinctions and interrelationships of the doctrinal principles that the various teachings above have clarified; reflect on them accordingly. Such are the numerous logical possibilities of the roots and ramifications of the many teachings, tied together to form a great net of teaching. The skillful means of the Great Sage continually nurture beings' opportunities for enlightenment, so that all are completely accommodated. Thus, this [*Flower Garland*] *Sutra* states, "Cast widely this great net of teaching, all the way across the ocean of samsara! Pull out humans, celestial beings, and dragons, and place them on the shore of nirvana!" This is what it means.

VI. The Sequence of the Emergence of the Teachings

Sixth gate: The sequence of the emergence of the teachings. Within this there are two parts. The first part clarifies the root teaching that accords with

Dharma. The second part clarifies the ramified teachings designed for practitioners.

A. Root Teaching in Accord with the Dharma

As to the first part, it is the Distinct Teaching of One Vehicle. It is what the Buddha taught in the second week after he first accomplished the Way, seated under the *bodhi* tree. Like the sun just coming up and first illuminating the tallest mountains, while remaining within the ocean-seal *samādhi* he expounded the infinitely manifold Dharma gate in which the interdependent arising of principal and attendants is complete, all-pervasive and autonomous, and inclusive of the realms of Indra's net and subtle particulars, throughout the nine times and the ten aspects of time. At that moment, all causes and results, principles and phenomena, and so on—all earlier and later Dharma gates, even such future phenomena as the circulating of buddha relics among the believers of later ages—were all together simultaneously manifest. What is the reason? It is because of the absolute autonomy of his rolling up and unrolling the teachings.[15] Unrolled, it is found in the nine times; rolled up, it exists in a single moment. This rolling up is precisely unrolling, and unrolling is also precisely rolling up.

What is the reason? It is because they interdependently arise together as one. It is because of their characteristic nonduality. The [*Flower Garland*] *Sutra* originally states, "Established within a single mote of dust are the three periods of time and all the Buddha's activities." It also states, "Within a single thought are all eight periods of the Buddha's life, even his nirvana and the
482c circulation of his relics." This is extensively explained in the sutra. Thus, according to this universal Dharma, all Dharmas of the Buddha were taught together in the second week. He taught at one time, in sequence; he taught sequentially, at one time. It is like the printed Dharma of this world: when we read the text, the sentences are in sequence, but as printed text, they are manifest simultaneously. Simultaneity and sequence are not contradictory in principle. You should understand that the principle of the Buddha's first teaching is also like this. Reflect on it accordingly.

B. Ramified Teachings Designed for Practitioners

The second part is the ramified teachings designed for practitioners. This refers to the three vehicles, and has two significances. One, the three vehicles were taught with the One Vehicle at one time but in different places; and two, the three vehicles were taught at different times and in different places. As to the former significance, it is the Common Teaching. The ramifications are not separate from the root; they are formed dependently on the root. As to the latter significance, the characteristics of the root and the ramifications are separate from one another; the ramifications are not one with the root. Each of these significances also has two kinds: the three vehicles and the Lesser Vehicle.

1. Taught at One Time but Different Places

[As to being taught at one time but different places], the *Sutra on the Warrior with the Hidden Tracks* explains that when the Buddha first attained the Way, upon completing the seven days of contemplation, then at Deer Park he adorned his Dharma seat with a multitude of treasures and gathered great assemblies of the three vehicles. A Brahmā king asked for a teaching, so the Buddha turned the wheel of the Dharma to the great benefit of the assemblies of the three vehicles, causing them to attain the Greater and Lesser results, and so on, as is extensively explained in that sutra. The *Larger Prajñāpāramitā Sutra* also states:

> When the Buddha first turned the Dharma wheel of the four noble truths at Deer Park, innumerable beings gave rise to the mind of the *śrāvaka*, innumerable beings gave rise to the mind of the *pratyekabuddha*, and innumerable beings gave rise to the mind of *anuttarā samyaksaṃbodhi* and practiced the six *pāramitā*s. Innumerable bodhisattvas attained tolerance of the understanding of the unproduced nature of dharmas and resided in the first bodhisattva stage, the second stage, and so on up to the tenth stage. Innumerable bodhisattvas in their final lifetime of benefiting beings became buddhas at once.

Interpretation: By means of this evidence from the teachings, you should understand that at the very beginning, in the second week after enlightenment, the Buddha taught the Dharma of the three vehicles simultaneously with the One Vehicle.

Second is the Lesser Vehicle. As the *Mahīśāsaka-vinaya* teaches, "the Buddha first accomplished the way and entered into *samādhi*. After seven days he turned the Dharma wheel at Deer Park." Thus we know that the Lesser Vehicle was also taught at the same time as the One Vehicle. In addition, the *Sutra on Universal Brilliance* states:

> In the second week five hundred merchants, such as Trapuṣa, offered the Buddha roasted grain and honey. The Buddha bestowed on them accounts of their future attainment of buddhahood.

Although the teachings of this sutra are shared with the teachings of the
483a three vehicles, its significance encompasses the Dharmas of the human and heavenly vehicles and was also taught at the same time as the One Vehicle.

Question: So, the times of teaching are same; how are the places of teaching different?

Reply: The Dharma is manifested for the perspectives of times and places, so there must be similarities and differences. Thus, the *Treatise on the Ten Stages* states, "The differences of time and place contrast to demonstrate the excellence of this teaching." Being taught at the same time manifests the Common Teaching. Being taught in a different place shows it is not the Distinct Teaching. As to the Distinct Teaching of One Vehicle being taught under the *bodhi* tree, it is to clarify that this very place of attaining *bodhi* is right where the Tathāgata taught the realized Dharma in accord with the root. It was taught without moving places. The Dharmas of the other three vehicles and so on are taught in different places to clarify that in designing teachings for practitioners of different capacities, changes are made. Moving the place to Deer Park to teach for the sake of practitioners shows that it is not the root teaching.

2. Taught at Different Times and Different Places

The latter significance is that of time and place both being different. Since the other vehicles do not have the same significance as the One Vehicle, the time and place are both distinct. Some Dharma was taught after three weeks, such as the *Lotus Sutra.* Some was taught only after six weeks, such as the *Four-part Vinaya* and the *Sarvāstivāda-vinaya-vibhāṣā.* Some was taught only after seven weeks, such as the *Sutra on Awakening of Practice.* Some was taught only after eight weeks, such as the teachings of *Vinaya in Ten Recitations.* Some was taught after fifty-seven days, as taught in the *Treatise on the Larger Prajñāpāramitā Sutra.* Some Dharma was not taught within a year, but during the second year five people were delivered, as taught in the *Sutra of the Buddha's First Twelve Years.* Someone has interpreted this as follows: "The fifty-seven days of the *Treatise on the Larger Prajñāpāramitā Sutra* are actually fifty seven-day weeks, the same as the one year of the *Sutra of the Buddha's First Twelve Years.*"

You should understand by means of this evidence from the teachings. Neither the teachings of the three vehicles nor those of the Lesser Vehicle were taught in the second week. For this reason, they are to be distinguished from the One Vehicle. They are designed to suit practitioners' capacities. You should understand the rest accordingly.

VII. Determining the Reasons for the Sequence of the Teachings

Seventh gate: Determining the reasons for the sequence of the teachings. It is difficult to understand the differences in the sequences of the various teachings. I will distinguish the reasons summarily in ten gates.

A. Lesser Vehicle Capacities

The spiritual capacities of some living beings are set from start to finish within the Lesser Vehicle of this world. They see the Tathāgata, from his beginning to his attainment of the Way and even his nirvana, as only teaching the Lesser Vehicle; they never see the turning of the Dharma wheel of the Great Vehicle. These are such as those of the various schools of the Lesser Vehicle who are attached to their views and do not have faith in the Great Vehicle.

B. Early Teaching Capacities

The spiritual capacities of some living beings are not set in the Lesser Vehicle of this world. Thus, they can advance into the initial teaching of the Great Vehicle and then their capacities are set. They see the Tathāgata first turning the Dharma wheel of the Lesser Vehicle in order to overturn the various heterodox ways, and later see him turning the Dharma wheel of the initial teaching of the Great Vehicle, which is emptiness, in order to convert the various Lesser Vehicle practitioners. This is as taught in the beginning of the *Treatise on the Middle Way.*

C. Final Teaching Capacities

The spiritual capacities of some living beings are set neither in the Lesser
483b Vehicle nor in the initial teaching of this world. Thus, they can advance into the Final Teaching and then their capacities are set. They see the turning of the Dharma wheel of the Lesser Vehicle in the first period, they see the turning of the Dharma wheel of the teaching of emptiness in the middle period, and they see the turning of the Dharma wheel of the teaching of nonemptiness in the later period. This is what is taught in such scriptures as the *Sutra on the Explication of Underlying Meaning.*

D. Sudden Teaching Capacities

The spiritual capacities of some living beings are not set in the Gradual Teaching. Thus, they can enter the Sudden Teaching, and then their capacities are set. They see that the first teaching shown by use of verbal explanation is not the ultimate, but rather the teaching later manifested by the severing of language is the ultimate. These are such beings as those who take the teaching of the *Vimalakīrti-sūtra,* in which the first thirty-two bodhisattvas and Mañjuśrī explain nonduality in words and then Vimalakīrti manifests it in the severing of words, to be the ultimate.

E. Capacity for Sudden Enlightenment

There are some living beings whose opportunity for sudden awakening has ripened in this world, and so their capabilities are set. They see that the Buddha did not teach a single word, from his starting-out to his attainment of the Way and even his nirvana. This is as taught in the *Laṅkāvatāra-sūtra.* Also, the *Nirvana Sutra* states, "If there is one who knows that the Tathāgata never taught the Dharma, that one is called a bodhisattva of great learning," and so on.

F. Three Vehicles Capacities

The spiritual capacities of some living beings are set in the three vehicles of this world. They see the Buddha teaching the Dharma of the three vehicles, and nothing else, from the beginning to his attainment of nirvana. This is as in the *Sutra on the Warrior with the Hidden Tracks* and the *Larger Prajñāpāramitā Sutra,* discussed above.

G. Capacity for the Common Teaching of One Vehicle

The spiritual capacities of some living beings are not set in the three vehicles of this world, so they are able to advance into the Common Teaching of One Vehicle. They see that the Dharmas of the three vehicles that they acquired all rely on the One Vehicle's inexhaustible arising of teachings; those Dharmas arc formulated as its skillful means, its Āgamas. Thus, all that they have cultivated is entirely converted into the One Vehicle. This is as in "the three returning to the one" [in the *Lotus Sutra*], and as in the three vehicles being taught at the same time as the One Vehicle, as in the citations above.

H. Capacity for the Distinct Teaching of One Vehicle

The spiritual capacities of some living beings are not set in the three vehicles of this world, so they are able to advance into the Distinct Teaching of One Vehicle. They know that the Dharmas of those three vehicles are originally no different from the Distinct Teaching of One Vehicle. How so? Because it is what they intend; because it is not a different matter. This is as in the Common Teaching of the *Lotus Sutra.*

I. Capacity of Samantabhadra

There are some living beings who have the full spiritual capacity of Samantabhadra in this world. They see that all the Dharmas of the Tathāgata, from the first accomplishment of the Way to the attainment of nirvana, are all within the first time of teaching, the ocean-seal *samādhi* of the second week, when in absolute autonomy he taught the repletion of the infinitely manifold interdependent arising of principal and attendants and the inexhaustible realms of Indra's net and of subtle particulars. Originally there was no teaching of the Dharmas of three vehicles or Lesser Vehicles to be seen. This is as in the Distinct Teaching of the *Flower Garland Sutra.* This is taught from the perspective of
the previous lifetime of seeing and hearing and the present lifetime of under- 483c
standing and practice in Samantabhadra's aspect of the teaching.

J. Already Accomplished

There are some living beings who have fulfilled the lifetime of understanding and practice in the Distinct Teaching of One Vehicle and have already realized entry into the ocean of result. They see the various teachings described above to be formed according to conditions from the infinite ocean of true nature, and they see that they are not a different matter [than the One Vehicle]. Thus, the various teachings are the universal illumination of the rich virtues of the infinite ocean of result, difficult to conceive, truly the inexpressible of the inexpressible. This is taught from the perspective of the extent of the realization that is entered into via the One Vehicle. The rest can be understood by this standard.

VIII. Comparison of their Formulations

Eighth gate: Comparing the formulations of the teachings. Now, the differences among these teachings are very many. I will summarize them in ten gates in order to manifest the infinitude of their differentiation. What are these ten differences?

A. Difference in Times

First is the difference in times. This One Vehicle must be taught in the second week of the first period, like the sun rising to first shine on the highest mountains. Thus, the *Treatise* [*on the Ten Stages*] states, "Because this is the most excellent Dharma, it is taught in the first period and at the most excellent place." But if this is so, "then why wasn't it taught in the first week? This was due to the Buddha contemplating the activity of causes and conditions [in order to become enlightened for the benefit of others]," as elucidated in that treatise. Moreover, this very time of teaching, because of Indra's net and so on, encompasses all times. Whether before or after incalculable *kalpa*s, the parameters of future and past are both encompassed within this single time. The teachings of the three vehicles are not so, because in order to accord with the capacities of practitioners and suit their times, their times are not fixed. Sometimes before and sometimes after, they are not taught at the one time that incorporates all *kalpa*s.

B. Difference in Locations

Second is the difference in places. This One Vehicle must be taught under the *bodhi* tree that is adorned with the multitude of treasures in the ocean of the lotus flower treasury worlds. This location encompasses the seven places and the eight assemblies, and even all the inexpressibly inexpressible oceans of worlds are within it, because this one place encompasses all places. Thus, the Buddha does not move from the tree of the Way even while ascending the six heavens: this is its significance. Furthermore, Indra's net pervades these flower treasury worlds, so this is true of every mote of dust within them. In this place that accords with the Dharma realm, the Buddha teaches the One Vehicle Dharma gate that accords with the Dharma realm. But the three vehicles are not so. Their Dharmas are taught under trees in the *sahā* world and such places, and they do not have the teaching of the one place that is identical to all places.

Question: If so, why are the *Sutra on the Buddha Stage* and such scriptures then taught in the Pure Land? 484a

Reply: Those scriptures only state that there are brilliant palaces in which the eighteen kinds of perfection [of the Buddha's *saṃbhogakāya* (reward body)] are complete, but they do not specifically indicate the kingdom of Magadha and so on. Because they teach the virtue of the buddha stage for the sake of those bodhisattvas in the stages, they teach that it exists in the enjoyment land beyond the triple world. This is taught in the Final Teaching of the three vehicles and the Common Teaching of One Vehicle. As to this Huayan teaching, however, it is said to be taught in the kingdom of Magadha that is within the flower treasury worlds, and so on. It is not said to be within the *sahā* world, and yet neither is it said to be beyond the triple world. Thus, we know it is distinct. You should understand the other significances accordingly.

C. Difference in Principals

Third is the difference in principals (i.e., sovereigns). With reference to this One Vehicle, the principal figure is necessarily Vairocana Buddha of the ten buddha bodies and their infinite teachings throughout the three times. As the "Samantabhadra's Practice" chapter of the *Flower Garland Sutra* states, "Buddhas teach, bodhisattvas teach, *kṣatriya*s teach, all living beings teach, everything of the three times teaches," and so on. This is not the same as the three vehicles' teachings of the principal figures being the transformation body and the enjoyment body. Understand the other significances accordingly.

D. Difference in Assemblies

Fourth is the difference in assemblies. That is, the One Vehicle scriptures begin by only listing assemblies of bodhisattvas such as Samantabhadra, and various divine kings of the buddha realms. It is not the same in the three vehicles scriptures, which sometimes have assemblies of only *śrāvaka*s and sometimes have the two assemblies of the Lesser and Great Vehicles.

Question: If so, for what reason does the eighth assembly [of the *Flower Garland Sutra*] include the *śrāvaka*s?

Reply: The reasons for which *śrāvaka*s are listed in that assembly are two. One, it illuminates the Dharma by making a contrast, manifesting the surpassing profundity of the Dharma of the One Vehicle by showing those *śrāvaka*s to be as if deaf and blind. Two, the six thousand *bhikṣu*s gathered by Mañjuśrī when he left the assembly are not those previously included in the assembly. All of these were already within the three vehicles. This teaching was made to cause beings to convert to the One Vehicle.

E. Difference in Sources

Fifth is the difference in sources. The arising of this One Vehicle teaching is necessarily based on the Buddha's ocean-seal *samādhi* from whence it came. This is different from the three vehicles, which are based on what came out of the wisdom the Buddha attained later.

F. Difference in Explanations

Sixth is the difference in explanations. This One Vehicle, at the time when it teaches from this one direction about one phenomenon, one significance, one type, or one assembly, always connects to and includes all the worlds of the ten directions; all share in this teaching. Principal and attendants together form one whole. For this reason, by pursuing any single word or single line of this scripture you can extend your understanding to the ten directions. By pursuing many words and many lines, you can also extend all of them to the ten directions. The three vehicles are not so; their explanations only pursue the single characteristic of a single direction. They do not have the pervasive thoroughness of the teaching of principal and attendants, and so on.

G. Difference in Ranks

Seventh is the difference in ranks. As to this One Vehicle, all its ranks, high and low, are equal, for each single rank encompasses all ranks within it. Thus, all ranks, even up to buddhahood, are within the initial rank of faith. The other ranks are also this way. Within the three vehicles, it is not so. One can only proceed with one's rank in the sequence, whether high or low, ascending or descending sequentially, never intermixing. The rest is as explained below.

H. Difference in Practices

Eighth is the difference in practices. In the One Vehicle, any one bodhisattva practice includes the six ranks, such as the ten stages of faith and so on. 484b
Within each and every rank, all definitive activities with their differences of concentration or distraction and so on are cultivated together at once. If while one is in the eastern realms one constantly enters into states of concentration, then in the western realms one constantly makes offerings to the buddhas. It is to be here in these realms of the ten directions fully exhausting the practices of the Dharma realm, even without dividing one's body. At one time all [ranks] are universally fulfilled. With one thought, all [activities] are universally cultivated. Within each and every thought it is also like this. From the fulfilled mind of the stages of faith and onward, each and every stage is cultivated thus. There can be no superior or inferior practices. Moreover, "one practice is all practices" and such principles pervade universally, like Indra's net. In the three vehicles it is not like this. Even the bodhisattvas of the stages have their respective distinctions; how much more so those who are prior to the bodhisattva stages! The rest is as explained below.

I. Difference in Dharma Gates

Ninth is the difference in Dharma gates. In summary there are ten kinds.

1. That has three buddhas, this has ten buddhas.
2. That has six supernatural powers, this has ten supernatural powers.
3. That has three kinds of insight, this has ten kinds of insight.
4. That has eight kinds of liberation, this has ten kinds of liberation.
5. That has four kinds of fearlessness, this has ten kinds of fearlessness.
6. That has five kinds of vision, this has ten kinds of vision.
7. That has three temporal worlds, this has ten temporal worlds.
8. That has four noble truths, this has ten noble truths.
9. That has four teaching abilities, this has ten teaching abilities.
10. That has eighteen special marks of a buddha, this has ten special marks.

The other gates are innumerable, as extensively explained in the scriptures.

J. Difference in Particular Phenomena

Tenth is the difference in particular phenomena. Follow any phenomenon, such as a house, a forest, a pond, some earth, or a mountain: all are Dharma gates, whether of practice, rank, or doctrine—but that does not destroy their phenomenality. Even within every single mote of dust, the Dharma realm with all its different phenomena is complete, and Indra's net and the simultaneous accommodation of subtle particulars are realized. Follow the arising of a single phenomenon: all are completely thus. In the three vehicles, however, it is not so. They only can teach that this phenomenon is empty, and truly thus, and so on, and so it is not the same as this One Vehicle teaching. Moreover, although they use spiritual insight of inconceivable power, what they encounter is but a momentary manifestation, not this Dharma's fundamental nature of thusness. The rest you can understand accordingly.

This is the end of the eighth section. Next, there are the two gates on explanations and doctrinal principles, completing the ten gates.

IX. Differences in their Explanations [of Essential Concepts]

484c Ninth gate: Clarification of the differences among the explanations of the various teachings. This will be summarized in ten gates. Because there are differences in their doctrines, it is apparent that the differences in what they can explain are numerous. The rest is as taught elsewhere (i.e., in the work of my teacher Zhiyan).

1. Fundamental consciousness
2. Clarification of buddha seed-nature
3. Distinctions in practices and ranks
4. Duration of cultivation
5. Embodied basis of cultivation
6. Distinctions in the severing of delusions
7. Conversion of the two vehicles
8. Characteristics of buddhahood
9. Worlds encompassed and transformed
10. Analysis and synthesis of buddha bodies

A. Fundamental Consciousness

First are the differences in the explanations of fundamental consciousness.

1. Lesser Vehicle

As to the Lesser Vehicle, it only has six consciousnesses. Their significance is divided into mind (*citta*), thought (*manas*), and consciousness (*vijñāna*). When the Lesser Vehicle treatises teach of the storehouse consciousness (*ālayavijñāna*) they only get to its name [and don't explain its significance], as taught in the *Incremental Āgama Sutra,* for example.

2. Early Teaching

As to the Early Teaching, with regard to the storehouse consciousness, it only attains one part of its significance—that is, that it is produced and extinguished. It is not yet able to see that it is thoroughly pervaded by true principle. It only teaches a reified [storehouse consciousness] that does not create the myriad dharmas. Thus, it just establishes storehouse consciousness among the interdependently arising phenomena of production and extinction. It is produced through the differentiation of the essence of karmic and verbal seeds. As the consciousness of the recompense of their different ripenings, it becomes the basis of various dharmas. It is a skillful means to gradually draw Lesser Vehicle practitioners toward true principle, so it teaches that all things, such as the permeating influence of karmic impressions and so on, are in fact empty. This is as explained in the *Sutra on the Explication of Underlying Meaning,* which states:

> If a bodhisattva, looking within and without, does not see the storing [of seeds], does not see the permeating influence of karmic impressions, does not see the storehouse, does not see storehouse consciousness, does not see appropriation (*ādāna*), does not see the appropriating consciousness (*ādānavijñāna*)—if there is one who can understand thusly, this one is called a wondrously skilled bodhisattva. The Tathāgata in this way established all the esoteric and wondrously skillful teachings of mind, thought, and sense consciousness.

In Yogācāra we also find this same teaching.

Interpretation: In this way, on the basis of not seeing [storehouse consciousness] and so on, mind, thought, and so on are established as teachings of wondrous skill. For this reason, you should know that all the characteristics of storehouse consciousness that are established in the Early Teaching, such as its production and extinction and so on, have esoteric intent, and are not to be taken literally. It ultimately returns to true thusness.

3. Final Teaching

485a As to the Final Teaching, it attains two parts of the significance of storehouse consciousness, which is that true principle and phenomenality both pervade it. The *Treatise* [*on the Awakening of Faith*] states only, "no production and no extinction, production and extinction—harmoniously combined, neither the same nor different: this is called storehouse consciousness." Because the Final Teaching recognizes that true thusness and the karmic impressions that permeate true thusness are harmonized and combined to form this original consciousness, it is not the same as the abovementioned teaching in which karmic and verbal seeds produce it. The *Laṅkāvatāra-sūtra* states, "The *tathāgatagarbha,* being what is permeated by beginningless evil habits, is called storehouse consciousness."[16] It also states, "The *tathāgatagarbha* receives suffering and pleasure and their causes; together they are born or they are extinguished." It also states, "The *tathāgatagarbha* is called 'storehouse consciousness,' and it exists together with ignorance and the seventh consciousness."

Also, *The Awakening of Faith* states, "The immaculate mind of self-nature, moved by the winds of ignorance, becomes the impure mind," and so on. Teachings like this are numerous.

Question: [According to you, the Final Teaching] has said that true thusness is a permanent dharma. How then can it teach that it arises and is extinguished in being permeated by karmic impressions? Having recognized that it arises and goes extinct, how can the [Final Teaching] also teach that it has reified permanence?

Reply: The permanence of true thusness spoken of is not permanence as posited in words. Why would the sages teach that true thusness is reified? This is because even when it produces various dharmas according to conditions, it does not lose its own essence; thus, it is taught to be permanent. This is no different from the permanence of impermanence, which is called "the inconceivable permanence." It is not saying that [the storehouse consciousness, being truly thus,] does not create myriad dharmas, as in the reified view posited by deluded sentience. Thus, the *Sutra of Queen Śrīmālā of the Lion's Roar* calls it "what is not defiled, and yet defiled." This clarifies the production of various dharmas according to conditions. "Defiled and yet not defiled" clarifies that it does not lose its self-nature when according with conditions. By the former significance, mundane truth is realized. By the latter significance, the absolute truth is also established. In this way the absolute and mundane truths have two significances, but do not have two essences. Interfused without obstruction, they are beyond the grasping of sentient beings. Thus, the *Commentary* [*on the Summary of the Great Vehicle*] states, "When beings in the darkness of the extreme myopia of cognitive hindrances talk about the absolute and the mundane, they form attachment to their separation," it refers to this.

These two significances of true thusness are the same as what was discussed above in the section on the Early Teaching. Because the Early Teaching takes the perspective of the Dharma gate of differentiated dharma characteristics, it only teaches the one reified aspect of the significance of true thusness. Within this Final Teaching, because it takes the perspective of the Dharma gate of the interfusion of essence and characteristics, it teaches the significance of the nonduality of both aspects of true thusness. This doctrine is broadly explained in my *Commentary on The Awakening of Faith.*

Also, it is as stated in the *Ten Stages Sutra,* "The triple world is delusion, only the creation of one mind." The *Summary of the Great Vehicle* and such texts take the perspective of the Early Teaching and explicate this [one mind] to be the various consciousnesses, such as the storehouse consciousness. The *Treatise on the Ten Stages* takes the perspective of the Final Teaching, explaining it to be the true mind of the ultimate principle.

It is furthermore as in the verses of the *Abhidharma Sutra,* in explanation of which the *Summary of the Great Vehicle* states, "As to 'this realm' (*dhātu*) and so on, 'realm' means cause; it is the consciousness that contains the seeds (i.e., storehouse consciousness)," and so on. The *Treatise on the Jewel Nature* interprets it from the perspective of the Final Teaching: "This nature is the nature of *tathāgatagarbha.* Depending upon this, the various destinies of sentient beings exist." As the *Sutra of Queen Śrīmālā* teaches, "Depending upon
tathāgatagarbha, birth and death exist; depending upon *tathāgatagarbha,* 485b

nirvana exists"; and so on, as extensively taught. For these reasons, you should understand that the two gates of the Early and Final teachings are distinct.

4. Sudden Teaching

According to the Sudden Teaching, all dharmas are only the one mind of true thusness. [The one mind] exhausts distinguishing characteristics, abandoning words and cutting off thoughts. It is inexpressible. As in the *Vimalakīrti-sūtra,* the Dharma gate of "not two" taught by the thirty-two bodhisattvas is the Final Teaching doctrine discussed above; that is, the nonduality of interfused impurity and purity. What Vimalakīrti manifests is the "not two" that abandons words; this is the Dharma gate of the Sudden Teaching. Because in this latter view all impure and pure characteristics are exhausted, there are no two dharmas that could be harmonized, and thus one cannot even explain them as being "not two."

5. Perfect Teaching

As to the Perfect Teaching, it takes the perspective of the perfect illumination of the ocean of original nature, the unobstructed freedom of the interdependent arising of the Dharma realm in which one is everything and everything is one and principal and attendants are perfectly interfused. Thus, it teaches the ten kinds of mind in order to manifest the infinite. This is as taught in the "Transcending the Mundane" chapter of the *Flower Garland Sutra,* and in the section on the ninth bodhisattva stage. Moreover, there is only one mind of the Dharma realm that arises from original nature, and it is replete with the Ten Virtues, as taught in the "Arising from Original Nature" chapter. These are based on the Distinct Teaching.

6. Common Teaching

If we take the perspective of the Common Teaching, it encompasses all the foregoing teachings of mind and consciousness. How so? Because they are its skillful means; they all flow out from it. The rest can be understood by this standard.

7. Explanation of Differences

Question: How can one mind have such different significances in the perspectives of the various teachings?

Reply: There are two significances to this. First, from the perspective of Dharma, all the teachings are completely included. Second, from the perspective of living beings' capacities, there are distinctions.

As to the first significance, five doctrinal gates originate from this extremely profound one mind of interdependent arising. Thus, a sage may encompass and transform all the living beings by means of the one gate appropriate to each. [They are as follows:] One: the gate that adumbrates the significance [of storehouse consciousness] in giving precedence to the name, as taught in the Lesser Vehicle. Two: the gate that adumbrates the true principle [of storehouse consciousness] in giving precedence to its phenomenality, as taught in the Early Teaching. Three: the gate of the nonobstruction of true principle and phenomena [with regard to storehouse consciousness], as taught in the Final Teaching. Four: the gate of reaching the end of phenomenality in order to reveal the true principle, as taught in the Sudden Teaching. Five: the gate of the ocean of original nature replete with virtues, as taught in the Perfect Teaching. This is how the unmoving root continually ramifies; without destroying the ramifications, the root is permanent. Thus, the characteristics of the five doctrines are fused in the evolutions of the one mind.

As to the second significance, it clarifies that there are distinctions in the Dharma from the perspective of living beings' capacities. There are beings who attain the name but do not attain the significance, as in the Lesser Vehicle teachings. Or, there are those who attain the name and attain one part of the significance, as in Early Teaching. There are those who attain the name and attain all parts of the significance, as in the Final Teaching. There are those who attain the significance but do not preserve the name, as in the Sudden Teaching. Or there are those who have the name and the significance together, infinitely, as in the Perfect Teaching. The other gates of doctrine are as taught in the "Essay on Consciousness Only."

B. Clarification of Buddha Seed-nature

Second is the difference in the explanations of the seed-natures.

1. Lesser Vehicle

According to the Lesser Vehicle view, there are six kinds of seed-natures. These are backsliding, concern [for backsliding], protection [of the progress one has gained], abiding [in the rank one has gained], ascension [to higher

ranks], and immovability. Within the immovable nature, there are three types.
485c The highest is buddha seed-nature, the middle is *pratyekabuddha*-nature, and the lower is *śrāvaka*-nature—for example, those such as Śāriputra. Although within this Lesser Vehicle it is taught that the Buddha alone has buddha seed-nature, this is not the great *bodhi*-nature, because it is not taught that the Buddha's meritorious activities include the arising of great salvific function unto the very limit of the future, and so on. You should understand that within this teaching, besides the one person of the Buddha, all the myriad beings are taught as not having great *bodhi*-nature. The rest of the doctrine is as taught in the Lesser Vehicle treatises.

2. Three Vehicles

According to the three vehicles teachings, there are in summary three explanations of the different seed-natures.

i. Early Teaching

One is from the perspective of the Early Teaching. That is, because seed-nature is established within created, impermanent dharmas, it can't extend to all sentient beings. Thus, within the five kinds of seed-nature there is one part of living beings without seed-nature. The *Treatise on Praise of the Sacred Teachings* states, "What is the reason for the five different kinds of seed-nature? It is because it is possible [even] given the differences of the many realms," and so on, to "If only in this present world [and not in other temporal worlds, one part of living beings] did not have the dharma of *parinirvāṇa,* that would not correspond to the true principle"; and so on, as extensively taught. Therefore, you should understand that by reason of things-as-they-are, from beginningless time there are five kinds of seed-nature for all sentient beings. But the fifth seed-nature lacks the meritorious cause of transcendence, and so [beings of this nature] never extinguish delusions and cross over [to the other shore]. Because of this principle, the buddhas' meritorious activity of benefiting sentient beings has no end.

Regarding the existence of natures, the *Treatise on Yogācāra Stages* states:

> Summarily, there are two kinds of seed-natures. One is what is originally inherent. Two is what is formed through habituation. As to what is originally inherent, it means that bodhisattvas have such a characteristic in the superior faculties of the six cognitive fields. Since beginningless time,

[this inherent nature] has evolved and continued, and is attained by virtue of things-as-they-are. As to what is formed through habituation, this refers to what is attained by the repeated cultivation of good roots from the past.

Within this statement, original nature is identified with the cognitive field of thought, which is considered to be most superior among the six cognitive fields. It is the originally awakened liberated nature within storehouse consciousness, which is seed-nature. Thus, the Liang *Summary of the Great Vehicle* states, "The permeating influences received harmonize with the liberated nature that is within storehouse consciousness. All the sages take this as their cause." However, the *Treatise on Yogācāra Stages* states, "those who have both kinds of nature are able to aspire to enlightenment." You should know that the two dharmas of inherent and habitual nature together form one seed-nature. For this reason, these two arise interdependently and are not two. If one is lacking, seed-nature is not complete. It does not teach that inherent nature is first and habituation is after; it only allows that they exist from the rank of the fulfillment of faith and above. Then, from the perspective of origin, [Yogācāra] teaches that there is inherent nature, while from the perspective of cultivation, it teaches habitual nature. Thus, there are two significances, but it is not two things. We can understand this from the above statement from the *Summary of the Great Vehicle:* the two significances are harmonized as one cause.

Question: What is the difference between these two seed-natures and [the explanation given by] the *Benevolent King* and *Basic Activities* sutras on the habituated seeds and inherent seeds among the six seed-natures?

Reply: Those sutras are mostly taught from the perspective of ranks. They 486a
consider what is there in initial habituation to be habitual seed-nature, and what is accumulated through long habituation to be inherent seed-nature. They teach that the habitual seed-nature exists in the ten abodes and the inherent seed-nature exists in the ten practices. Before the stage of the three worthy sets of practices, those sutras only refer to good destinies and do not refer to seed-nature.

In the *Treatise on Yogācāra Stages,* long habituation is called habitual seed-nature, while from the perspective of origin, it is called inherent seed-nature;

of these two seeds, however, neither is first, nor middle, nor last. Thus, scripture teaches that inherent nature forms because of habituation. The treatises explain it as habituation arising dependent upon nature. Truly this is because these two form mutually and arise interdependently, without any characteristic of duality. The scriptures and the treatises complement each other to provide the full significance. At the same time, the scriptures teach that seed-nature exists after the aspiration to enlightenment, while in the treatises it is taught that seed-nature exists before the aspiration to enlightenment. It is like this because the effective power [of seed-nature] only manifests when the respective rank is attained. For this reason, the scriptures teach that it exists at the rank of the three worthy sets of practices. But its effective power must depend on something. For this reason, in the treatises it is explained as existing before the rank is attained. The effective power must become manifest for it to be said to exist: the scripture does not contradict the treatises. The nature must exist for it to give rise to effective power: the treatise does not contradict the scripture. They uphold each other, and the meaning is thoroughly interfused.

Question: By what reason am I to understand that seed-nature exists at the rank of fulfillment of faith?

Reply: You can understand it by means of the teaching in the treatises that seed-nature must necessarily include both inherent and habitual natures. If there is already habituation, there must be practice. If there is already practice, the fulfillment of faith must be attained. If one does not cultivate these repeated habituating practices from the rank of ignorance until reaching the fulfillment of faith, then at what rank will one cultivate it? Because in the rank of ignorance one has not yet cultivated habituation, and since after attaining this rank is the second abode, then for these reasons you should understand that from the rank of ignorance one [first] cultivates repeated habituating practices. Upon reaching the rank of fulfillment of faith, repeated habituation is then accomplished, and so the inherent nature and habitual nature are thoroughly fused to become seed-nature.

Question: If inherent nature is taught as necessarily following habituation, then given that those at the rank of ignorance have not yet cultivated habituation, shouldn't they lack inherent nature? If they don't have it then, they shouldn't have it later, because something that does not exist before but does exist later would not be inherent. If they do have it, then this is having inherent nature without habituation, which does not accord with the principle stated above, and is not what the treatises teach.

Reply: These two both arise interdependently, so that when there is no habitual nature, there is likewise no inherent nature. Through this they establish that there are sentient beings who have no inherent nature. As to your claim that what does not exist before and does exist later would not be inherent, you are not correct. Based on the fact that habituation is accomplished, it is certain that the natures existed before. Because there is still no habituation [of good practices] at the rank of ignorance, the natures are not taught [to exist]. Of beings that later give rise to the habituation [of good practices], it cannot be said that there is no habituation. For this reason, the natures are taught to exist after habituation is accomplished. When practices pertinent to the respective vehicle have been repeatedly habituated, then at that time those natures are said to originally exist.

Question: If it is like this, then there is only one indeterminate nature. How could it be that there are five differentiated natures?

Reply: It is because of this significance (i.e., the interdependent arising of the two kinds of seed-nature) that we securely establish five natures. How is that? 486b
Having cultivated the six perfections [of the Great Vehicle] through repeated habituation, upon attaining the rank of fulfillment of faith, one forms bodhisattva seed-nature. If one has habituated Lesser Vehicle practices and attained the rank of endurance, one forms *śrāvaka*-nature. Thus, the *Treatise on the Larger Prajñāpāramitā Sutra* states, "'Warmth,' 'pinnacles,' 'patience,' and so on (i.e., the four roots of goodness) are names for the stage of nature." The *Sutra on the Good Moral Discipline of Bodhisattvas* states, "If one attains the world's highest (i.e., fourth of the roots of goodness), this is named 'the second rank.'" Thus, you should know that the first three roots of goodness belong to the rank of seed-nature. According to the *Abhidharmakośa-bhāṣya,* seed-nature is taught to exist at the rank where one attains the good root of the cause leading to liberation. Thus, that treatise states:

> As to the cause leading to liberation, this is the good root that determines one's ability to experience the result of nirvana. Having produced this good root, those sentient beings are said to have the dharma of nirvana in their life.

The *pratyekabuddha*s should also be understood by this standard. The three vehicles teaching on seed-nature is established in this way. So, if one cultivates any one of the three practices and has not yet arrived at the basic rank, at this time one establishes indeterminate seed-nature. If one has not yet cultivated any of the three practices, at this time no seed-nature is established. By this you should fully understand that the seed-natures of the various vehicles are all taught as pertaining to habituation.

Question: If in the rank of ignorance there is no habituation and therefore no [seed-]nature,[17] then later, even if one gives rise to habituation, how could it be that one has it?

Reply: When habituation exists, it is not the rank of no habituation. Thus, if habituation exists, then [seed-nature] exists eternally. If habituation does not exist, [seed-nature] has never existed. One does not take nonhabituation and make it into habituation; likewise, one does not make non-nature become nature. This is because of the difference in rank. As the *Nirvana Sutra* states:

> Of the three kinds of people, those who will die in the end [without reaching nirvana] are compared to *icchantika*s, who lack buddha-nature. Good sons, whether those who are *icchantika*s meet good friends, buddhas, and bodhisattvas, and hear them teach the profound Dharma, or whether they don't meet them, either way they do not depart from the mind of *icchantika.* Why? Because their good roots are severed. Yet those who are *icchantika*s may attain the mind of *anuttarā samyaksaṃbodhi.* By means of what? If they can aspire to *bodhi*-mind, then they are no longer named *icchantika*s. Good sons, under what conditions are *icchantika*s said to attain *anuttarā samyaksaṃbodhi*? Those who are *icchantika*s in fact do not attain *anuttarā samyaksaṃbodhi* [as *icchantika*s], like those whose life span is ended.

And so on, as extensively taught. You should understand from this that the existence or nonexistence [of seed-nature] is eternally fixed in regard to one's position relative to the ranks. [Habituation and nonhabituation] do not depend on each other.

ii. Final Teaching

Two is from the perspective of the Final Teaching. Because it establishes seed-nature within the nature of true thusness, all living beings have seed-nature—each and every one. The *Treatise on the Larger Prajñāpāramitā Sutra* states:

> White stones have the nature of silver, yellow stones have the nature of gold, water is of the nature of wetness, and fire is of the nature of heat. All living beings have the nature of nirvana.

This is because among all beings of deluded consciousness, there are none who cannot return to their own true nature, as the sutra teaches when it states: 486c

> Living beings are thus: they all have minds; each being that has a mind will definitely realize *anuttarā samyaksaṃbodhi.* Because of this principle, I have always taught that all living beings have buddha-nature.

Question: What if a critic were to say, "All beings possessing minds attain *bodhi,* and buddhas also have minds, so buddhas also should definitely attain *bodhi.* If you say that buddhas have minds, but have nothing further to attain, then that would mean that although living beings without nature have minds, they also have nothing to attain."

Reply: In the scripture, in order to prevent such confusion, it only states that living beings have minds, and does not state the same about buddhas. Those who receive births in various realms are called living beings. They are not the same as buddhas.

Question: If all beings have [buddha-]nature, why establish those without nature among the five kinds of nature?

Reply: The treatises have exegeses on this. The *Treatise on the Jewel Nature* states:

> It has been taught that *icchantika*s do not have the nature of nirvana and do not enter nirvana. What is the significance of this? It is meant to show

> that the cause [of having no buddha-nature] is slandering the Great Vehicle. What significance does this clarify? It is meant to convert the minds of those who would slander the Great Vehicle, because in reality they do have the pure buddha-nature. [The scripture] made this teaching in consideration of the immeasurable time [of *icchantika*s' debasement, to frighten slanderers].
>
> Moreover, the *Treatise on Buddha-nature* states:
>
> Question: If it is as you say, why did the Buddha teach that living beings in whom the nature does not abide will never gain *parinirvāṇa*?
>
> Reply: If there are beings who spitefully turn against the Great Vehicle, that dharma is the cause of becoming *icchantika*s. It is meant to make living beings abandon that dharma. If they fall into the cause of becoming *icchantika*s, then they will turn over and over in the long night without respite. For this reason, the scripture makes this teaching. But according to true principles, all of the myriad living beings originally have pure buddha-nature. There is no basis for the idea that some do not attain *parinirvāṇa.* Thus, buddha-nature definitely originally exists. It is beyond existence and beyond nonexistence.

Interpretation: An earlier passage of this treatise extensively refutes the nonexistence of nature, down to the end of the passage, which states:

> As to the third point, its mistake is the same as in the heterodox ways—that existence is originally fixed as existence and nonexistence is originally fixed as nonexistence, existence being imperishable and nonexistence being improducible. Such errors and mistakes originate in your perverse attachment to the doctrine of naturelessness.
>
> And so on, as extensively taught.

Question: The Early Teaching, as explained above, definitely teaches that there are living beings without [buddha-]nature. Now in this Final Teaching, they all have [buddha-]nature. How can these statements be reconciled?

Reply: The treatises again have exegeses on this. The second fascicle of the *Treatise on Buddha-nature* states:

Why do the scriptures repeatedly state that, among living beings, *icchantika*s definitely do not have the nature of *parinirvāṇa*? If it is so, then the two scriptures contradict each other. How can the two explanations be reconciled? One is complete and one is incomplete, so there is no contradiction.

Interpretation: According to the Lesser Vehicle, only the one person of the Buddha has buddha-nature, and all the rest of the people cannot be said to 487a have it. According to the Early Teaching of the three vehicles, it is slightly different and many people have it, but still it is not completely different from the Lesser Vehicle teaching; it still allows that one part of beings have no buddha-nature. For this reason, in the treatises it is judged as being the provisional and incomplete teaching.

Question: According to the Final Teaching, all living beings will definitely become buddhas. Although living beings are many, they will come to a final end. If it is so, then when the last one becomes a buddha there will be nothing left to transform. Because there is nothing to transform, the practice of benefiting others [which constitutes buddhahood] is absent, and becoming a buddha when the practice of benefiting others is absent does not correspond to true principles. Moreover, the merits of the buddhas' activities of benefiting others would be severed completely. If it is the case that all beings without exception will become buddhas, and yet the teachings say that living beings are ultimately infinite, then this is a fallacy of the words themselves contradicting each other, because if they are endless they will never all become buddhas. Furthermore, if one buddha crosses over innumerable beings, is there a decrease in the realm of living beings? If there is a gradual decrease, then there must be a final end. If there were a decrease without an end, that would not accord with reason. If there is no decrease, then there is no extinction and crossing over. If there were extinction without decrease, that would not accord with reason. Given such principles as these, the *Treatise on the Sutra on the Buddha Stage* and such texts establish the concept of sentient beings without buddha-nature to avoid the various mistakes above. What is the meaning of all this?

Reply: In reference to the teaching that living beings come to an end, due to having buddha-nature and thus becoming buddhas together, this is to give rise to the partial view that mistakenly maintains there is decrease within the realm of living beings. If there is decrease in the realm of living beings, there must be increase in the realm of buddhas; this is to give rise to the partial view that mistakenly maintains there is increase in the buddha realm. Such partial views of decrease and increase are not the correct view. Thus, the *Sutra on No Increase and No Decrease* states, "Śāriputra, as to the greatly mistaken view, it is to see increase in the realm of living beings, or to see decrease in the realm of living beings," and so on, as extensively taught. In order to avoid this mistaken view, the teachings establish this one division of sentient beings without buddha-nature as those which do not increase or decrease. But that teaching ultimately cannot avoid the partial views of increase and decrease. Why? Because seeing all those beings who do have buddha-nature and become buddhas together gives rise to annihilationism and the partial view of decrease; seeing those beings who do not have buddha-nature and do not become buddhas, it gives rise to eternalism and the partial view of increase. This is because they do not apprehend the realm of living beings. For this reason, the sutra states:

> All ignorant ordinary people do not truly understand the absolute Dharma realm. Because they do not truly see the absolute Dharma realm, they give rise to mistaken views, believing that the realm of living beings increases or decreases.

Furthermore, *Mañjuśrī's Sutra on Prajñāpāramitā* states:

> Even if one buddha dwells in the world, whether for one *kalpa* or more than one *kalpa;* even if, as in that one buddha world, there are myriad buddhas like that one buddha, as innumerable as the boundless sands of
> 487b the Ganges River; even if each and every buddha, whether for one *kalpa* or more than one *kalpa,* teaches the Dharma day and night without resting their heart for a moment, crossing over each and every one of the living beings, who are as innumerable as the grains of sand of the Ganges River, so that they all enter nirvana—even so, the realm of living beings does not increase or decrease. All the buddha worlds of the ten directions are also like this. Every single one of the myriad buddhas teaches the Dharma and causes the transformation of living beings. Each crosses over living

> beings as innumerable as the grains of sand of the Ganges so that they all enter nirvana, and in the realm of living beings there is neither increase nor decrease. How so? Because a fixed characteristic of living beings [by which to count them] is not obtainable.

To expand upon the significance of this, the realm of living beings is like an empty sky. Suppose that innumerable conquering deities pass through it, each flying across the empty sky for innumerable *kalpa*s in search of the boundaries of the sky. Yet ultimately they cannot reach the end of it. It is not the case that because the sky has no limit, they can't roam across it; it is not the case that by roaming across it they will reach its boundaries. You should understand that the true principle within this [teaching on no increase or decrease] is likewise. It is not the case that because living beings will attain buddhahood they will come to an end; it is not the case that because they have no end, there are some who do not attain buddhahood. Thus, none of the various criticisms are unaccounted for.

Moreover, in order to make the point that a buddha's merits of benefiting others are never severed or exhausted, the teachings established one division of living beings without buddha-nature. This means that those buddhas would have only the merits of benefiting others through their transformation bodies, while the various merits of their enjoyment bodies would be severed, because there would be no bodhisattvas to attest to the various bodhisattva stages. Furthermore, among the beings transformed, there would only be beings of coarse capacities while those beings of subtle capacities would be severed and extinguished, because there would be not one person to attain the uncontaminated mind of the two vehicles. Furthermore, as to the buddhas of this time and after, there would not be one buddha to reach the point of teaching the three vehicles teachings, because none would have the opportunity to attain sagehood. This would sever the buddhas' great compassion and empathetic identity with all beings.

Furthermore, if you insist that because all beings have buddha-nature they will certainly all come to an end, and you fear that the very last buddha would then lack the practice of benefiting others, and so you establish one part of living beings to be fixed without buddha-nature, still, that last buddha's practice of benefiting others would not be perfectly fulfilled in the end, because among those beings they tried to transform there would be not one sentient being to attain the result of sagehood. Only benefiting others, among the two benefits of the buddhas and bodhisattvas, is the greatest. How could there be one who does not cause even a single being to attain the result of sagehood and yet attains buddhahood in their own body?

Furthermore, originally all buddhas make the great vow, saying, "I will cause all living beings to attain *bodhi.*" Thus, by causing them to attain it, this original vow is not in vain. And yet the realm of living beings cannot be emptied, so the original vow is not severed. If it was not like this, they would be contradicting their original vow, and the practice of the vow would be vain. To become a buddha through vain practice does not accord with true principles. For this reason, although [the authors of the texts you mention] wished to avoid the above mistakes by establishing beings without buddha-nature, they did not realize that they fell into those very errors within this tenet. For this reason, [the existence of beings] without buddha-nature is not to be taken as the ultimately realized significance of the doctrine.

487c Question: When discussing seed-nature, it must be discussed as a created phenomenon. How can this teaching make a claim about seed-nature from the perspective of true thusness?

Reply: It is because when true thusness accords with conditions and is harmonized with impurities to become root consciousness (i.e., storehouse consciousness), then within that true thusness there is an original awakening without contamination, influencing living beings as the cause of their turning against the current [of samsara]; so there is seed-nature. The Liang *Summary of the Great Vehicle* teaches it as the nature of liberation within storehouse consciousness. *The Awakening of Faith* teaches it as original awakening, being among the two significances of storehouse consciousness. In that treatise, the *tathāgatagarbha* is completely without contamination, eternally influencing living beings as the cause of pure dharmas. Also, the *Treatise on the Jewel Nature* states:

> As to "and that nature of true thusness," it is as stated in the *Sutra on the Accumulations of the Six Senses,*[18] which teaches that the six sense faculties are thus since the beginningless beginning, ultimately becoming the essence of all dharmas.

Interpretation: Although true thusness pervades all dharmas, the text here excludes nonsentient beings. From the perspective of those numerous living beings who do possess the six sense bases, the principle of ultimate true thusness is to be taken as the inherent nature. This is the same in name as what is taught in Yogācāra, but that only teaches it from the perspective of the Early Teaching in terms of its coarse characteristics, true principle being secondary to particular phenomena. Thus, within the perspective of phenomena, it clarifies seed-nature. The *Bodhisattva Stages Sutra* states, "The coarse characteristics of seed-nature I have already summarily taught." It refers to this. The *Treatise on the Jewel Nature* takes the perspective of this Final Teaching, in which phenomena are secondary to true principle, to teach its profound subtleties. This is thusness clarifying the inherent nature. For this reason, the *Treatise on Buddha-nature* states, "The mind of pure self-nature is named 'the truth of the way' (i.e., the way to extinguish affliction, fourth of the four noble truths)." Also, the *Nirvana Sutra* states, "As to buddha-nature, it is what is called emptiness in its primary significance. Emptiness in its primary significance is called wisdom." These are both just the wisdom of the nature of original awakening, taught as inherent nature. The habitual seeds are likewise formed by following from true thusness. The *Summary of the Great Vehicle* states, "The habituating influence of hearing the Dharma flows from the most pure Dharma realm," and so on.

Moreover, in *The Awakening of Faith* the two great aspects of true thusness, essence and characteristics, are taken as the causes of internal permeating influence, while the great aspect of function of true thusness is the condition of external permeating influence. These are harmonized with the impure dharmas of ignorance, and thus the three great aspects of thusness are taught in terms of internal and external permeating influence. When ignorance is eliminated due to the power of permeating influence, they are profoundly joined and nondual, only one true thusness.

iii. Sudden Teaching

Third is clarification from the perspective of the Sudden Teaching. Only the one true thusness, beyond characteristics that could be described in words, is called seed-nature. The Sudden Teaching does not distinguish between inherent nature and habitual nature, because all dharmas are without dualistic characteristics. For this reason, the *Sutra on the Emptiness of All Dharmas* states:

> How can this phenomenon be called seed-nature? Mañjuśrī, all living beings are of one characteristic. Ultimately they are not produced and are beyond all naming. Sameness or difference cannot be obtained. This is called seed-nature.

You should understand according to this standard. This is the end of the above section on the perspectives of three vehicles teachings.

3. One Vehicle

488a Third is from the perspective of the One Vehicle, containing two teachings.

i. Common Teaching

One clarifies seed-nature by encompassing all the previous teachings; together they form the tenet in which principal and attendants are complete. Because this is the Common Teaching, it encompasses them as skillful means.

ii. Distinct Teaching

Two, according to the Distinct Teaching, seed-nature is very profound, such that cause and result are nondual. It pervades circumstantial and direct karmic compensation throughout the three times. It includes all the various Dharma gates of principle and phenomena, understanding and practice, and so on. It is always already fulfilled and completely realized. Thus, the great [*Flower Garland*] *Sutra* states in reference to this, "The seed-nature of the bodhisattvas is profound and vast, equal to the Dharma realm and empty space." If it manifests according to the Dharma gates (i.e., as provisional teachings), then the six determining factors of each of the ranks among the five ranks are called seed-natures. It is this dharma that is named the result-characteristic (one of the three characteristics of the storehouse consciousness), because cause and result are of a common essence and a single nature. This is as extensively taught in the scripture. The rest can be understood accordingly.

4. Explanation of Differences

Question: Why is seed-nature differentiated in dissimilar ways by the various teachings?

Reply: There are two significances to this. One is the analysis of the mutual inclusion of its hidden and manifest facets from the perspective of Dharma. The other is the clarification of distinctions in the dharmas attained from the perspective of beings' spiritual capacities.

As to the former significance, it consists of five gates of significance by which we can understand how this seed-nature arises interdependently without obstruction. The various teachings each describe one gate, according to beings' capacities to accept and be transformed by the teaching. The doctrines do not contradict each other. What are the five? One is the gate of nonexistence of seed-nature, following from consideration of attachment, as explained in the Lesser Vehicle. Two pursues the gate of deficiency and fullness of seed-nature, following from consideration of its phenomenality, as explained in the Early Teaching. Three is the gate of seed-nature's universality in sentient beings, following from consideration of true principle, as explained the Final Teaching. Four is the gate of cutting off characteristics and going beyond language, as explained in the Sudden Teaching. Five is the gate in which seed-nature is endowed with myriad virtues, as explained in the Perfect Teaching. Although there are five significances, seed-nature is all-pervasive and universally inclusive. The hidden and manifest facets are equally present.

As to the second [significance], the clarification of distinctions in the dharmas attained from the perspective of beings' spiritual capacities: sometimes all things lack seed-nature, with the one exception of the Buddha, as in the Lesser Vehicle teachings. Sometimes all things have it, except for herbs and trees and such, as explained in the Final Teaching. Sometimes it both exists and does not exist, because one division of beings without nature is recognized, as explained in the Early Teaching. Sometimes it neither exists nor does not exist, as explained in the Sudden Teaching, because it is beyond characteristics. Sometimes the doctrine of seed-nature consists of all the preceding four explanations, being taught as the One Vehicle's skillful means. Sometimes it is both cause and result pervading the three times, as explained in the Perfect Teaching. The rest can be understood by this standard.

C. Distinctions in Practices and Ranks

Third are the distinctions in practices and ranks. All of the various teachings will be summarized by means of three significances: clarification of the characteristics of the ranks, clarification of the stage of nonreturning, and clarification of the characteristics of practices.

1. Lesser Vehicle

First, according to the Lesser Vehicle, there are four ranks: skillful means, insight, cultivation, and the ultimate. It teaches that the twelve abodes of the Lesser Vehicle are to be considered the ultimate. It also teaches the triple world, the nine stages, and the eleven stages, and so on, as extensively taught in the Lesser Vehicle treatises. Second, as to nonreturning, within this teaching those who practice up to the rank of patience (i.e., third of the four good roots) attain the status of nonreturning. The characteristics of their practices
488b are as taught in those various treatises.

Question: For what reason are the characteristics of the Lesser Vehicle practices and ranks not broadly explored in this discussion?

Reply: The intention of this is to show that the teachings are not the same by means of obvious differences in their doctrines. There can be no doubt that the Lesser Vehicle teaching differs from the true principles of the Great Vehicle, so it does not need further explanation.

2. Early Teaching

As to the initial teaching, it will also be made clear by means of the three significances (i.e., ranks, nonreturning, and practices).

First, the characteristics of ranks. This contains two parts. One is the teaching of the conversion of mind, which is made to draw in the followers of the two vehicles of the ignorant teaching and convert their minds. It also has only four ranks—insight and cultivation and so on—and the nine stages and so on, of which the names are the same as in the Lesser Vehicle. Or, it establishes five ranks, which are included in the seven expedient attainments before the path of insight. Among the seven, the first three kinds are separated out as the rank of preparation because they are distant skillful means, while the latter four, the roots of goodness, are designated as the rank of applied practices, being the near skillful means. The other names are the same as above.

The Early Teaching also teaches the stage of dry wisdom and the other ten stages. The ninth is named the bodhisattva stage; the tenth is named the buddha stage. This is to attract the two vehicles practitioners who wish to advance and are not satisfied, so that they may gradually progress in practices until reaching the result of buddhahood. Now, as to buddhahood being a stage within the ten stages and not beyond them, it is taught this way in order to draw in those two vehicles practitioners by the skillful means of appearing similar to their own teachings, because in the two vehicles people attain the result of sagehood in this present life, and not after it. Furthermore, the characteristics of these ranks and practices are extensively expounded in the "Decision" section on *śrāvaka*s in the *Treatise on the Yogācāra Stages* and in the *Treatise on the Collected Abhidharma.*

Question: Why are the characteristics of the practices and ranks clarified in the *Treatise on Yogācāra Stages* and the other works not the same as those in the Abhidharma?

Reply: There are two significances to their different characteristics. One is in manifesting the incompleteness of the teaching of the various dharmas among the ignorant people of the Lesser Vehicle. Two is in using skillful means to gradually draw them into the Great Vehicle. The dharmas of the practices and ranks that these works clarify are all skillful means to get beings to enter into the teachings of the Great Vehicle, so they are not the same. These beings are not those of the Lesser Vehicle of the ignorant teaching, and also not the bodhisattvas; so we know they are of the *śrāvaka* vehicle within the teachings of the three vehicles.

The second part of the characteristics of ranks in the Early Teaching is about the people who advance directly into the Great Vehicle. When demonstrating the characteristics of the ranks for them, they are taught the differences among the ten bodhisattva stages. Moreover, the ten bodhisattva stages are explained to be the path of insight and the path of cultivation, and together with the ranks that precede the ten bodhisattva stages they are considered to be the meaning of the twelve abodes of the Great Vehicle. Why? This is in order to appear similar to the Lesser Vehicle. Furthermore, those ranks before the bodhisattva stages include the forty levels of mind, since the ten stages of faith are established as a rank therein; this also is done in order to be similar to the four skillful means prior to the way of the Lesser Vehicle. Thus, the Liang *Summary of the Great Vehicle* states:

There are four ranks before *śrotaāpanna* (stream-enterer), which are warmth, pinnacles, patience, and the world's highest Dharma. The four ranks before the bodhisattva stages are also like this; they are the ten stages of faith, the ten understandings, the ten practices, and the ten conversions of merit (i.e., the forty levels of mind).

Likewise, in order to be similar to the teaching of the conversion of mind, the stages of faith and the rest of the four ranks are considered to be the rank
488c of preparation. After the ten conversions of merit, it separately establishes the four roots of goodness as the rank of applied practices. The path of insight and so on are the same as the above.

Question: Why do many of the names of the ranks in this Early Teaching appear like those of the Lesser Vehicle?

Reply: It is in order to draw in the Lesser Vehicle practitioners by the skillful means of appearing similar, because it has superior skillful means. If the names were entirely different, they would find it difficult to believe and accept. If the names were completely the same, it could not be called drawing them in to the Great Vehicle.

Question: If it is taught for the sake of drawing in the followers of the two vehicles, it can certainly be similar to their teachings, but if it is for the sake of people who advance directly into the Great Vehicle, why should it imitate the Lesser Vehicle?

Reply: There are two meanings for its resemblance to the Lesser Vehicle. One, because the spiritual capacities of the people of the Early Teaching who advance directly into the Great Vehicle are coarse and shallow, they are unable to completely receive the profound Dharma of the Great Vehicle. For this reason, the Dharma characteristics of the ranks that are shown to them do indeed resemble those of the Lesser Vehicle, but the doctrinal principles are in fact different. Two, whenever the Great Vehicle is taught in a way that is similar to the Lesser Vehicle, there are two significances: one is in order to draw in the followers of the Lesser Vehicle, and the other is in order to teach those beings of shallow capacity. For these reasons, these characteristics of ranks are taught in the Early Teaching.

Now, as to the significance of all this, it is as taught in the *Treatise on Yogācāra Stages,* which states:

> What are the characteristics of the realized *pudgala* (individual person)? This refers to those *śrāvaka*s who have already repeatedly habituated good dharmas. If they dwell a while in lower-level maturation, at that time they will have lower-level desires and lower-level application of practice, and they will tend toward evil destinies. In this present state they will not confirm the result of śramaṇahood, and in this present state they will not attain *parinirvāṇa.* If they dwell a while in the middle-level maturation, at that time they will have middle-level desires and middle-level application of practices, and they will not tend toward evil destinies. In this present state, they will confirm the result of śramaṇahood, but in this present state they will not attain *parinirvāṇa.* If they dwell for a while in the higher-level maturation, at this time they will have higher-level desires and higher-level application of practice, and they will not tend toward evil destinies. In this present state they will confirm the result of śramaṇahood, and in this present state they will attain *parinirvāṇa.* It is taught like this of the *śrāvaka*s, and for the *pratyekabuddha*s it is also so. Why? Because this path is the same as that of beings with *śrāvaka* seed-nature.

And so on, as extensively taught. In order to make the bodhisattva rank appear similar to the two vehicles, three kinds of accomplishment are established within it like this. So the treatise states:

> If bodhisattvas dwell in the stage of superior understanding and practice, that is called lower-level accomplishment. If they dwell in the stage of pure, superior aspiration, that is called middle-level accomplishment. If they dwell in the decisively ultimate stage, it is called the higher-level accomplishment. If bodhisattvas dwell in the lower-level maturation, they will tend toward evil destinies. This exhausts [their rebirths in] the first incalculable great *kalpa.*

And so on, as extensively explained. The other two great *kalpa*s are paired with the other two levels of accomplishment. There are numerous other textual examples like this. The rest can be understood according to the standard of the above.

Second is the characteristics of nonreturning. According to the *Treatise on Buddha-nature,* when *śrāvaka*s reach the stage of tolerance of suffering, when *pratyekabuddha*s reach the world's highest Dharma, and when bodhi-
489a sattvas reach the ten conversions of merit, then they all are nonreturners. You should understand within this that these *śrāvaka*s and *pratyekabuddha*s are not those ignorant of Dharma. For this reason, they are all people of the three vehicles' Early Teaching. Moreover, all those before the bodhisattva stages can be explained as returners, because they still may fall into evil destinies. As the *Treatise on Yogācāra Stages* states, "If the bodhisattvas dwell in the stage of superior understanding and practice, they will still tend toward evil destinies. This exhausts [their rebirths in] the first incalculable great *kalpa,*" and so on.

Third is the clarification of the differences between the practices of the ranks. As the *Treatise on Yogācāra Stages* states:

> When the bodhisattvas, dwelling in superior understanding and practices, evolve spiritually, what are their practices and what are their characteristics? Sometimes, they are replete with wise intelligence, and are able to accept and uphold all dharmas, and are able to fully awaken into the doctrinal principles. But sometimes they cannot do this at one time. Sometimes for a time they are replete with remembrance [of their vows], sometimes for a time they become forgetful. With regard to the various living beings, these bodhisattvas have not yet been able to completely understand the skillful means of disciplining them; with regard to their own cultivation of Buddha-Dharma, they have likewise not yet completely understood how to capably apply skillful means in accordance with true reality. To explain the Dharma for others, they instruct and admonish, diligent in transmitting the teachings. But although they are diligent in transmitting the teachings, they have not been able to understand them in accordance with true reality. Sometimes their efforts are wasted, like shooting arrows in the dark, sometimes hitting the target and sometimes not, because their actions are formed from their desires. Sometimes for a time great *bodhi* has awakened in their minds, but later they turn back and abandon it. Due to their inner inclination for enjoyment they desire to enjoy themselves; due to their analytical thoughts, they desire to make others joyful. Sometimes,

> when for a time they hear the teaching of the profound and vast Dharma, they become afraid and doubtful. Those who are like this dwell in what is named superior understanding and practice.

Interpretation: These are the characteristics of practice in the second abode of the twelve abodes. The characteristics of the practices of the first, the abode of seed-nature, are even more deficient. The characteristics of the practices of the bodhisattva stages are all as taught [in the Yogācāra treatise].

3. Final Teaching

According to the Final Teaching, the differences of the ten bodhisattva stages are also taught, but not by such names as the path of insight and the path of cultivation. Furthermore, prior to the bodhisattva stages there are only the three worthy sets of practices, because the stages of faith are only considered to be practices and not ranks; they are not yet said to be the attainment of nonreturning. The *Sutra on Basic Activities* states, "Prior to ascending to the abodes there are the ten kinds of mind." They are not called ranks. It also states:

> Beginning from the stage of ordinary being to the time of encountering buddhas and bodhisattvas, to give rise to a single thought of faith in any of the correct teachings of the Dharma is to aspire to *bodhi*-mind. This person at that time is called a bodhisattva with the characteristic of faith prior to the abodes. This person is also called a provisionally named bodhisattva and a bodhisattva in name only. This person, in summary, cultivates the practices of the ten minds, which are faith, endeavor.

And so on, as extensively taught in that text. The *Sutra for Benevolent Kings* also states, "Before the habituation of the five kinds of tolerance, the bodhisattvas practicing the ten good abstentions advance and retreat, like delicate hairs following the wind to the east or west."

In these practices they pass through tens of thousands of *kalpa*s and enter
the rank of the ten abodes, where they attain nonreturning. At the beginning 489b
of the ten abodes there is no returning or falling down into the stages of the two vehicles, much less evil destinies or the stages of ordinary beings. Although the *Sutra on Basic Activities* teaches that some beings regress from the sixth mind of the ten abodes, *The Awakening of Faith* explains this passage

as showing regression for the sake of urging on the minds of the lazy and lax, while in reality bodhisattvas who have entered the abodes of awakened mind have already attained nonreturning.

As to the characteristics of practices, *The Awakening of Faith* teaches that at the beginning rank of the three worthy sets of practices, one will partially attain a view of the Dharma body and be able to benefit the living beings of the worlds of the ten directions with manifestations of the eight aspects of a buddha's life. Moreover, by the power of vow one will freely accept rebirth into a delimited body, but will not be bound by karmic ties. On the basis of *samādhi,* one will attain a partial view of the Buddha's reward body, and one's practices will all comply with true nature. This means "understanding that the essence of dharmas is without stinginess or greed, and therefore, in compliance with it, cultivating *dāna-pāramitā* (perfection of generosity)" and so on, as extensively taught in that text. Also, in the Liang *Summary of the Great Vehicle,* the ten stages of faith are named the stages of "ordinary bodhisattvas," while the ten understandings are called the stages of "sage bodhisattvas." By this standard you can understand that the characteristics of the practices of the bodhisattva stages are even more superior. For these reasons, you should understand that the characteristics of practices and ranks within this Final Teaching and those of the Early Teaching discussed above are obviously different in terms of shallowness and depth.

Question: Why does this teaching not similarly draw in the followers of the two vehicles? Why are the practices and ranks of the Final Teaching not similar to those of the Lesser Vehicle?

Reply: From this point on, the various teachings are all profoundly superior. Those beings drawn in from the two vehicles are pure, mature, and of highly superior capacity, so it does not need to imitate those Lesser teachings.

4. Sudden Teaching

According to the Sudden Teaching, all practices and ranks are inexpressible because they are beyond characteristics. Not one thought is produced: this is buddhahood. If one sees distinctions in the characteristics of practices and ranks, this is inverted thinking. If one were to show it by putting it in words, it is as the *Laṅkāvatāra* states: "The first stage is in fact the eighth stage." It even states that "none of them exist at all, so how could there be a sequence among them?" Also, the *Sutra on the Questions of Viśeṣacinti Brahmā* states:

> If people learn the true nature of these dharmas, studiously practicing and endeavoring as they are taught, they do not go from one stage to another stage. If they do not go from one stage to another stage, these people do not dwell in samsara or in nirvana.

And so on.

5. Perfect Teaching

According to the Perfect Teaching, there are two significances to the distinctions in practices and ranks. One, it encompasses all the previous practices and ranks as illuminated by the various teachings, because they are all the skillful means of this [Common Teaching]. Two, according to the Distinct Teaching, there are the three significances (i.e., ranks, nonreturning, and practices).

First [the Perfect Teaching] is shown from the perspective of ranks attained. That is, beginning from the ten stages of faith and going on up to the stage of buddhahood, there are six ranks, which is not the same as in the other vehicles. Upon attaining one rank, one attains all ranks. How so? Because [all the ranks] include the six characteristics; because of the interdependent arising of principal and attendants; because of mutual intersection; because of mutual identification; because of perfect interfusion. The [*Flower Garland*] *Sutra* states, "Within one stage, the merits of all the various stages are universally encompassed." Thus, in the sutra, "Upon the fulfilled mind of the ten stages of faith, when one is advancing to the next stage, one attains all 489c
ranks up to the stage of buddhahood" is in reference to this. Moreover, all the various ranks up to the stage of buddhahood are mutually identified, and so on. This is the nonduality of cause and result, the nonobstruction of beginning and end. At each and every rank one is a bodhisattva, and one is a buddha. This is its significance.

Second, the characteristics of the ranks are clarified from the perspective of karmic recompense. In this there are only three kinds of rebirths. One is to be born at the rank of seeing and hearing, which means seeing and hearing this inexhaustible Dharma gate and forming indestructible diamond seeds, as taught in the "Arising from Original Nature" chapter [of the *Flower Garland*

Sutra]. Two is to be born at the rank of understanding and practice, which refers to those who have already departed from evil ways, such as the Prince of Tuṣita Heaven. In a single lifetime they attain the tolerance of the understanding of the unproduced nature of dharmas upon the ten bodhisattva stages, and the realms of the ten kinds of vision and the ten kinds of hearing and so on, before attaining the *samādhi* beyond defilements. This is extensively taught in the "Lesser Characteristics" chapter [of the *Flower Garland Sutra*]. It is also like Sudhana, who went from the ten stages of faith and on through the ten bodhisattva stages, completely fulfilling all these practices and ranks of Samantabhadra in one birth and one body with the support of the good friends in the Dharma that he found; this is its significance. Three is the rank of verification of the ocean of result (i.e., buddhahood). That is, for example, when Maitreya said to Sudhana, "When I accomplish correct awakening in the time to come, you shall see me." You should understand that this is divided from the perspective of the cause and result into two ranks: before and after [awakening]. Thus, at the rank of "before," there is only the cause, while the perfected result exists in the rank of "after." So he says, "You shall see me."

Third, the ranks are clarified from the perspective of practice. There are only two parts: the initial part of the stage and the part of advancing to the next stage. This Dharma gate is taught on the basis of the understandings and practices of all the various ranks above, and the distinctions in the dharmas thereby attained. It is like those such as the prince Universal Adornment, whose body dwells above the tenfold worlds, such as the original nature worlds. This must be the rank of the wheel-turning king of the pure white jewel net. Attaining the universally seeing eyes of flesh, he sees the oceans of worlds of the ten buddha lands, as innumerable as motes of dust. But the eyes of flesh of the three vehicles are not like this. The *Treatise on the Larger Prajñāpāramitā Sutra* states, "Eyes of flesh only see things within the three thousand worlds. If they could see outside the three thousand worlds, why make use of the heavenly eyes?" This is so you know they are not the same.

Also, within a single thought, they can transform inexpressibly inexpressible multitudes of living beings, causing them all to come up to the *samādhi* beyond defilements at once. Within all of their other thoughts it is also like this. They perfectly reflect the good fortune reaped from this, like Dīpaṃkara's crystal mirror, illuminating the oceans of worlds of the ten buddha lands as innumerable as motes of dust. You should understand that these are the characteristics of practice within the rank of understanding and practice, among the previously described three kinds of rebirth. This is shown from the perspective of the Dharma gate of causation. From the perspective of the ranks attained by the fulfillment of faith and beyond, however, all practices and functions arise everywhere throughout the Dharma realm. As the [*Flower Garland*] *Sutra* states:

> [Bodhisattvas] can cover the great thousandfold worlds with one hand, from that hand producing offerings equal to the Dharma realm that is as vast as empty space, at one time offering nourishment to the infinite numbers of various buddhas, doing great Buddhist works for the enrichment 490a
> of living beings. These practices and functions are inexpressible.

This as is extensively taught in the scripture passages on the ranks of faith. It also states:

> Without leaving one world, without rising from one seat, [bodhisattvas] can yet manifest all the practices of innumerable bodies, and within a single thought can become the buddhas turning the Dharma wheels in the worlds of the ten directions at once.

And so on, as extensively taught. For these reasons you should understand that it is completely different from those teachings of the three vehicles. Why? Because the practices and ranks of the three vehicles are created from the perspective of trusting and understanding the teachings of the Āgamas, so they are explained like this.

Question: Previously in the section on the Final Teaching you said that at the time of nonreturning one also attains these eight characteristic actions of a buddha and other such functions. How is that different from this?

Reply: That Final Teaching shows that when buddhahood is realized in this given rank, it is not freely realized in all the latter ranks, because they have not yet been attained. Only the transformations appropriate to the present rank arise for the short time one is in it. This Perfect Teaching is not so. When these functions arise within the initial rank, they also arise together at the same time within later ranks; they have all already been attained, because this is true practice, which includes all six ranks.

Question: Then the significances are not the same. Why are they nevertheless taught to be the same in terms of arising these functions upon the superior advancement portion of the rank in the fulfillment of faith?

Reply: The desire to expediently manifest this One Vehicle teaching of the fulfillment of faith and the achievement of buddhahood makes it easy to believe and receive; so, this teaching was made first in that Final Teaching.

Question: So all the ranks are within the first rank, and with the mind of fulfilled faith one already attains buddhahood. Why must the Distinct Teaching also teach the various ranks that come after?

Reply: It teaches that the various latter ranks are indeed, all of them, within the initial rank. As it is with the initial rank, so it is with the latter ranks.

Question: If it is the case that the initial rank includes the latter ranks, and upon attaining the initial rank one attains the latter ranks, then can it also be that the latter ranks likewise include the initial rank? Shouldn't it be that if one does not attain the latter ranks then one doesn't attain the initial rank?

Reply: It is in fact so. Just by attaining the initial rank, all of the latter ranks are attained; thus, there is no one who would attain the latter rank and yet not attain the initial rank.

Question: If it is as you say, how can it teach that there is advancing and descending in sequence among the various ranks?

Reply: There are two skillful reasons within this scripture by which the various ranks are securely established. One, from the perspective of characteristics and with regard to the doctrinal gates, the ranks are divided in sequential order to be similar to the three vehicles, to draw those practitioners into this Common Teaching by skillful means. Two, from the perspective of essential substance and with regard to Dharma, the ranks that come before and after are mutually intersecting. This [state of] perfect interfusion and autonomy is different from the teaching of those three vehicles; this is the Distinct Teaching. However, because as doctrinal gates they are unmoving, their eternal characteristics are not destroyed, and so they are eternal in their sequence. For this reason, the two significances interfuse and do not contradict each other.

Question: If it is so that the initial gate [of the stage of faith] is identical with all ranks, then why does the Distinct Teaching not teach that all ranks are attained in the initial mind of the ranks of faith, rather than teach that all are attained in the fulfilled mind of faith?

Reply: If this were considered from the standpoint of the Distinct Teaching, then indeed, accomplishment does not depend on ranks. But our discussion here is according to the explanation of the ranks in the Final Teaching of the three vehicles. Within that teaching, upon reaching nonreturning, in the ful- 490b
fillment of faith, one attains entry into the ranks. Now, in the case of this Distinct Teaching, those who have attained entry into the ranks attain all the characteristics of the practices of the various early and later ranks at once. It does not teach that they all are attained in the initial mind of faith, because one who has not yet attained nonreturning has not yet achieved the characteristics of the ranks; it is only a matter of practice.

Question: If it is so, then shouldn't we say that buddhahood is accomplished in the rank of the abodes? Why is it called "fulfillment of faith"?

Reply: By the very reason that faith is formed, this is the buddhahood of practice, not the buddhahood of rank. The rest of the significance you should understand accordingly.

D. Duration of Cultivation

Fourth is the explanation of the duration of cultivation.

1. Lesser Vehicle

According to the Lesser Vehicle, there are three kinds of people. "Lower-level spiritual roots" refers to the many *śrāvaka*s, those who are most swift in attaining the result of arhatship within three lifetimes. That is, in their first lifetime they plant the causes of liberation; in the second lifetime they pursue decisive insight; in the third lifetime contamination by goal-orientation is eliminated and the result is attained. The latest arrive in sixty *kalpa*s. "Middling spiritual roots" refers to *pratyekabuddha*s; those who are most swift attain the result in four lifetimes, while the slowest take a hundred *kalpa*s. "Higher-level spiritual roots" refers to buddhas, who are certain to fulfill buddhahood in three *asaṃkhyeya kalpa*s, within which there are numerous *kalpa*s. Taking the *kalpa* that ends in fire, the *kalpa* that ends in water, and the *kalpa* that ends in wind each as one *kalpa* makes one count. Ten of these combined as one makes the second count. Multiplying like this until the sixtieth makes one *asaṃkhyeya kalpa.* This is the way to count three *asaṃkhyeya kalpa*s.

Question: Why is it that those of lower-level spiritual roots take less time, but those of higher-level spiritual roots take more time?

Reply: To be able to cultivate the practices of training the spiritual roots over a long period of time is considered the more difficult, so more time is taken.

Moreover, according to the *Mahāvibhāṣā-śāstra,* in a bodhisattva's achievement of buddhahood there are two bodies. One is the Dharma body, two is the living body. As to the Dharma body, this refers to the five parts of morality, concentration, wisdom, and so on (i.e., morality body, concentration body, wisdom body, liberation body, and awareness of liberation body). The cultivation of this Dharma body includes four time periods. One is the time of cultivating the four *pāramitā*s with contamination by residual goal-orientation for three *asaṃkhyeya kalpa*s. Second is cultivating the activities that produce the primary and secondary characteristics of buddhahood for a hundred *kalpa*s. Third is the time of leaving home to become a mendicant, ascetic practices, and cultivating *dhyāna* concentration. Fourth is the time of achieving correct awakening under the *bodhi* tree. As to the living body, in only one hundred *kalpa*s of cultivating the activities that produce the primary and secondary characteristics of buddhahood, with the final bodily lifetime in the royal family of King Śuddhodana of Gaya, he was reborn in the reward body and ascended to the way of awakening in the kingdom of Magadha. The rest is as taught in the Lesser Vehicle.

2. Early Teaching

According to the Early Teaching, the cultivation and attainment of buddhahood definitely takes three *asaṃkhyeya kalpa*s, but these *kalpa*s are not the same as those of the Lesser Vehicle. How so? The Early Teaching takes the *kalpa* that ends in fire, the *kalpa* that ends in water, and so on to be great *kalpa*s; counting these up to a hundred thousand, they then count these units a hundred thousand times to make a complete *koṭī:* this they call the first count. Counting in this way to complete a *koṭī,* and then counting a *koṭī* of

these units makes the second count. In this way they multiply them by the number counted until they reach one hundred, and call it an *asaṃkhyeya kalpa*. This is the first of the ten great *kalpa*s. One fulfills three *asaṃkhyeya* 490c
*kalpa*s in this way of counting.

Even the life of Śākyamuni fits into this doctrine, within this Early Teaching. As the *Sutra on Upāsaka Precepts* states:

> I, long ago, at the place of Ratnaśikhin Buddha fulfilled the first *asaṃkhyeya kalpa;* at the place of Dīpaṃkara Buddha I fulfilled the second *asaṃkhyeya kalpa;* at the place of Kāśyapa Buddha I fulfilled the third *asaṃkhyeya kalpa.* I, long ago, at the place of Śākya[muni] Buddha, first gave rise to the mind of *anuttarā samyaksaṃbodhi.*

Also, according to the *Sutra on Basic Activities,* although there may be a hundred *kalpa*s of cultivating the activities that produce the primary and secondary characteristics of buddhahood, this is only for the sake of transformation, and not the true cultivation. Moreover, by means of a single verse in praise of Puṣya Buddha, [a bodhisattva] skipped over nine *kalpa*s, becoming a buddha in only ninety-one *kalpa*s.

Question: If after three innumerable *kalpa*s of cultivating the myriad true practices one should achieve the reward body, why does the Early Teaching still teach it to be the transformation body?

Reply: This is because this Early Teaching is taught for those of lower spiritual capacity; it is for the two vehicles. It is because the transformation body is what they can see and understand. This teaching was made as a provisional teaching.

3. Final Teaching

According to the Final Teaching, there are two significances. One, the duration of practices is fixed as three *asaṃkhyeya kalpa*s, because it is from the perspective of a single transformative method of teaching (i.e., appropriate only to this present world). Within this teaching, cultivation of true practice results in achievement of the true reward body. This is not taught from the perspective of the transformation body. Thus, the *Lotus Sutra* states, "Since I truly became a buddha, immeasurable and boundless hundreds of thousands of millions of *asaṃkhyeya kalpa*s have passed." Also, the [*Diamond*] *Sutra* states, "In the place of Dīpaṃkara Buddha I received assurances of future buddhahood," and so on. These are to be discerned as skillful means.

The Final Teaching also maintains that there are no hundred *kalpa*s of cultivating the activities that produce the primary and secondary characteristics of buddhahood. How so? Because within the Lesser Vehicle only the part of the path to enlightenment that is based on wisdom is cultivated, while the part of the path that is based on cultivation of good fortune is not cultivated; so, at the time when one is about to achieve buddhahood, there is yet another hundred *kalpa*s of separately cultivating activities that generate good fortune. The Early Vehicle draws in those Lesser Vehicle practitioners, so it teaches the same doctrine as theirs in this regard, which is still the teaching of the transformation body. Within this Final Teaching, when it discusses true practice, the parts of the path based on merit and wisdom are both cultivated from the first intention for enlightenment; thus, at the time of becoming a buddha there is no other cultivation.

The other [significance] is that the duration of cultivation is not fixed as three *asaṃkhyeya kalpa*s. This has two significances: practice extends through other various kinds of temporal worlds, as taught in the *Sutra of King Pravaradeva;* and practice is based on the infinitude of the Buddha's virtues. As the *Jewel Cloud Sutra* states:

> My good sons, the bodhisattvas cannot conceive of the realm of the Tathāgata. The realm of the Tathāgata cannot be comprehended. It is only for the sake of the shallow minds of the myriad beings that I teach of *bodhi* attained by practicing for three *asaṃkhyeya kalpa*s, but for you I teach the truth that the duration of practice since truly aspiring for enlightenment
> 491a cannot be calculated.

Interpretation: As to that which "cannot be calculated" in this passage, it is incalculable *asaṃkhyeya kalpa*s; there are not only three.

Question: Why does the preceding teaching fix the duration of practices as three *asaṃkhyeya kalpa*s, while this teaching has fixed and nonfixed durations of practices?

Reply: The preceding Early Teaching is immature. This Final Teaching is mature. The teaching is made like this as a skillful means to gradually turn those practitioners of the three vehicles toward the One Vehicle.

4. Sudden Teaching

According to the Sudden Teaching, all times and divisions of durations of practice are inexpressible. Not one thought is produced—just that is buddhahood. That one thought is the absence of thought. As to time, it is the absence of time. The rest can be understood accordingly.

5. Perfect Teaching

According to the Perfect Teaching, all times and divisions of durations of practice are entirely unfixed. How so? Because all *kalpa*s mutually intersect; because they are mutually identified. They thoroughly pervade all the myriad worlds, such as Indra's world and so on. Thus, in accordance with each situation, the duration of practices may be one thought or it may be infinite *kalpa*s, but it does not contradict the teachings of times. Use this standard to reflect upon the rest.

E. Embodied Basis of Cultivation

Fifth is the embodied basis of cultivation.

1. Lesser Vehicle

According to the Lesser Vehicle, there is only the delimited body up to ultimate rank, and the Buddha is also the same. The buddha body is a real body, not the transformation body.

2. Early Teaching

According to the Early Teaching, in order to bring about the conversion of mind of the *śrāvaka*s, the teaching is that there is the delimited body up to the ultimate rank, and that the buddha body is likewise, but this buddha body is the transformation body, not a real body.

As to the bodhisattvas who advance directly into the Great Vehicle, there are two explanations within this Early Teaching. One: According to the rank of the practitioner, it shows the different characteristics of the two ranks—coarse and fine, effort and effortlessness—within the ten bodhisattva stages. It teaches that in the seventh stage and below one has a delimited body while in the eighth stage and above one has a mutable body. Two: With regard to the true reward body, it explains that the delimited body exists at all stages up to the diamond stage (i.e., completion of the bodhisattva stages). Because the seeds of the afflictive hindrances have not yet been eternally severed within the ten bodhisattva stages, they remain even up to the diamond stage. As there are delusive hindrances, how could it be that such a one would not receive a delimited body?[19] Thus, the *Ten Stages Sutra* states, "There are beings in the state of intermediate existence [between life and death] up to the tenth stage." This is what it means.

Question: At the eighth stage and above, all bodhisattvas have long since subdued the afflictive hindrances and do not act them out. Since the result of uncontaminated wisdom continues forever, they are like arhats, without any occurrence of delusion. Why should they receive delimited bodies?

Reply: If we were referring to ordinary beings, those beings would receive rebirth by the occurrence of delusions fertilizing their karmic seeds. Sages are not like this. Only the [unfertilized] seeds of delusion remain to be used in receiving rebirth. As stated in the *Treatise on the Collected Abhidharma,* "All the sages are bound to continuous rebirth by the latent power [of unfertilized karmic seeds]." Also, the Liang *Summary of the Great Vehicle* states:

> Because they differ from ordinary beings, they are able to eternally subdue the delusions of advanced states of mind. Because they differ from the practitioners of the two vehicles, they retain their seeds.

Interpretation: The rebirth of sages is not based on the occurrence of delusion fertilizing seeds, but they do retain seeds.

491b [Question:] So why don't they receive delimited bodies? If you say that at the eighth stage and above cognitive hindrance is the condition of receiving a mutable body, then the seeds of delusion that remain would have no function. Why wouldn't it be that the seeds of affliction are destroyed forever starting in this eighth stage?

[Reply:] It isn't like that. So, what does this mean? If we consider it from the perspective of those *śrāvaka*s who turn toward *bodhi* and have already cut off afflictions, then they can receive mutable bodies by means of those cognitive hindrances, and pass through the various ranks.

Question: If this is so, why do the sacred teachings explain that at the eighth stage and above it is solely one's cognitive hindrances that serve as the basis for receiving the mutable body?

Reply: These teachings are meant to be compared with the teachings of the two vehicles, to show the respective superiority and inferiority of the teachings. The scripture explains it thus, but this comparison depends on the differences between the perspectives on the ranks in all the various sacred teachings. I will summarize them in ten gates, as follows.

One: It is taught that arhats are identical to buddhas, so the ranks are not divided. For example, in the Vinaya it is taught that when the Buddha delivered five people, he said, "With the Buddha included, there are six arhats who have gone out of the mundane world" and "they sat together," and so on. You should understand that this is from the perspective of the Lesser Vehicle teaching.

Two: Arhats are separated out from the buddha stage. For example, the *Treatise on the Collected Abhidharma* teaches that at the time of attaining *bodhi* the afflictive hindrances and any cognitive hindrances are suddenly cut off, so practitioners suddenly become arhats and tathāgatas. Although in this teaching the perspective is that "arhat" is the name for one who has eliminated afflictions, it is for the sake of producing superior aspirations within the minds of the *śrāvaka*s. It accordingly divides buddhahood into greater and lesser.

Three: The tenth stage is called arhat; as the buddha stage is transcendent, it is not that arhat stage. For example, in explaining the four kinds of reliable supports, the *Nirvana Sutra* states, "As to arhats, they dwell in the tenth stage." This matches the causes to the different results to divide them into greater and lesser. The two gates above are taught from the perspective of the Early Teaching converting the adherents of the two vehicles.

Four: The seventh stage and below are ascribed together to the arhats, while eighth stage and above are ascribed to the bodhisattva ranks. As the *Sutra for Benevolent Kings* states:

> Bodhisattvas at the seventh bodhisattva stage, which is called "distant traveling," subdue the habituated causes of the triple world. Having extinguished the karmic results, in their last [delimited] body, they reside in the seventh stage at the rank of arhat.

This places the ranks of autonomy and the ranks of not-yet-autonomous within the causal state to divide them into greater and lesser. This is from the perspective of the Early Teaching taught for the directly advancing bodhisattvas. Within this, since it ascribes the stages up to the seventh to the *śrāvaka*s, the afflictive hindrances and delimited body are present up to that rank. The eighth stage and onward are ascribed to these bodhisattvas; their practices and ranks are superior to those before. Thus, they have only the cognitive afflictions and the mutable body.

Five: The first, second, and third stages are attributed to the mundane world, because in them one attains the four kinds of meditation of the mundane world. The fourth stage is ascribed to the *śrotaāpanna*s, because they attain the factors conducive to the path of enlightenment, and because it is the first
491c attainment of the supramundane. The fifth stage is ascribed to the *śrāvaka* arhats, because they have attained the Dharma of the four noble truths. The sixth stage is ascribed to the *pratyekabuddha*s, because they attain the Dharma of twelvefold dependent origination. The seventh stage and onward are ascribed to the bodhisattvas, because they attain the tolerance of the understanding of the unproduced nature of dharmas. This is as taught in the *Sutra on Basic Activities.* The foregoing is taught solely from the perspective of the three vehicles, since the One Vehicle Dharma has not yet been separated out.

Six: Worldly beings and practitioners of the two vehicles, as in the previous, reach the sixth stage. The seventh stage is ascribed to bodhisattvas of the three vehicles, because they have still not attained autonomy. The eighth stage and onward are ascribed to the One Vehicle practitioners because they attain autonomy. This is as taught in such texts as the Liang *Summary of the Great Vehicle.* This is taught from the perspective of separating the characteristics of the One Vehicle from those of the three vehicles.

Seven: Within the initial stage, practitioners have already surpassed the mundane world and the two vehicles. This is taught in such texts as the *Treatise on the Bodhisattva Stages.* It is taught from the perspective of the distinction between inferential and direct realization within the three vehicles.

Eight: Before the bodhisattva stages, the rank of the three worthy sets of practices already surpasses the stages of the two vehicles, as taught in *The Awakening of Faith.* And the *Sutra for Benevolent Kings* teaches, "There are ten kinds of mind within the habitual seed-nature, which already surpass all the beneficial stages of the two vehicles." This is taught from the perspective of nonreturning in the Final Teaching.

Nine: After the mind of fulfilled faith, one surpasses all the ranks of the Lesser Vehicle and the three vehicles, as taught in the "Bhadraśrī" chapter [of the *Flower Garland Sutra*]. This is taught from the perspective of the One Vehicle.

Ten: When the mind of a practitioner first aspires to enlightenment, in the initial stage of ordinary beings, this already surpasses the two vehicles. As taught in the *Treatise on the Larger Prajñāpāramitā Sutra,* "The arhat *bhikṣu* knew that the *śrāmaṇera* had aspired to enlightenment, and put the *śrāmaṇera* ahead of himself." This is taught in both the One Vehicle and the three vehicles.

You should understand the order of the various teachings by this standard, through the comparison of dharmas in such gates as these.

3. Final Teaching

According to the Final Teaching, practitioners retain delusions and receive 492a
the delimited body prior to the bodhisattva stages. Within the first bodhisattva stage all the seeds of afflictions are forever severed, and they are not divided into discriminatory and inborn seeds. Moreover, within cognitive hindrances, one part of the coarse afflictions proper are cut off. For this reason, those in the bodhisattva stages receive the mutable body up to the diamond stage. The rest of this doctrine is as explained below in the section on severing delusions.

Question: If those in the bodhisattva stages do not retain afflictions, how could they embrace the suffering of living beings with great compassion and cooperation?

Reply: Because prior to entering the bodhisattva stages and within the Early Teaching, the power of their wisdom and vows is weak, so they retain afflictions and receive the rebirth that helps them fulfill their vows. But now this is not the case. Because their vow-wisdom is superior they can freely commune with living beings.

Question: It is taught that above the eighth stage there are, in summary, two kinds of bodhisattvas: those of higher compassion and those of higher wisdom. Those of higher compassion retain delusions and receive the delimited body.

Those of higher wisdom subdue delusions and receive the mutable body. What does this doctrine mean?

Reply: I'm afraid that explaining it like this is not quite right. Why? If their compassion is higher, their wisdom must be inferior; if inferior wisdom guides their compassion, their compassion must be clouded by false views. How could compassion clouded by false views be called "higher"? Even if compassion and wisdom are equally balanced, then it can't be called "higher compassion." As it is with inferior wisdom guiding compassion yet calling it higher, so it is with those of higher wisdom. Their compassion must be inferior; inferior compassion guides their wisdom, and their wisdom must be clouded by quiescence. How could the wisdom clouded by quiescence be called "higher"? All bodhisattvas differ from ordinary beings from the beginning, so their compassion and wisdom guide each other. With every thought they cultivate both—like the two wheels of a cart, like the two wings of a bird. How could we say that they are higher or lower?

You should understand by this that the two teachings of Early and Final differ in their coarseness and fineness. There are two kinds of bodies in birth and death (i.e., the delimited and the mutable), but this is not due to either compassion or wisdom being higher. If you say that those bodhisattvas of higher wisdom have Lesser Vehicle habits and have forever subdued their afflictions out of fear of afflictions, or that prior to the bodhisattva stages they have not yet verified true thusness, then from the perspective of original habituation one could permit the existence of this kind of practitioner, because they are not yet pure and mature. According to this Final Teaching, however, from the initial stage on up their practices and understandings are pure and mature; they have the same realization, the same practice, the same cultivation, the same severing of afflictions. How could there be such distinctions? Thus, *The Awakening of Faith* states, "There are no differences among either the seed-nature, the aspiration to enlightenment, or the practices cultivated by bodhisattvas in the stages." Moreover, within this Final Teaching, the mutable
492b body in the stages is not the same with regard to the ranks. There are four kinds, as indicated below.[20]

4. Sudden Teaching

According to the Sudden Teaching, all practices and ranks are inexpressible.

The allotted body on which the practices depend is likewise to be understood by this standard. This is as extensively taught in the *Larger Prajñāpāramitā Sutra* in the part on the bodhisattva Nāgaśrī.

5. Perfect Teaching

In the Perfect Teaching, the mutable body is not taught, but the delimited body reaches up to the tenth stage prior to the concentration beyond defilements. Because upon reaching that rank one attains the universally seeing eyes of flesh, we understand that this is the delimited body. It is also like Sudhana, who exhausted the ranks of causation by means of his delimited body.

Question: Why does this Perfect Teaching not teach the mutable body?

Reply: Bodies such as those of the original nature worlds and above, being extremely subtle and transcending the many heavens, must be the same as the mutable body. But because this teaching does not separate the coarse and fine characteristics of birth and death—instead considering them together with regard to transgression and misfortune as being of one realm until the fulfillment of faith, after which practitioners suddenly overturn that realm—it doesn't teach it. The rest can be understood accordingly.

F. Distinctions in the Severing of Delusions

Sixth are the distinctions in the explanations of severing delusions.

1. Lesser Vehicle

The teaching according to the Lesser Vehicle is as taught elsewhere.

2. Three Vehicles: Early and Final Teachings

According to the three vehicles, there are two kinds of significance. One, the characteristics of extinguishing delusions are clarified from the perspective of ranks. Two, the characteristics of ranks are shown according to the kinds of delusion that pertain to them.

i. Characteristics of Extinguishing Delusions

As to the former, in the Early Teaching the three vehicles' teachings of the differences among the means of severing delusions are fully complete, because it is the origin of the other three vehicles teachings. There are two kinds of hindrances, afflictive and cognitive. First I will discuss the two vehicles'[21] explanations of severing afflictive hindrances, within which there are two parts. First are the names and numbers of the hindrances; second is the result attained upon severing the delusions.

a. Afflictive Hindrances

Within the first part, there are two general categories of afflictions: those produced from discrimination [in this life], and those that are born together with the body (i.e., inborn; retained from a previous life). In all, there are ten kinds:

1. Craving
2. Aversion
3. Ignorance
4. Pride
5. Doubt
6. False view of the existence of an independent self
7. Extreme views
8. Perverse views
9. Attachment to views
10. Attachment to precepts

Within these, four kinds arise only as afflictions produced from discrimination: doubt, perverse views, attachment to views, and attachment to precepts. The other six are of both of the two kinds, discriminated and inborn. The five consciousnesses give rise to the first three; they are both discriminated and inborn. Within *mano* consciousness (i.e., mental consciousness, the sixth consciousness), the afflictions produced from discrimination arise through the functioning of their three causes, which are false teachers, [false teachings, and false thinking]. The *mano* consciousness has all ten kinds of affliction; the four discriminated kinds and the six that are of both kinds. The *manas* (seventh consciousness) only includes four of the inborn afflictions. Of the six inborn afflictions, aversion and extreme views are excluded. Aversion is excluded by being unwholesome, because impeded moral indeterminacy is the quality of the *manas* consciousness. There are no extreme views because of the propensity of the *manas* to perpetuate similar characteristics in dependence on the eighth consciousness, and its continual attachment to self. Moreover, because the four discriminated afflictions are produced in connection with their three causes, *manas* consciousness does not have them and they do not arise. Also, because of the condition of eternal continuity of characteristics, [the afflictions of the *manas*] are not drawn from the sixth consciousness and are not the same as those of the five consciousnesses. Thus, there are only four afflictions included. In the eighth consciousness (i.e., storehouse consciousness) none of them arise, because it consists only of the variable ripening of karmic seeds, and has the quality of unimpeded moral indeterminacy.

These discriminatory and inborn kinds of affliction are all found throughout
the triple world. Aversion is only found in the desire world, because the afflic- 492c
tions of the upper two worlds all have the quality of impeded moral indeterminacy. As to those which arise because of discrimination, each of the four noble truths of the desire realm has the ten defilements, making forty kinds of afflictions. The upper two worlds exclude aversion, so their noble truths each have nine kinds, totaling seventy-two. Combining these with those of the desire world makes one hundred and twelve altogether. As to those which are inborn, the desire world includes six. The upper two worlds exclude aversion, so each has only five; combining them makes sixteen, and with the discriminatory afflictions above that makes altogether one hundred and twenty-eight.

Question: How is it that within the previous Lesser Vehicle of the ignorant teaching, all ten defilements do not cause confusion about the four noble truths, but within this Early Teaching all of them do?

Reply: This has two significances: it is because within the three vehicles the power of afflictions has gradually expanded, obstructing everything; and it is also because confusion and such ideas pervade all objects of mind.

As to the results attained upon severing delusions, first we will clarify the severing of discriminated delusions in terms of the three kinds of people who do so. The first kind of person goes from being fully bound by delusion into the path of direct insight; in an instant they suddenly sever the discriminatory afflictions of the four noble truths of the triple world and attain the result of stream-entry. The second kind of person abandons a double portion of the afflictions of the desire realm; they enter the path of true insight and at the same time abandon a double portion of the afflictions of the desire realm, attaining the result of once-returner. These who "abandon a double portion of the afflictions of the desire realm" are those who cultivate the severing of the nine classes of delusion while they are ordinary beings in the desire world; since they have already suppressed the former six of the nine (i.e., two-thirds), they are called those who "abandon a double portion of the afflictions of the desire realm." When they enter the path of insight they sever the previously suppressed afflictions forever, and in this way attain the result of once-returner. The third kind of person has already gone beyond the realm of desire; they enter the path of true insight and simultaneously sever the nine classes of delusion, attaining the result of non-returner. As the *Treatise on Yogācāra Stages* explains, the results of entering the path of true insight are of three kinds; they will verify the three results according to what they deserve.

Next are the results attained upon severing inborn afflictions. The inborn afflictions of the sixth consciousness have nine classes at each of the nine levels. Moreover, there are two kinds of people who advance into the path of cultivation. The first [kind] is those who gradually depart from the mundane and completely sever the afflictions of the first six classes of the nine classes of the desire world attain the result of once-returner. Those who completely sever the nine classes attain the result of non-returner. Those who completely sever the afflictions of the upper two worlds attain the result of arhatship. The second [kind] is those who suddenly depart from the mundane are those who attain the initial result (i.e., stream-enterer) and then suddenly sever the afflictions of the triple world. They gradually eliminate the afflictions of the nine classes, and attain the result of arhatship. Then there is no further result. Why is this so? Because in the cultivation of severing the afflictions of the nine classes of the desire world together with those of the upper two worlds, there are three kinds of the nine classes, each with its own first class. These practitioners suddenly sever them at once, so I say they suddenly sever the afflictions of the triple world. When this is discussed temporally, each one of the nine classes is separately severed, so I say they are gradually eliminated. If this is so, why are there some who sever afflictions gradually? This is because they cannot suddenly apprehend all the dharmas of the triple world. The *Treatise on the Collected Abhidharma* states:

> Those who suddenly abandon afflictions are those who have already
> 493a entered the clear observation of the four noble truths. With their basis in

> incomplete concentration, they aspire to depart from the mundane way. Suddenly severing all the afflictions of the triple world, and separately severing afflictions class by class, they only establish the two kinds of result. This refers to the result of stream-enterer and the result of arhatship.

And so on, as explained in the widely cited *Fingertip Sutra.*[22]

Regarding the extremely subtle characteristics of the activity of the afflictions of the *manas,* the aforementioned two kinds of people, the gradual and the sudden, all suddenly sever afflictions at once with the delusions of the nonideation level (the ninth of the nine levels). Thus, the *Treatise on Yogācāra Stages* states:

> The *manas* is associated with the carried-over (i.e., inborn) afflictions, which are only severed together with the afflictions of the nonideation level. Being severed suddenly and all at once, they are not like the other delusions that are gradually severed in sequence.

Question: Why do the previous two vehicles of the ignorant teaching not have the teaching of sudden transcendence, while this Early Teaching does have it?

Reply: In order to demonstrate the inferiority of the previous teachings, this teaching surpasses it. The two vehicles of the ignorant teaching do not have this superior wisdom. Demonstrating the inferiority of that teaching is a skillful means to gradually draw in two vehicles practitioners and inspire superior desires in them. This teaching was made to cause them to renounce the Lesser and follow the Great.

As to the absence in the Lesser Vehicle of the teaching of extinguishing the delusions of the *manas,* you can understand it accordingly.

b. Cognitive Hindrances

Above was the two vehicles' explanation of severing afflictive hindrances. As to their teaching on cognitive hindrances, those who proceed into quiescence sever all the hindrances at once when they enter into nirvana of no remainder. This is the nonanalytical extinction. As to all the rest of the practitioners, some sever cognitive hindrances and some do not. The people who have been liberated by their wisdom do not sever them, while of those who have been liberated by both wisdom and concentration, some of them sever some of the hindrances. That is, the hindrance to the eight liberations, which is undefiled ignorance, is counteracted by cultivating the eight superior liberating understandings. As the *Treatise on Yogācāra Stages* explains, the various liberations are what is manifested through the liberation from cognitive hindrances, because *śrāvaka*s and *pratyekabuddha*s attain liberation with the mind of cognitive hindrances. You must understand that this Early Teaching exists in order to gradually draw those ignorant of the Dharma toward the Great Vehicle; thus, this teaching was established as profoundly superior to that Lesser Vehicle. Thus, the cognitive hindrances are indeed severed in part, but the above severed delusions are not the same as those of the ignorant teaching, since those practitioners only sever the acquisition of the afflictions. These practitioners of the Great Vehicle are not so; they sever the seeds of the afflictions. So when those bodhisattvas who advance directly into the Great Vehicle sever delusions, they sever both kinds of hindrances, afflictive and cognitive.

Moreover, within the afflictive hindrances, the perspective on dividing the classes among the realms is not the same as that of the two vehicles. Of the two kinds of hindrances, the occurrence of that kind of hindrance that arises from discrimination is subdued prior to the bodhisattva stages. At the time of entering the initial bodhisattva stage on the path of true insight, in one instant the seeds of the hindrances are suddenly severed. Those afflictive hindrances among the inborn hindrances can be freely severed from the initial bodhisattva stage and onward; yet in order to be retained, they are not severed. Why is that? It is because bodhisattvas nourish continued rebirth in order to embrace and transform all beings. In order to sever their cognitive hindrances, in order to attain great *bodhi,* they do not pursue the levels of the two vehicles.

For this reason, the *Summary of the Great Vehicle* states, "Through retaining delusions up to the end of delusion, buddhas verify all wisdom." Interpretation: As to ending delusion, it is ending cognitive hindrances. Superior practice arises through retaining afflictive hindrances. Attaining ranks up to this, one
493b verifies the result, which is buddhahood. Also, the Liang *Summary of the Great Vehicle* states, "They retain seeds." Thus, you should understand that the seeds of afflictive hindrances exist up to the diamond rank.

The activity of the cognitive hindrances is subtle, evidently obstructing the bodhisattva way. Stage by stage, they are severed in part. One must reach the stage of buddhahood, at which point they are altogether ended. Because of this, [the Early Teaching] teaches that the cultivation of severing the delusions of the two kinds of hindrances exists up to the stage of buddhahood. The *Treatise on the Collected Abhidharma* states:

> The many bodhisattvas, while at the rank of cultivating the way on the ten stages, only cultivate the way of counteracting the cognitive hindrances but not the afflictive hindrances. When they attain *bodhi,* they suddenly sever the afflictive hindrances and the cognitive hindrances, suddenly becoming arhats and tathāgatas.

The activity of the inborn afflictions of the *manas* is subtle, and as in the above discussion, this activity exists up to the stage of buddhahood and then is ended.

Question: The cultivation of severing the delusions of these two kinds of hindrances corresponds to the various levels of consciousness. How is their occurrence in the bodhisattva stages similar or different?

Reply: Within the afflictive hindrances, the delusions of the sixth consciousness are already ended upon entering the bodhisattva stages. Because these are ended, bodhisattvas retain the cognitive hindrances. Thus, whether in occurrence or as seeds, they are governed by wisdom. They are used to form superior practice and do not give rise to transgression or misfortune. It is like a poisonous snake that is governed by the power of an incantation, so that it does not cause death. Not giving rise to transgression or misfortune, but becoming otherwise useful: such is the skillfulness of the bodhisattvas in retaining their delusions. Thus, the *Summary of the Great Vehicle* states, "It is like making an incantation for controlling the damage done by poison." For this reason, you should understand that those afflictions, whether they are in the state of occurrence or of seed, may all be freely employed.

The nature of afflictions in the seventh consciousness is not to fertilize rebirth, so they are not retained. Their activity is subtle. At the seventh bodhisattva stage and below they sometimes briefly appear and interrupt contemplative wisdom. All these cognitive hindrances may arise in later stages or may arise in previous stages. Sometimes occurring, sometimes as seeds, they are separately severed stage by stage.

Question: If this is so, why are there places that explain that the contaminated mind arises at the seventh bodhisattva stage and below?

Reply: According to the perspective that afflictive hindrances within the sixth consciousness are considered to be contaminating, because that consciousness has retained delusions, it appears to be contaminated [but isn't really]. According to the perspective that the cognitive hindrances are considered to be contaminating, it is truly contaminated. These two kinds of hindrances pervade the ten bodhisattva stages. If the afflictions of the *manas* are truly contaminated, then up to the seventh bodhisattva stage their existence or nonexistence is indeterminate, because bodhisattvas at that stage sometimes briefly give rise to the contaminated mind. You should understand the rest of this doctrine according to this standard.

Also, as to distinctions in the extinction of delusions and the arising of wisdom within this teaching, they are as follows. At the time when the seeds of delusion are extinguished, wisdom is then produced; they revert into each other at the same time. It is like the common idea that what goes up must come down, and what goes down must come up. This is as extensively explained in the *Treatise on the Collected Abhidharma.* Moreover, the dharma of these hindrances is empty, with nothing by which to be discriminated, because it depends on consciousness and lacks self-nature. This is the significance of these hindrances. As the *Vimalakīrti-sūtra* states, "The five aggregates, as objects of attachment, are thoroughly penetrated by emptiness, giving rise to nothing. This is the significance of suffering." The significance of these hindrances can also be understood by this standard.

493c According to the Final Teaching, all *śrāvaka*s are still unable to sever the afflictive hindrances; they can only suppress them. How, then, could they sever the cognitive hindrances? Thus, the *Treatise on the Sutra of the Questions of Maitreya* states, "None of the *śrāvaka*s and *pratyekabuddha*s can truly cultivate the four immeasurable minds, nor can they finally sever all their afflictions; they can only suppress all their afflictions." A passage in the *Laṅkāvatāra-sūtra* also explains it as above.

Question: Why is this explanation different from the earlier teaching?

Reply: The earlier teaching is made to draw in the practitioners of the two vehicles; it is not yet a profound explanation. Thus, in making the higher teaching approximate the lower one, the afflictive hindrances are the same as those of the two vehicles up to the stage of buddhahood, at which point they are ended. In making the lower teaching the same as the higher, however, it also maintains that the practitioners of the two vehicles completely sever the delusive hindrances and partially sever the cognitive hindrances. Now, this Final Teaching approaches true reality. Because the practitioners of the two vehicles of the ignorant teaching do not have expansive minds, so it can also be maintained that they are not finally able to sever their afflictive hindrances. The previous explanation was from the perspective of *śrāvaka*s within the three vehicles. This includes the perspective of the ignorant teaching, so it is not the same.

The Final Teaching on bodhisattvas does not divide the two kinds of hindrances (afflictive and cognitive) into inborn and discriminatory; it only includes afflictions proper and habituated energies. Prior to the stages, bodhisattvas subdue the occurrence of afflictions. At the initial stage they sever the seeds of afflictions. Ascending through the stages, they remove habituated energies, and at the buddha stage they are finally pure. However, prior to the stages, they are in the ranks of the three worthy sets of practices, so from the beginning they do not sink into the stages of the two vehicles. They can freely sever or retain the afflictive hindrances; so, to retain them, they do not sever them, in order to remove cognitive hindrances. Thus, the Liang *Summary of the Great Vehicle* states, "After the ten understandings, one attains the pure mind of the supramundane." It also states, "Having reached the ten understandings, one is named a sage, and does not sink into the stages of the two vehicles." The *Sutra for Benevolent Kings* states, "Prior to the stages, one attains insight into the emptiness of one's person, but does not reach realization." Also, *The Awakening of Faith* expounds that upon attaining a partial glimpse of the Dharma body, a bodhisattva can perform the eight characteristic actions of a buddha, and so on. These passages all have this significance. Because of this [freedom to sever or retain afflictive hindrances], bodhisattvas only fear the cognitive hindrances, and so they cultivate the contemplations of consciousness only and true thusness, to suppress and sever those hindrances. However, they not only do not fear afflictive hindrances, they do not even cultivate the practice of counteracting them. They even retain [afflictive hindrances] to help them achieve superior practice. Once they have

reached the initial bodhisattva stage, they sever the coarse part of the cognitive hindrances and do not further retain afflictive hindrances. Thus, the two kinds
494a of hindrances are not divided between the paths of insight and cultivation. When bodhisattvas arrive at the initial stage, the afflictions proper are both eliminated. Thus, the *Treatise on the Sutra of the Questions of Maitreya* states:

> He asked, "If a *śrāvaka* first severs the afflictions that are severed on the path of insight, and later gradually severs the afflictions that are severed on the path of cultivation, why don't bodhisattvas do the same as *śrāvaka*s?"
>
> The Buddha replied, "The people who are bodhisattvas have done beneficial deeds for the sake of living beings for immeasurable generations. Later, seeing the Dharma realm of the sweet dew of true thusness, they observe the lives of all those myriad living beings, and realize this world is truly not different from the place they sought. Thus, for bodhisattvas, all the afflictions within the paths of insight and cultivation can obstruct the activity of benefiting living beings, and so upon the path of insight they are all severed together."

These passages are confirmation.

The coarse parts of the afflictions of the *manas* consciousness are likewise severed at the initial stage, and later the remnant fine parts are removed. Thus, Asvabhāva's *Commentary on the Summary of the Great Vehicle* states:

> Transforming the defiled *manas,* one attains the wisdom of the equality of all things. At the time of the initial insight into reality, one has already attained realization. In the ranks of the path of cultivation, the *manas* evolves further toward purification.

Interpretation: Evolving toward purification means removing habituated energies, because the afflictions proper were severed before. As to what happens after, the text refers to evolving toward purity, and does not mention severing afflictions.

[Question:] According to this statement, at the time of entering the path of true insight these afflictions are briefly subdued and do not arise; they are not actually severed. But in this case the *manas* should not be said to evolve further toward purification. As the afflictions are not yet completely severed, why is this called "evolving toward purity"?

[Reply:] According to the Early Teaching, such an explanation may be permitted. But you should understand that in this Final Teaching, in the bodhisattva stages one only removes the habitual energies.

The *Treatise on the Jewel Nature* states:

> Impurity is the afflictive hindrances, which all ordinary beings have. Defilement is the cognitive hindrances, which all the *śrāvaka*s and *pratyekabuddha*s have. Taint is the habitual energies of the two kinds of hindrances, upon which all bodhisattvas and *mahāsattva*s depend.

Interpretation: The treatise explains that those in the bodhisattva stages are named *mahāsattva*s; thus, we understand that they have only the hindrance of habitual energies. Within this, habitual energy follows from severing the seeds of the afflictions proper. Habitual energy may be present immediately. Why? When the seeds are not yet severed, there is no delicate residue (i.e., habitual energy). When the seeds are severed, then their delicate residue may immediately be present. The treatise explains it as "the immediate production of habitual energy."

Question: How is it that within the bodhisattva stages the afflictions proper are ended, and yet one does not sink into the stages of the two vehicles?

Reply: The power of their wisdom is superior, and they have already eliminated the afflictions proper of the cognitive hindrance. For example, when altruistic people of the Early Teaching and Lesser Vehicle suddenly depart from the mundane, completely severing the delusions of the six classes of the desire realm, they must in the same way completely sever the delusions of the six classes of the upper two worlds, and yet they never attain the result of once-returner. How exceptionally superior, then, is the power of this bodhisattva way! It is even more the case because of the afflictions proper of cognitive hindrance that have already been severed. If we were referring to those beings prior to the stages or followers of the Early Teaching, we could permit that loss of progress. But it does not exist within this Final Teaching. Moreover,
within this teaching, at the time of actually severing delusions, wisdom arises 494b
and delusion is extinguished. It is not at the beginning, at the middle, or after, because before, middle, and after are all taken [together]. You ask, how is it extinguished? Like the original purity of the empty sky: it is extinguished

thus, as extensively explained in the *Treatise on the Ten Stages*. Moreover, within this teaching, dharmas such as afflictions are all created from true thusness according with conditions. Thus, they are no different from true thusness. This is the significance of affliction, as taught in *The Awakening of Faith*. Moreover, the [*Vimalakīrti-*]*sūtra* states, "All dharmas are thusness," and so on. Afflictions meet this standard. Thus, you should understand that this doctrine is not the same as that which the various teachings above have postulated; you should understand it appropriately.

ii. Delusions Pertaining to Various Ranks

Second, the characteristics of ranks are shown via the pertinent kinds of delusion. All the explanations of the sacred teachings are summarized in eighteen gates.

One: Two ranks are shown via the two kinds of hindrances. This refers to the division of the hindrances into two, delusive and cognitive, to show the two ranks, which are inferential and direct realization. The Liang *Summary of the Great Vehicle* states, "Prior to the bodhisattva stages one gradually removes afflictive hindrances. In the stages one gradually removes the cognitive hindrances." It also states, "After the ten understandings one attains the pure mind of the supramundane." It also states, "Although one attains insight into one's own selflessness prior to the stages, because one has not yet realized the selflessness of dharmas, one is not yet pure; realizing one's own selflessness is therefore not purity." It also states, "Before, one is attached to one's sense of self; within the ten understandings it has been removed. Now there is only the attachment to the selfhood of dharmas to extinguish."

Also, the *Sutra for Benevolent Kings* states, "After the stage of habitual seed-nature one enters the rank of realizing the emptiness of one's own birth, and attains the nature of sagehood." The *Sutra on Basic Activities* and *The Awakening of Faith* have these same explanations.

Two: The three *asaṃkhyeya kalpa*s are shown via the three kinds of delusion; that is, of the flesh, and so on. The Liang *Summary of the Great Vehicle* states:

> In the first of the three *asaṃkhyeya kalpa*s one severs the afflictions of the outer skin; in the second *asaṃkhyeya* one severs the afflictions of the inner flesh; in the third *asaṃkhyeya* one severs the afflictions of the heart.[23]

Three: Three different minds of each of the stages are shown via these same three delusions. As in the explanation of the thirty-three *asaṃkhyeya kalpa*s in the Liang *Summary of the Great Vehicle,* in each stage, with the entering mind one removes afflictions of the outer skin, with the abiding mind one removes afflictions of the inner flesh, and with the departing mind one removes afflictions of the heart.

Four: Three ranks are shown via the fineness or coarseness of the two kinds of hindrance. As the *Bodhisattva Stages Sutra* states, "The two kinds of hindrance pervade the three places, which refers to the time prior to the stages, the bodhisattva stages, and the stage of buddhahood."

Five: The three bodies are shown via the coarseness or fineness of the defiled mind in the three ranks. As taught in the *Sutra of Golden Light:*

> In relying on the path of suppressing afflictions, when the mind that gives rise to phenomena ends, one attains the manifestation of the transformation body. In relying on the path of severing attachment to dharmas, when that which depends on the root mind ends, one attains the manifestation of the response body. In relying on the path of superior uprooting [of hindrances], when the root mind ends, one attains the manifestation of the Dharma body.

Someone has interpreted this as follows:

> The path of suppressing afflictions is prior to the stages. The mind that gives rise to phenomena is the sixth consciousness. The path of severing attachment to dharmas is the bodhisattva stages. The mind that depends on original root mind is the *manas,* because it is conditioned by the root mind, which is the *ālaya* (storehouse) consciousness. The path of superior uprooting is the diamond rank. The root mind is the storehouse consciousness.

Six: The three bodies are shown directly as pertaining to the three kinds of hindrances. Thus, that same sutra (i.e., *Sutra of Golden Light*) states:

Upon purification of the afflictive hindrances one can manifest the response 494c
body. Upon purification of the karmic hindrances one can manifest the transformation body. Upon purification of the cognitive hindrances one can manifest the Dharma body.

Seven: The three bodies are shown via the afflictions arising from confusion about the three kinds of naturelessness. Thus, that same sutra states:

> All ordinary beings, on account of the three characteristics, have bonds and hindrances; so they are far from the three bodies, and do not reach the three bodies. What are the three characteristics? One is the characteristic of being discriminated by thought. Two is the characteristic of arising dependent on other factors. Three is the characteristic of completion. Because of these three characteristics, ordinary beings are unable to unbind themselves, unable to extinguish suffering, unable to be pure. Thus, they do not reach the three bodies. But these three marks can be unbound, extinguished, and purified. Thus, all buddhas reach the three bodies.

Interpretation: What can be unbound is that nature of attachment to what is entirely imagined; one has only to understand it. What can be extinguished is the defiled part of other-dependent nature; one must sever and extinguish it. What can be purified is the bound aspect of the true thusness nature; one cultivates oneself so as to purify it.

Eight: Four ranks are shown via the four kinds of hindrance. This has two significances. First, from the perspective of afflictions proper, the four ranks, four practices, four causes, and four recompenses prior to the stages are shown. Why are there four? One refers to the *icchantika*s; when they have extinguished the afflictions proper of the hindrance of faithlessness, they turn it over to manifest the rank of the ten stages of faith, complete the practices of faith and joy in the Great Vehicle, and form the cause of the virtue of purity. They are rewarded as kings who turn the iron wheel. Two is the followers of heterodox ways; when they have extinguished the afflictions proper of the hindrance of attachment to self, they turn it over to manifest the rank of the ten understandings, complete the practices of *prajñā,* and form the cause of the virtue of self-mastery. They are rewarded as kings who turn the copper wheel. Three is the *śrāvaka*s; when they have extinguished the afflictions proper of the hindrance of the fear of suffering, they manifest the rank of the ten practices, complete the *samādhi* that breaks through emptiness, and form the cause of the virtue of enjoyment. They are rewarded as kings who turn the silver wheel. Four is the *pratyekabuddha*s; when they have extinguished the afflictions proper of the hindrance of renouncing great compassion, they manifest the rank of the ten conversions of merit, complete the practices of great compassion, and form the cause of the virtue of permanence.

They are rewarded as kings who turn the golden wheel. Further, the four practices obtained upon overturning the previous four hindrances constitute the four purposes of the children of buddhas. Overturning the initial hindrance forms the seeds of faith and joy in the Great Vehicle as cause, which is just like a father. Overturning the second hindrance forms *prajñā* as conditions, which is just like a mother. Third, the concentration of breaking through emptiness leaves behind the attachments of the Lesser Vehicle and solidifies the Dharma body, just like a womb. Fourth, great compassion benefits living beings, just like a mother's milk. By completing these four conditions, from prior to the bodhisattva stages one attains rebirth in the initial stage and above in the home of the buddhas, so one is named a child of the buddhas. Moreover, these four kinds are harmoniously joined like the wheels of a cart, able to carry the cart forward to reach the realm of liberation. It is like the wheel of a sage king that is equipped with four elements: hub, rim, spokes, and axle. You should understand the four purposes by this sequence.

Second, the four ranks, four concentrations, four virtues, and four recompenses of the bodhisattva stages are shown via the habitual energies of the four kinds of hindrance. One: In the first, second, and third stages, one extinguishes the *icchantika* habit of faithlessness and manifests the characteristics of this one rank, which are the same as those of the mundane world. One 495a
also attains the *samādhi* of the brilliant illumination of the Great Vehicle, and being accomplished in the virtue of purity, eliminates the recompense of the mutable body of the birth and death of causes and conditions. Two: In the fourth, fifth, and sixth stages, one extinguishes the heterodox habit of attachment to self and manifests the characteristics of this one rank, which are the same as those of the two vehicles. One attains the *samādhi* of the king of accumulating fortune and virtue and, being accomplished in the virtue of self-mastery, eliminates the recompense of the birth and death of skillful means. Three: In the seventh, eighth, and ninth stages, one extinguishes the *śrāvaka* habit of fear of suffering and manifests the characteristics of this one rank, which are the same as those of the Great Vehicle. One attains the *samādhi* of Bhadrapāla and, being accomplished in the virtue of joy, eliminates the recompense of the birth and death of phenomenal existence. Four: From the tenth stage to the stage of buddhahood, one eliminates the *pratyekabuddha* habit of foregoing great compassion and manifests the perfection of causes

and fulfillment of results of this one rank. One attains the *śūraṃgama samādhi* (the *samādhi* that destroys afflictions) and, being accomplished in the virtue of permanence, eliminates the recompense of the birth and death of nonexistence. Because the fourth virtue is perfect, the cycle of birth and death is eternally ended, and it is said to not exist. These tenets are extensively taught in such texts as the *Sutra on Unsurpassed Refuge,* the *Sutra on Basic Activities,* the *Treatise on Buddha-nature,* the *Treatise on the Jewel Nature,* and the Liang *Summary of the Great Vehicle.* Furthermore, within these four, the former two pertain to both kinds of hindrance, while the latter two only pertain to cognitive hindrance. The afflictions proper are removed prior to the bodhisattva stages, while the habitual energies are purified within the stages. These passages are authentic proof.

Nine: Characteristics are distinguished within the ten bodhisattva stages. Up to the final state of mind of the third bodhisattva stage, among the two kinds of hindrance, all the afflictions proper of the delusions encountered in cultivation are completely severed. From the fourth stage and onward, there are only the subtle habitual energies. Why? Because the characteristics of the prior three stages are the same as those of the mundane world, while those of the fourth stage and onward are supramundane. Thus, the final passage on the third stage of the *Ten Stages Sutra* states:

> All the bonds of desire evolve into a state of greater subtlety (i.e., as residual energies). All the bonds of form evolve into greater subtlety. All the bonds of existence evolve into greater subtlety. All the bonds of ignorance evolve into greater subtlety. The many bonds of false views have already been completely removed before.

The *Treatise on the Ten Stages* states:

> As to the statement "All the bonds of desire evolve into greater subtlety," and so on, it means severing all of the afflictions of the realms of desire, form, and formlessness on the path of cultivation, along with their causes; the same as the habitual energies of ignorance, which are all subtle and detached. As to the many bonds of false views (i.e., afflictions proper), on the path of insight of the first stage they have already been severed.

Interpretation: As to the words "with their causes," this means the seeds of the afflictive hindrances. As to "habitual energies of ignorance," this means the seeds of cognitive hindrances. Because the seeds of the two kinds of hindrance are detached at the same time, the word "same" is used. For this reason, you should understand that the afflictions proper of the delusions encountered in cultivation of both the two kinds of hindrance are all completely ended in this stage.

The divisions above are explained for the most part from the perspective of the Final Teaching.

Ten: Via further distinguishing characteristics within the ten bodhisattva stages, distinctions are shown between the three ranks of the mundane, the two vehicles, and the bodhisattvas. The *Sutra for Benevolent Kings* states:

> In the initial three stages one severs the afflictions of form of the triple world. In the fourth, fifth, and sixth stages one severs the afflictions of mind of the triple world. In the seventh, eighth, and ninth stages one severs the habitual energies of form of the triple world. In the tenth stage and the stage of buddhahood one severs the habitual energies of mind of the triple world.

Interpretation: By means of the final rank of the third stage, one attains the 495b
concentrations of the upper realms (i.e., the form and formless realms, excluding the desire realms). At the utmost, one reaches the four empty concentrations, beyond the forms of the lower stages. So it says "severs the afflictions of form." Because at the fourth stage and onward one attains the uncontaminated supramundane rank of the two vehicles, mundane form and mind are completely ended. The seventh stage and onward is the bodhisattva rank; because the afflictions have gradually become subtler than before, that rank is shown on the basis of extinction of the habitual energies of form and mind.

Eleven: Two ranks are distinguished within the bodhisattva rank, in order to show the autonomous and not-yet-autonomous states. The seventh rank and below pertain to extinguishing the afflictions of form and mind of the triple world along with their resultant recompense. The eighth stage and onward pertain to extinguishing the ignorance of the two kinds of habitual energies of form and mind. Thus, the *Sutra on Basic Activities* states:

> In the seventh stage and below one extinguishes the two kinds of habitual energy and resultant recompense of form and mind of the triple world, extinguishing them without remainder. In the eighth stage the habitual ignorance of form is ended. In the ninth stage the habitual ignorance of mind is extinguished and removed. In the tenth stage the two kinds of habitual ignorance are extinguished completely.

Twelve: According to the *Treatise on the Three Kinds of Naturelessness,* the difference between the two ranks of insight and cultivation is shown via the extinguishing of two kinds of nature. Thus, the treatise states:

> Through the path of insight, one realizes that the discriminated nature is nonexistent, so it is said to be unattained. Through the path of cultivation, the other-dependent nature is extinguished, so it is said to be unseen.

Thirteen: According to such texts as the *Treatise on the Collected Abhidharma,* the difference between the paths of insight and cultivation is shown via the two kinds of affliction, discriminated and inborn. How can this be understood? The difference is only in the attribution of the ranks [as understood within the Early Teaching], and not in true severing. It is like how the discriminated view of self is a sign of the three conditions of the production [of discriminated affliction]—that is, false teachers, false teachings, and false thinking—the blind projection of a self that is identical to the aggregates or beyond the aggregates, and so on. If they were disciples of the Buddha, in spite of living in the rank of ordinary beings they would rely on correct teachers, correct teachings, and correct thinking; they would not only stop giving rise to such attachments as the identity of self with aggregates, they would even wish to realize the nonexistence of self-nature. How could these people have already severed their afflictions and yet not have entered the path of insight? If you say that although their seeds have not occurred they still have seeds, so they have not entered the path of insight, and having not occurred, they should enter the earlier ranks of preparation and applied practice—well, the significance is not so. For this reason, you should understand that in order to show the principle of selflessness in the path of insight, those sideways and upside-down coarse delusions are attributed to it [in the Early Teaching]. Furthermore, because the fine afflictions that arise spontaneously (i.e., inborn afflictions) are difficult to sever, they are used to show that the rank of cultivation is different in terms of gradual progress. As to the true significance, there is only one affliction, which has coarse and fine aspects. In the rank of insight one severs the coarse and in the rank of cultivation one severs the fine. As to afflictions of the *manas,* one severs them throughout both ranks. As the *Treatise on the Nonexistence of Characteristics* states:

> The second attached consciousness and corresponding dharmas are completely extinguished upon reaching the rank of arhat. As to the consciousness of afflictions and the mental dharmas that are encountered within the path of insight into the truth, at the time when one attains the sixteenth mind of the supramundane way, they are finally severed and extinguished. Unfinished remnants only belong to the category of thoughts. This is named the second [attached] consciousness.

Asvabhāva's *Commentary on the Summary of the Great Vehicle* teaches 495c
this same thing. You can understand this as with the citations above.

Fourteen: The distinctions between the three worthy sets of practices prior to the stages are shown on the basis of the three conditions that prefigure the discriminatory delusions. This refers to the elimination of false teachers and so on in the course of the ten understandings, etc. By their order you should understand that this is taught from the perspective of the directly advancing bodhisattvas. Moreover, the suppression of the delusions to which false teachers and false teachings give rise is attributed to the rank of preparation, because their activity is coarse. The suppression of the delusions to which false thinking gives rise is attributed to the rank of applied practice, because their activity is fine. This is taught from the perspective of the conversion of the minds of the two vehicles practitioners.

Fifteen: Within the inborn afflictions, the delusions of the sixth and seventh consciousnesses that exist in the state of occurrence (i.e., not as latent seeds) pertain up to the seventh bodhisattva stage. From the eighth stage and onward they are eternally subdued and do not arise. This teaching was made to provide a basis for showing the difference between the ranks of interrupted and uninterrupted entry into contemplation.

Sixteen: Again, the afflictions of the sixth consciousness pertain up to the fourth stage, and the afflictions of the *manas* pertain up to the seventh stage. At the eighth stage and onward there are only the cognitive afflictions. This teaching is also made in order to show the ranks of the mundane, the two vehicles, and the bodhisattvas.

Seventeen: The difference between the ten stages and the buddha stage is shown via recourse to the eleven kinds of ignorance.

Eighteen: The two kinds of wisdom of each stage—the true and the conventional—are shown via the twenty-two kinds of ignorance. For example, the *Sutra on the Explication of Underlying Meaning* states, "Because of these twenty-two kinds of foolishness and the eleven kinds of heavy bonds, the various stages are posited." It states "posited" so we know they are attributed in this way to be shown [to practitioners, not because these ranks are real in an ultimate sense].

These various significances are extensively explained in such treatises as the *Yogācāra Stages,* the *Treatise on the Collected Abhidharma,* the "Essay on Consciousness Only," and the *Summary of the Great Vehicle.* The divisions above are mostly explained from the perspective of the Early Teaching. All the various gates above are also gates of the Āgamas. The differences in the characteristics of the ranks are shown via the overturning of delusions. Why? In order to maintain the ten stages; in order to cause living beings to go beyond their conceited attachments within the ten stages. The characteristics of the ranks are profound and extremely difficult to understand. Showing the ranks on the basis of delusions produces pure faith. Reflect on the rest of the doctrine according to this standard and it will be evident.

3. Sudden Teaching

According to the Sudden Teaching, all afflictions are originally and innately beyond [discursive thought]. One cannot speak of severing them, nor of not severing them. As the *Sutra on the Essential Nature of Entering the Dharma Realm* states:

> The Buddha told Mañjuśrī, "Tell what teaching causes the good children [of buddhas] to awaken *bodhi*-mind." Mañjuśrī said, "I teach the arising of the mind of self-view. Why? The removal of self-view is *bodhi.*"

You should understand it according to the evidence of this passage.

4. Perfect Teaching

According to the Perfect Teaching, the essential nature of all afflictions is inexpressible; to speak only from the perspective of their function, they are profound and vast. Because the dharmas that are obstructed are each identified with every one, replete with the interdependent arising of principal and attendants, then those delusions that obstruct are also like this. For this reason, they are not divided into defilements proper and habitual energies, or into seeds and the occurrence of seeds. In the Dharma realm the attainment of one is the attainment of all. For this reason, with afflictions, severing one is severing all. Thus the "Samantabhadra['s Practice]" chapter [of the *Flower* 496a *Garland Sutra*] clarifies that to be obstructed by one is to be obstructed by everything, while the "Manifestation of the Tathāgata" chapter clarifies that to sever one is to sever everything. This is their significance.

There are four kinds of distinctions of this severing of delusion, according to a thorough examination of the scriptural passages. One, from the perspective of realization, refers to severing afflictions within the ten bodhisattva stages. Two, from the perspective of ranks, refers to severing afflictions after reaching the ten abodes. Three, from the perspective of practice, refers to severing afflictions in the final state of mind of the ten minds of faith. Four, from the perspective of true reality, refers to the teaching that there is nothing that could be severed, because everything is originally pure. This is as extensively explained in the scripture.

Moreover, as to the three vehicles' various gates of severing delusions discussed previously, if to be obstructed by one affliction were to be obstructed by all afflictions, and to sever one affliction were to sever all afflictions, then that teaching would be included in this Perfect Teaching. If one is to pursue the severing of afflictions via gates in a sequence of before and after, it is the three vehicles. This is said from the perspective of the Distinct Teaching. According to the perspective of all-encompassing skillful means, that which is clarified by the previous teachings is all together enclosed within this Perfect Teaching, because they are its skillful means; because they are its outflow and its contents. This is the standard for the rest of the doctrine.

Here ends the gate of distinctions in the severing of delusions.

G. Conversion of the Two Vehicles

Seventh is the conversion of mind of the two vehicles practitioners. There are six kinds of teachings.

1. No Conversion (Lesser Vehicle)

It may be taught that of all the practitioners of the two vehicles, none convert their minds, because they believe there is nothing more to seek, as those among the Lesser Vehicle teach.

2. All Beings Converted (Final Teaching)

It may be taught that all of the practitioners of the two vehicles convert their minds, because they all have the power of buddha-nature as the cause of permeating influence within, and because they do not relinquish the external condition of the power of the Tathāgata's great compassion. Because their root ignorance is not yet ended, the nirvana of the Lesser Vehicle is not final. Thus, of all the practitioners, none fail to convert their minds toward great *bodhi.* This is the perspective of the Final Teaching.

Question: As the *Treatise on Yogācāra Stages* and the *Treatise on Praise of the Sacred Teachings* explain in the exposition of the four logical possibilities of mature and immature consciousnesses, in the *śrāvaka*s and *pratyekabuddha*s who enter nirvana without remainder, the storehouse consciousness and all the evolving consciousnesses do not mature. Since the root consciousness and the evolving consciousnesses are all extinguished without remainder, what would be the cause by which a mind is produced later? To produce a result without a cause does not accord with reason.

Reply: Those treatises are based on the gate of the Early Teaching to draw in the Lesser Vehicle practitioners, so the characteristics of the storehouse that they establish are coarse and do not arise from true reality; thus, they explain that the storehouse may be extinguished. Moreover, in order to comply with the Lesser Vehicle, they also grant that their nirvana may be final. So they explain that having entered nirvana there is no further arising of mind. Now, in the Final Teaching, it is taught in accord with reality that root ignorance permeates the *tathāgatagarbha* to form storehouse consciousness. Those of the two vehicles have not yet severed root ignorance, nor realized *tathāgatagarbha*—by what cause could they attain extinction of the storehouse consciousness? And because they have neither severed nor verified these two dharmas, how could the nirvana they attain be final? The analogy of the unreal city [in the *Lotus Sutra,* which the Buddha makes appear and disappear to represent the unreal nirvana of the Lesser Vehicle] would then be mistaken. It is because of the four causes mentioned above that one attains the production of mind.

Question: What do you say about the distinctions in the time of production of mind and conversion to the Great Vehicle?

Reply: Because spiritual roots are unequal, there will be those who are slow 496b
and those who are quick. The slow ones pass through *kalpa*s and then give rise to faith in the Great Vehicle. Thus, the *Laṅkāvatāra* states:

> Those who have tasted the joy of *samādhi* abide peacefully in the uncontaminated realm. They have no concern for the final reward, but they also do not retrogress. Attaining the various bodies of the *samādhi*s, even for the duration of a *kalpa* they do not awaken. They can be compared to drunken people, who awaken later, after the wine is digested. This dharma of awakening is likewise. [After awakening from deluded awakening] they attain the unsurpassed buddha body.

Interpretation: This passage only explains the general characteristics. To explain it according to specific differences, depending on the sharpness or dullness of their spiritual capacities: each within their own time arrives at the rank of the mind of *anuttarā samyaksaṃbodhi.* As the *Nirvana Sutra* states, "Because *śrotaāpanna*s are still not fixed on the path to final nirvana, they pass through eighty thousand *kalpa*s and then are able to attain the mind of *anuttarā samyak-saṃbodhi.*" It also states, "*Pratyekabuddha*s pass through ten thousand *kalpa*s and attain the mind of *anuttarā samyaksaṃbodhi.*"

Interpretation: This clarifies that the dullest *śrotaāpanna*s receive seven rebirths before they enter nirvana and extinguish mind and dharmas of mind. If they enter the concentration of total extinction, they further pass through eighty thousand *kalpa*s and then attain the production of mind, receive the Buddha's transformative teaching, and aspire to *bodhi*-mind. If in one lifetime they attain the second result (i.e., of once-returner), receive their second rebirths and then enter nirvana, they will pass through sixty thousand *kalpa*s and then they can aspire to *bodhi*-mind. If in one lifetime they attain the third result (i.e., of nonreturner), do not return to the desire realm, and then enter nirvana, they will pass through forty thousand *kalpa*s and then aspire to *bodhi*-mind. If in one lifetime they attain arhatship and manifest the concentration of total extinction, they will pass through twenty thousand *kalpa*s and then they can aspire to *bodhi*-mind. If the spiritual capacities of the *pratyekabuddha*s are sharp, they will pass through ten thousand *kalpa*s and then they can aspire to *bodhi*-mind. When these five kinds of people aspire to enlightenment, they then enter the bodhisattva ranks of the ten stages of faith. This is called "aspiring to the mind of *anuttarā samyaksaṃbodhi*."

This has some further significance. The previous five kinds of people follow the ordinary and attain the lesser result; after they enter nirvana they give rise to the converted mind and cultivate the practices of the ten stages of faith. When they have fulfilled the ten minds of faith and until they can enter the initial aspiration to enlightenment of the ten abodes, they each pass through those *kalpa*s depending on the sharpness or dullness of their spiritual capacities. It isn't necessarily that they are within nirvana all along as they pass through such a number of *kalpa*s. Like the people who advance directly into the Great Vehicle, having passed through ten thousand *kalpa*s and fulfilled the cultivation of practices to be able to aspire to *bodhi*-mind, those *pratyekabuddha*s whose capacities are sharpest likewise pass through ten thousand *kalpa*s. There are many distinctions among the time to final nirvana of the other four kinds, who have dull capacities, because there are many differences among them. The above clarifies the slow ones. As to the most quick, it is as the *Lotus Sutra* states:

> After my extinction and crossing over, if there are still disciples who do not hear this sutra, who do not understand, and who do not awaken to the practices of the bodhisattva; if they produce thoughts of extinction and crossing over from the merits they have themselves attained, and are about to enter nirvana, then in another kingdom I will become a buddha with a different name. Although this person has produced thoughts of extinction
> 496c and crossing over and entered into nirvana, even so in that other land they will seek the Buddha's wisdom and get to hear this sutra. It is only by means of the buddha vehicle that one can attain extinction and crossing over. There is no other vehicle. The merely expedient teachings of the Tathāgata have been removed.

The above is all taught from the perspective of the Final Teaching.

3. Some are Converted, Some are Not (Early Teaching)

It may be taught that of all the practitioners of the two vehicles, some convert and some do not convert. That is, those whose seed-nature is predetermined attain quiescence and do not convert, while those whose seed-nature is not predetermined all turn toward the Great Vehicle, as taught in the "Decision" section on *śrāvakas* in the *Treatise on Yogācāra Stages.* This is taught from the perspective of the Early Teaching, drawing in the two vehicles practitioners.

4. Neither Conversion nor Nonconversion (Sudden Teaching)

It may be that there is neither conversion nor nonconversion, because [realization] is beyond characteristics, as taught in the *Mañjuśrī's Sutra on Prajñāpāramitā* and so on. This is taught from the perspective of the Sudden Teaching.

5. Preceding Theories are Skillful Means (Common Teaching)

It may be that the preceding four teachings are included together, because they are the skillful means of the great Dharma. This is taught from the perspective of the One Vehicle encompassing skillful means.

6. Preceding Theories are All Severed (Distinct Teaching)

It may be that the preceding five teachings are all completely cut off. This has two aspects. One, there is nothing to which all those beings of the two vehicles could convert, because from the point of view of the One Vehicle, it's clear that all is empty and there is nothing to which one could be converted. This is what is meant by "as if deaf and blind" in the scriptures. Two, all of those two vehicles practitioners have already been completely converted, and there is no further conversion. This is as in the scripture where, when seen with the eyes of Samantabhadra, all living beings have already attained the ultimate. These are taught from the perspective of the Distinct Teaching of One Vehicle.

Question: Tell us about the distinctions of the Dharma gates attained via conversion by the One Vehicle's all-encompassing skillful means versus conversion by those of the three vehicles.

Reply: If one converts within the three vehicles, one enters the gate of the ten stages of faith and goes on to cultivate the *bodhi*-mind and great compassion, advancing by degrees. If one converts within the One Vehicle, it is as in the following paraphrase of a passage [from the *Flower Garland Sutra*]: Śāriputra and Indra, and all the six thousand wise *bhikṣus*, converted their minds alongside Mañjuśrī and thereupon attained the ten great Dharma gates, and such realms as the ten eyes, the ten ears, and so on. The significance of this is just that this body of understanding and practice is present throughout the dharmas of the five ranks. The rest of the doctrine is as taught elsewhere.

H. Characteristics of Buddhahood

Eighth are the characteristics of the doctrines of resultant buddhahood. Within this there are two sections. First, I will clarify the doctrines of the permanence and impermanence of the characteristics of buddhahood. Second, I will clarify the differences among the teachings regarding the primary and secondary characteristics of buddhahood.

1. Permanence and Impermanence

i. Lesser Vehicle

Within the first section, according to the Lesser Vehicle, the characteristics of buddhahood are only impermanent, because it does not teach the merits of original nature. As the *Treatise on Buddha-nature* states, "Because in the Lesser Vehicle there is no buddha-nature as a virtue of original nature, there is only that nature that exists as a virtue of cultivation."

ii. Early Teaching

According to the Early Teaching of the three vehicles, the Dharma body is permanent, because of its self-nature. It is also impermanent, because it is beyond and not beyond [birth and death]. The merit produced from cultivation is impermanent, because it is produced in accordance with causes and conditions; it is created, though uncontaminated. It also can be permanent, because it is without interruption and arises continually. The *Treatise on the Adornment of the Great Vehicle* states, "Self-nature, uninterruptedness, and continuous arising: these three permanently abide in the buddhas."

iii. Final Teaching

According to the Final Teaching, there are two significances. First I will clarify the characteristics of buddhahood separately, and then I will explain
497a them generally. Within the clarification of separate characteristics, the merits produced by cultivation are impermanent, because they are produced by

cultivation; they are also permanent, because once they are attained they are the same as true thusness. Why is this? Because they originally emanate from true thusness, and when ignorance is ended, they return to the essence of true thusness. The Liang *Summary of the Great Vehicle* states, "There is nothing that does not emanate from this Dharma body. There is nothing that does not return to realize this Dharma body." The *Treatise on the Jewel Nature, The Awakening of Faith,* and other such texts fully establish this doctrine. You should understand it as they teach it. Also, the *Treatise on the Larger Prajñāpāramitā Sutra* states:

> *Sarvajña* (omniscience) does not coincide with the three times. Why not? Because the time of the past and so on are empty illusions; they are produced and extinguished. *Sarvajña* is the real Dharma, which is neither produced nor extinguished.

Interpretation: *"Sarvajña"* means the wisdom of everything, so we know that the perfect wisdom of the buddha stage is the same as thusness; it is neither produced nor extinguished. Also, the *Summary of the Great Vehicle* states:

> It is like empty space that thoroughly pervades the parameters of all forms, without production, abiding, extinction, or change. The wisdom of the Tathāgata likewise pervades all that is known, without confusion and without change.

Thus, you should understand that *sarvajña* is not permanent simply because of uninterrupted severing; it is permanent because it is the same as unchanging thusness.

The Dharma body is permanent, because even when it is according with conditions it does not change in self-nature. It is also impermanent, because it responds to beings' opportunities for enlightenment in accord with impure conditions. Why is this? Because the various meritorious deeds are all already the same as true thusness, the arising of function is only an effect of true thusness. In *The Awakening of Faith* it is explained that the two bodies, the reward body and the transformation body, belong to the great function aspect of true thusness. That treatise also states, "When the minds of living beings are pure, the reflection of the Dharma body appears," and so on. It also states:

> Furthermore, when original awakening accords with impurities, discrimination produces two characteristics, neither of which is detached from that original awakening. The first is the characteristic of pure wisdom, and the second is the characteristic of inconceivable karmic activity.
>
> And so on, as widely explained.

Second, the general explanation. Due to the significance of the Dharma body according with conditions, the teaching about differences in merit is formed. Due to the significance of the Dharma body not changing, there is no merit that is not identified with true thusness. As its entire essence accords with conditions completely, and the characteristics in their totality are without change, these two significances are interfused without obstruction. Thus, the resultant buddhahood is both permanent and impermanent. The four logical possibilities are complete, or the four logical possibilities are negated. You should understand according to these significances.

Question: If that is so, how can it be said that [the buddha bodies] are neither identical nor different?

Reply: According to the Early Teaching, because true thusness is universal and wisdom verifies thusness, they are not different. Because created and uncreated are not the same, they are not identical.

According to the Final Teaching, there are two doctrines of merit. One is the doctrine that buddhahood itself directly manifests interdependent arising, because the merit of the three incalculable *kalpa*s of cultivation is not void. Two is the doctrine that buddhahood has no self-nature, because apart from true thusness it has no essence of its own. Within these, the former doctrine coincides with
497b the teaching of the Dharma body that accords with conditions, while the latter doctrine coincides with the Dharma body that does not change. These are not different Dharma gates, because their totality is completely received into the teaching. Moreover, the former significance coincides with the teaching of the Dharma body that does not change, while the latter doctrine coincides with the teaching of the Dharma body that accords with conditions. These Dharma gates are not one, because the significances are different. This is to clarify nonidentity without moving from nondifference. Reflect on it and you can see.

iv. Sudden Teaching

According to the Sudden Teaching, because characteristics are ended and beyond thought, there is only one body of the nature of reality. All is equal, so one cannot speak of differences in merit, and one cannot speak of permanence or impermanence. If one were to show it by putting it into words, it would be as the [*Mahāparinirvāṇa-*]*sūtra* states, "This my present body is the Dharma body." The [*Flower Garland*] *Sutra* also states, "All the bodies of the various buddhas are only this one Dharma body." Understand it by this standard.

v. Perfect Teaching

According to the Perfect Teaching, there are three explanations regarding the doctrine of the permanence of resultant buddhahood. First, from the perspective of function, buddhahood already pervades all the dharmas of the three times; thus it includes all of the four logical possibilities of permanence. Second, from the perspective of virtues, buddhahood already includes four significances: (1) they are produced from cultivation, (2) they are originally present, (3) what is originally present is produced from cultivation, (4) what is produced from cultivation is originally present. These significances are perfectly interfused without obstruction, so buddhahood is equipped with infinite virtues. Thus, the four logical possibilities of permanence also apply. Ponder the significances of the two kinds of four possibilities above and you will see. Third, from the perspective of essence, it is also demonstrated through the four logical possibilities. That is, in this [*Flower Garland*] *Sutra,* because its purpose is to manifest the inexpressible, buddhahood is permanent; because it corresponds with the basic teachings, it is impermanent. These two significances are without obstruction and so both exist. Because of the parameters of interdependent arising, they are both negated.

In the above three significances, if one points out essence, they are all identified with essence, and so on; if one points out function, they are all identified with function. Because they are interfused and mutually encompassing without obstruction, they all exist, and so on, without obstruction. Reflect upon this.

2. Differences in Primary and Secondary Characteristics

Second is the clarification of the differences in primary and secondary characteristics of buddhahood.

i. Lesser Vehicle

According to the Lesser Vehicle, there are thirty-two primary characteristics and eighty kinds of special qualities. These are considered real dharmas.

ii. Early Teaching

Within the three vehicles, it may likewise be taught that there are only thirty-two primary characteristics and eighty kinds of special qualities. These are the characteristics of the transformation body. However, the significance of the characteristics is that they are empty, as taught in the *Diamond Sutra,* the *Treatise on the Collected Abhidharma,* and so on. This is taught from the perspective of the Early Teaching that draws in the Lesser Vehicle practitioners.

iii. Final Teaching

Or, it may be that the reward body is taught to have eighty-four thousand characteristics. These are its real virtues. This is taught from the perspective of the teaching for the directly advancing bodhisattvas and the Final Teaching.

Question: Why does the *Treatise on the Larger Prajñāpāramitā Sutra* and such texts discuss the transformation body in terms of the effects brought about by past karma, as in the stories about the Buddha being hurt by a splinter and fed horse feed? Each of the thirty-two characteristics likewise emerges from its cause in these explanations.

Reply: In order to draw in the two vehicles practitioners, it is taught in a way similar to the lower teaching. To show that the results of karma do not perish, the sacred way severs delusions but does not extinguish their recompense. It is like the story of the arhat eating sand. The stories about being hurt by a splinter and so on are the same. The Lesser Vehicle took this [buddha body] to be real. The Early Teaching teaches it to be empty, because it is a skillful means, as taught in the *Sutra on the Skillful Means of the Great Vehicle.*

497c There are two significances of the teaching that the primary characteristics and special qualities emerge from causes. First is that it is a skillful means to draw in the two vehicles practitioners. It shows superior causes and results within this buddha body, because the real reward body is not that which those two vehicles practitioners see. Second is that these are indeed the characteristics of the true reward body. Because they are manifested while the Buddha confers his presence in the transformation body, we get the teaching of its emergence from causes.

Question: Why is it taught in the *Summary of the Great Vehicle* that the thirty-two primary characteristics go into the category of the merits of the Dharma body?

Reply: This also has two significances. First is that it is taught gradually as a skillful means in order to convert the beings of the two vehicles. It is feared that the truly real Dharma body would be too difficult for them to believe. Because of this, these merits are taught to be part of the Dharma body to make it easy to believe and accept according to their expectations. Second, because the two vehicles consider [other] merits to be the Dharma body, the primary characteristics are encompassed among those. The above is all taught from the perspective of the Early Teaching. Also, the thirty-two primary characteristics are not produced and natureless; they are just the Dharma body of true thusness. This is taught from the perspective of the Final Teaching.

iv. One Vehicle

According to teachings of the One Vehicle, there are characteristics of buddhahood as numerous as the motes of dust of the ten oceans of lotus flower treasury worlds. Each and every characteristic pervades the Dharma realm. The karmic function is also like this. As to the teaching that there are ten of them, this is intended to show their infinitude. This is as taught in the chapter on "The Oceans of Characteristics" [of the *Flower Garland Sutra*]. Also, in the *Sutra on the Samādhi of Contemplating Buddha,* the characteristics and special qualities of buddhas are divided from the perspective of the tenets of the three vehicles, to make three levels. Thus, that sutra states:

As to the summary of the summary [of the buddhas' forms and bodies], I will now for the sake of this present great assembly and King Śuddhodana summarize the teachings of the primary characteristics and special qualities. The Buddha was born among humans to show he shares the human situation. Because he shares human characteristics, he teaches the thirty-two primary characteristics. Because he is superior to all the heavenly beings, he teaches the eighty kinds of special qualities. For the sake of the bodhisattvas, he teaches all eighty-four thousand miraculous characteristics and special qualities. As to the real characteristics and special qualities of buddhas, they were taught at the place of quiescence in Magadha where he first attained the way, for the sake of such great bodhisattvas as Samantabhadra and Bhadraśrī. This has been extensively distinguished in the *Miscellaneous Flowers Sutra.*

Interpretation: In this, the thirty-two primary characteristics are meant to be the summary of the summary, for the sake of humans, deities, two vehicles practitioners, and so on. This is meant for the beginning level. The significance of the eighty-four thousand is meant to be only a summary, for the sake of the three vehicles bodhisattvas. It is meant to be the next level. The real characteristics and special qualities of buddhas are as taught in the *Miscellaneous Flowers Sutra,* where their significance is extensively explained. This refers to the explanation of the "Oceans of Characteristics" chapter of the *Flower Garland Sutra.* This chapter explains the characteristics of buddhahood in the Distinct Teaching of One Vehicle. It is meant to be the last level, because the *Miscellaneous Flowers Sutra* is precisely the *Flower Garland Sutra.* The rest of the doctrine you can understand accordingly.

I. Worlds Encompassed and Transformed

Ninth is the clarification of the distinctions among the realms to be encompassed and transformed by the teachings.

1. Lesser Vehicle

In the Lesser Vehicle, this very *sahā* world of disorder is the buddha's reward land. Within it, here on this continent of Jambudvīpa is where the reward buddha is located, while the other ten billion lands are distinguished as the realms to be transformed.

2. Three Vehicles

Within the three vehicles, there are the Dharma-nature land and the land of the Buddha's self-enjoyment. They will not be discussed here at present.
498a As to Śākya Buddha's pure land of real reward that is provided for others' enjoyment, it is sometimes said to be in Maheśvara Heaven (the highest level of the form realm), while the ten billion Jambudvīpas completely filled by the transformation body are distinguished as the realms to be transformed. This is as taught in the *Brahmā's Net Sutra* and the *Treatise on the Collected Abhidharma.* You should understand that this is taught from the perspective of the Early Teaching. Why is this so? Since the two vehicles teaching considers Śākyamuni's body to be the real reward body, this turns it over by establishing a separate real reward body in that heaven to show that Śākyamuni's body is in fact the transformation body. It is also taught due to concern

that the practitioners of the two vehicles would not believe that there could be a real pure land outside of the mundane world, so the pure land is attributed to the most excellent place within the world. As to the transformation body only completely filling ten billion lands and so on, this also complies with their teaching.

It is sometimes said that Śākya Buddha's reward land is outside of the triple world. The *Nirvana Sutra* states:

> In the west, as many buddha lands from here as the grains of sand of thirty-two Ganges Rivers, there is a world named Unsurpassable. This is the pure land of Śākya Buddha's real reward.

This is taught from the perspective of the Final Teaching. Because it is not taught according to the lower understanding of the two vehicles practitioners, it is meant to show that the *sahā* world is only the realm of the transformation body. For this reason, you should understand that the body of the highest heaven of the form realm is also not the real reward.

It is sometimes said that there are not merely ten billion transformation realms, as in the *Treatise on the Larger Prajñāpāramitā Sutra.* Considering a great trichiliocosm to be one count, count up to the number of grains of sand of the Ganges River; this is one original nature world. Count these again up to the number of grains of sand of the Ganges; this is one ocean world. Count these again up to the immeasurable sands of the Ganges; this is one seed world. Count these again up to the innumerable sands of all the Ganges Rivers of the ten directions; this defines one buddha world to be transformed. This is also taught from the perspective of the Final Teaching, because the realms to be encompassed and transformed have been gradually expanded from the previous. This is also taught solely from the perspective of the world of Mount Sumeru, because it is situated in this world and doesn't yet explain the tree-shaped world [of the *Flower Garland*], and so on. So, this is not the One Vehicle.

3. Common Teaching

It is sometimes said that Śākyamuni's reward land is on sacred Vulture Peak. As the *Lotus Sutra* states, "I exist eternally on sacred Vulture Peak," and so on. The author of the treatise on the *Lotus Sutra* (i.e., Vasubandhu) explicates this as referring to the *bodhi* of the reward body. You should understand that this is taught from the perspective of the Common Teaching of One Vehicle. How so? Because the *Lotus Sutra* manifests the One Vehicle; its places accord with the teaching such that impurity returns to purity, so the place where the *Lotus Sutra* was taught is the real reward land. It is like considering the place where the *Flower Garland Sutra* was taught under the *bodhi* tree to be the ten buddha realms of the lotus treasury; the *Lotus Sutra* is like this. Because it has superficial commonality with this [Huayan teaching], it is the Common Teaching. However, it does not yet teach that that place is the ten lotus treasury worlds, or the realm of Indra's net, so it is not the Distinct Teaching.

It is sometimes said that this body of Śākyamuni is to be considered the enjoyment body of the real reward, as the beginning of the *Sutra on the Buddha Stage* explains. This text explicates that Śākya Buddha possesses
498b twenty-one kinds of merits of the real reward. Its treatise explicates this as the enjoyment body. This is also taught from the perspective of the Common Teaching. How so? This Śākya Buddha, in the three vehicles, is only a transformation body, but in the Distinct Teaching of One Vehicle, he is the ultimate body of the ten buddhas. Now, this is a provisional explanation as a skillful means for the three vehicles practitioners, to show that Śākyamuni's body is not only the transformation body. Fearing it would be difficult for them to believe and accept this, that sutra teaches from the perspective of the location of the profound merit of resultant buddhahood. To clarify that the buddha body accords with teaching as the provisional returning to the real, it is explained as the reward body. This is the manifestation of skillful means. At the time of teaching the Dharma of the Huayan One Vehicle, this body of Śākyamuni also accords with that teaching and is identified with the body of the ultimate Dharma realm of the ten buddhas. For this reason, that is included within the Common Teaching.

4. Sudden Teaching

Sometimes it is said that this body of Śākyamuni is the Dharma body. As the [*Nirvana*] *Sutra* states, "This my present body is the Dharma body." This is the perspective of the Sudden Teaching, taught by putting it into words, although in reality it exhausts characteristics and is beyond thoughts.

5. Distinct Teaching

According to the Distinct Teaching of One Vehicle, this body of Śākyamuni is not only the three bodies but is also the ten bodies. [The number] "ten" is given in order to show that it is inexhaustible. The realms of those ten buddhas have two bases. One [basis] is the perfect interfusion and absolute freedom of the oceans of lands; it is inexpressible. If it is to be shown in the Dharma, it is as explained at the beginning of the second assembly [in the "Names of the Tathāgata" chapter of the *Flower Garland Sutra*].

The second [basis] is the oceans of worlds, of which there are three categories. One is the oceans of adorned worlds of the lotus flower treasury, where the teaching of the interdependent arising of principal and attendants is complete and Indra's net is all-pervasive. This is the realm proper to the ten buddhas.

Two, outside of the trichiliocosm, there is a tenfold ocean of worlds:

1. Original nature worlds
2. Ocean worlds
3. Wheel worlds
4. Fulfillment worlds
5. Discrimination worlds
6. Orbital worlds
7. Revolving worlds
8. Lotus worlds
9. Sumeru worlds
10. Characteristic worlds

This must be understood as the realm of the wheel-turning king with more than ten thousand children.

Three, worlds of immeasurably heterogeneous categories all are omnipresent throughout the Dharma realm. Like the one category of Mount Sumeru worlds, the area and borders of which reach the ends of space and extend throughout the Dharma realm; like the one category of tree-shaped worlds, and even to worlds that have the shapes of all living beings—all of these are in this way completely omnipresent in the Dharma realm without obstructing each other.

The above three ranks are together the places to be encompassed and transformed by the ten bodies of Vairocana Buddha. Moreover, the root and ramifications of these three ranks are perfectly interfused and mutually inclusive without obstruction. How so? According with each world, whether it is coarse or fine, it will have these three. You should understand that this is completely distinct from and not common to the teachings of the three vehicles.

J. Analysis and Synthesis of Buddha Bodies

Tenth is the analysis and synthesis of the bodies of buddhas, in which there are two sections. First are the doctrines, followed by the enumerations.

1. Doctrines

Within the section on doctrines, first I will discuss the perspectives on the Dharma body.

i. Dharma Body

a. Early Teaching

Sometimes only the realm of true thusness is considered to be the Dharma body, as in the *Treatise on the Sutra on the Buddha Stage,* in which the stage
498c of great awakening is encompassed among the five kinds of Dharma. The Dharma realm of purity encompasses the Dharma body, and the four kinds of wisdom encompass the other bodies. This is taught from the perspective of the Early Teaching.

b. Final Teaching

Sometimes, only marvelous buddha wisdom is considered to be the Dharma body, because it is the wisdom of original awakening, and cultivated wisdom is the same as original awakening. For example, the *Treatise on the Larger Prajñāpāramitā Sutra* considers undefiled, unobstructed wisdom to be the Dharma body. In the *Sutra of Golden Light,* the four kinds of wisdom encompass the three bodies, because mirror-wisdom encompasses the Dharma body. Or, wisdom and its object are combined as the Dharma body, because wisdom and its object are both characterized by thusness. As the Liang *Summary of the Great Vehicle* states, "Only thusness and the wisdom that perceives thusness exist; this is named 'the Dharma body.'" The above two possibilities are taught from the perspective of the Final Teaching.

c. Sudden Teaching

Sometimes, the elimination of both wisdom and its object is considered to be the Dharma body. Scripture states, "The Dharma body of the Tathāgata is not mind and it is not objects of mind." This is taught from the perspective of the Sudden Teaching.

d. One Vehicle

Sometimes, all the preceding logical possibilities are synthesized, because all their virtues are included. Sometimes, the preceding five are completely cut off, because of perfect interfusion without obstruction. These two possibilities are as taught in the "Arising from Original Nature" chapter [of the *Flower Garland Sutra*]. This discussion takes the perspective of the One Vehicle.

ii. The Body of Śākyamuni

Next I will clarify the doctrines separately in terms of perspectives on the body of Śākyamuni. This body of Śākyamuni sometimes is the transformation body, not the Dharma body or reward body, as taught in the Early Teaching. Sometimes it is the reward body, and not the Dharma body or transformation body, as taught in the Common Teaching of One Vehicle and in the Lesser Vehicle. These are only different in terms of depth or shallowness. Sometimes it is the Dharma body and not the reward body or the transformation body, as taught in the Sudden Teaching. Sometimes it is both the Dharma body and the reward and transformation bodies, as is generally taught in the three vehicles. Sometimes it is not the Dharma body, and not the reward body or the transformation body, as in the Distinct Teaching of One Vehicle, because it is the ten buddhas.

2. Enumerations

The enumerations of the analysis and synthesis of the doctrines of the bodies of the buddhas are as follows.

i. One Buddha

Some teachings establish one buddha, which is the one buddha of real nature. This is the perspective of the Sudden Teaching.

ii. Two Buddhas

Some teachings establish two buddhas. There are three kinds. First is the living body and the transformation body. This is taught from the perspective of the Lesser Vehicle. Second is the living body and the Dharma body. This refers to merging the body of others' enjoyment and the transformation body, and calling it the living body, while the self-enjoyment body and the Dharma body are merged and called the Dharma body. This is as taught in the *Treatise on the Sutra on the Buddha Stage.* It is taught from the perspective of the Early Teaching. Third is the Dharma body of self-nature and the Dharma body of response and transformation. This is as taught in the *Sutra on Basic Activities.* It is taught from the perspective of the Final Teaching.

iii. Three Buddhas

Some teachings establish three bodies of buddha, as usually taught. This is taught throughout the two teachings, Early and Final.

iv. Four Buddhas

Some establish four buddhas. Within this there are three kinds. First, within the three bodies, the enjoyment body is further divided into the two bodies of self-enjoyment and others' enjoyment, which makes four. This is as taught in the *Treatise on the Sutra on the Buddha Stage.* This is the Early Teaching. Second, outside of the three bodies, the body of self-nature is separately established, in order to clarify that the Dharma body is the Dharma of meritorious deeds as numerous as the grains of sand of the Ganges River. For this reason, the Liang *Summary of the Great Vehicle* states, "The body of self-nature is the basis for the creation of the Dharma body." Third, within the reward body, the parts based on the cultivation of good fortune and the cultivation of wisdom are separated as two, making four. As the *Laṅkāvatāra-sūtra* states, "One is the buddha of responsive transformation, two is the buddha of meritorious deeds, three is the buddha of wisdom, four is the
499a buddha of thusness." This is taught from the perspective of the Final Teaching.

v. Ten Buddhas

Some establish ten buddhas, to show the inexhaustible. This is as taught in "Going Beyond the Mundane" chapter of the [*Flower Garland Sutra*].This is taught from the perspective of the Perfect Teaching of One Vehicle.

X. Distinctions in Doctrinal Principles

In the tenth gate, of distinctions in the doctrinal principles, there are four gates. One is the similarities and differences in the doctrines of the three natures. Two is the teaching of the six significances of the causal aspect of interdependent arising. Three is the ten mysterious Dharma gates of unobstructed interdependent arising. Four is the doctrine of the perfect interfusion of the six characteristics of conditioned phenomena.

A. Similarities and Differences in the Three Natures

As to the explanation of the similarities and differences in the three natures, there are two sections. First, they are clarified specifically, and then explained generally.

1. Specification

Within the section on specific clarification, there are also two parts: the unelaborated explanation, and the determination of what is correct.

i. Direct Explanation of Natures and their Aspects

Within the former, each of the three natures has two significances. The two significances within the fully perfected nature are the significance of not changing and the significance of according with conditions. The two significances of the other-dependent nature are the significance of appearing to exist and the significance of self-naturelessness. The two significances of the nature of attachment to what is entirely imagined are the significance of [conventional] existence to sentient beings and the significance of nonexistence in principle.

Due to the unchanging aspect of full perfection, the self-naturelessness aspect of other-dependency, and the nonexistence in principle aspect of attachment to imagination—due to these three aspects of their significance, the three natures are of one domain, the same without difference. This does not destroy the ramifications and the root is permanently maintained. The [*Vimala-kīrti-*]*sūtra* states, "Living beings are precisely nirvana. There is nothing further to be extinguished." Moreover, from the perspective of the according with conditions aspect of full perfection, the appearing to exist aspect of other-dependency, and the existence to sentient beings aspect of attachment to imagination—due to these three significances, they are also without difference. This is not moving the root and permanently maintaining the ramifications. The [*Sutra on No Increase and No Decrease*] states, "The Dharma body flowing and revolving in the five destinies is named 'living beings.'" Therefore, these three significances and the previous three significances are not one gate. For this reason, the true includes the delusory ramifications, and the delusory ramifications suffuse the wellspring of the true; the essential natures and their characteristics are thoroughly interfused without hindrance and without obstruction.

Question: How could other-dependency appearing to exist, and so on, possibly be the same as attachment to imagination being existent to sentient beings?

Reply: They are not different for two reasons. One, the "attachment" of that attachment to imagination is to take what merely appears to be as the truly real; so, the dharmas in question are no different. Two, if one were beyond attachment to imagination, the appearance of existence would not arise. The according with conditions aspect within the fully perfected nature should be understood likewise, because without attachment to imagination there is no according with conditions.

Question: How is it that each of the three natures has these two significances and yet they do not contradict each other?

Reply: Because these two significances are not essentially different. How are they not different? Consider full perfection; although it too forms impurity
499b and purity in accordance with conditions, it never loses its immaculate self-nature. It is only because it does not lose its immaculate self-nature that it is able to form impurity and purity in accordance with conditions. This is like a bright mirror revealing impurity and purity: although it reveals impurity and purity, the bright purity of the mirror [itself] is never lost. Only because the bright purity of the mirror is never lost can it reveal the characteristics of impurity and purity. By the reflection of impurity and purity, you know the pure brightness of the mirror. By the brightness of the mirror, you know its reflection of impurity and purity. Thus, the two significances are of one nature. Though it reflects pure dharmas, that does not add to the brightness of the mirror. Though it reflects impure dharmas, that does not stain the purity of the mirror. And not only is it not stained—on the contrary, it is because of this that the bright purity of the mirror is manifest. You should understand that the principle of true thusness is likewise. Not only does the unmoving pure nature form impurity and purity; it is because it forms impurity and purity that it manifests its pure nature. Not only do undestroyed impurity and purity illuminate the pure nature; it is because of the purity of its nature that it forms impurity and purity. Thus, the two significances are totally mutually inclusive, of one nature, nondual. How could they possibly contradict each other?

Within other-dependency, although again due to causes and conditions, its aspect of appearing to exist manifests, this appearance of existence certainly has no self-nature, because all conditionally produced phenomena have no self-nature. If it was not self-natureless, then it would not depend on conditions.

If it did not depend on conditions, it would not [falsely] appear to exist [as itself]. If the appearance of existence is to form, it must follow from myriad conditions. Since it follows from myriad conditions, it certainly has no self-nature. For this reason, due to its lack of self-nature, the appearance of existence is formed. Because the appearance of existence is formed, therefore it has no self-nature. Thus, the *Treatise on the Larger Prajñāpāramitā Sutra* states:

> Contemplate all dharmas. They are produced following from causes and conditions. Because they are produced following from causes and conditions, they have no self-nature. Having no self-nature, they are ultimately empty. As to ultimate emptiness, it is named *prajñāpāramitā.*

Thus, through conditioned production, naturelessness is manifested. The *Treatise on the Middle Way* states, "Because of the significance of emptiness, all dharmas attain their formation. This clarifies conditioned production through the teaching of naturelessness." The *Nirvana Sutra* states, "Dharmas exist because of causes and conditions. They are empty because they are natureless." This means naturelessness is just causes and conditions, causes and conditions are just naturelessness. This is the Dharma gate of not two; not only do the nature's two significances not contradict each other, rather they totally include each other and are ultimately nondual.

Within the nature of attachment to what is entirely imagined, although again phenomena appear to exist to the evaluating and grasping of sentient beings, when understood by true principles they are ultimately empty, because they exist only within baseless projection. It is like falsely imagining the existence of a ghost in a tree stump, when ultimately there is no ghost in the tree stump. If the tree stump did have a ghost, then this would not be called falsely imagining the existence of a ghost, because there would be something not created by baseless projection in the tree stump. Now, this act of false projection clarifies the aspect of nonexistence in principle. Because of non- 499c
existence in principle, the false projection is formed. Because projection is formed, you can understand nonexistence in principle. For this reason, they are nondual, only a single nature. You should understand that the true principle of attachment to imagination is also like this.

This concludes the direct discussion [of natures and their aspects] from above.

ii. Determination of Correct Understanding

Next is determination of what is correct through questions and answers, within which there are three gates. First, I attempt to maintain the attachments of discriminating consciousness. Second, I show the error of such attachment. Third, I demonstrate the significance.

a. Maintaining Attachments

The first gate, of maintaining attachments:

[The fully perfected nature:][24]

Question: Does true thusness exist?

Reply: No. Because of accordance with conditions.

Question: Does true thusness not exist?

Reply: No. Because it is unchanging.

Question: Does it both exist and not exist?

Reply: No. Because it does not have two natures.

Question: Does it neither exist nor not exist?

Reply: No. Because it is replete with virtues.

Question, again: Does it exist?

Reply: No. Because it is unchanging. How so? Because it is unchanging, it manifests in accordance with conditions.

Question: Is it nonexistent?

Reply: No. Because it accords with conditions. How so? Because it accords with conditions, it is unchanging and permanently abiding. The other two possibilities of the logical sequence can be understood in this way.

Question: Again, does it exist?

Reply: No. Because it is beyond what it is posited to be. The subsequent three logical possibilities are consistent with this example.

Question: Again, does it exist?

Reply: No. Because of the emptiness of true thusness.

Question: Does it not exist?

Reply: No. Because of true thusness that is not empty.

Question: Does it both exist and not exist?

Reply: No. Because it is beyond contradiction.

Question: Does it neither exist nor not exist?

Reply: No. Because it is beyond such frivolous discourse.

Question: Again, does it exist?

Reply: No. Because it is beyond false thought.

Question: Does it not exist?

Reply: No. Because it is the basis of sacred wisdom and practice. Make this the standard for the other possibilities of the logical sequence.

The other-dependent nature:

Question: Does other-dependency exist?

Reply: No. Because interdependent arising is self-natureless.

Question: Does other-dependency not exist?

Reply: No. Because naturelessness is interdependently arisen.

Question: Does it both exist and not exist?

Reply: No. Because it is essentially nondual.

Question: Does it neither exist nor not exist?

Reply: No. Because it has many gates of significance.

Question, again: Does it exist?

Reply: No. Because of interdependent arising. How so? Because all interdependently arisen phenomena are all without self-nature.

Question: Does it not exist?

Reply: No. Because it is natureless. How so? Because it is natureless, it is formed by interdependent arising. The other two possibilities of the logical sequence can be understood like this. Moreover, because interdependent arising is beyond the four logical possibilities, and because of naturelessness, [the other-dependent nature] is also beyond the four logical possibilities.
500a Both can be understood by this.

Question: Again, does other-dependency exist?

Reply: No. Because from the perspective of contemplation it is excluded.

Question: Does it not exist?

Reply: No. Because it can manifest naturelessness. You can thus understand that the subsequent two possibilities of the sequence are that it is beyond contradiction and beyond frivolous discourse.

Question: Again, does it exist?

Reply: No. Because it differs from full perfection. Also, because it is part of attachment to imagination, and because it is beyond what it is posited to be.

Question: Does it not exist?

Reply: No. Because it differs from attachment to imagination, and because it is part of full perfection. Also, because it is the object of wisdom. Make this the standard for the other possibilities of the logical sequence.

The nature of attachment to what is entirely imagined:

Question: Does attachment to imagination exist?

Reply: No. Because of nonexistence in principle.

Question: Does it not exist?

Reply: No. Because it exists to sentient beings.

Question: Does it both exist and not exist?

Reply: No. Because it does not have two natures.

Question: Does it neither exist nor not exist?

Reply: No. Because of the nature of attachment to what is entirely imagined.

Question: Again, does it exist?

Reply: No. Because it lacks true principle.

Question: Does it not exist?

Reply: No. Because it lacks true principle. Make this the standard for understanding the other possibilities of the logical sequence.

Question: Again, does it exist?

Reply: No. Because attachment exists.

Question: Again, does it not exist?

Reply: No. Because attachment exists.

Question: Does it both exist and not exist?

Reply: No. Because attachment exists.

Question: Does it neither exist nor not exist?

Reply: No. Because attachment forms it.

Question: Again, does it exist?

Reply: No. Due to its absence of characteristics.

Question: Again, does it not exist?

Reply: No. Because it is the objective realm of the contemplation of characteristiclessness. Make this the standard for the other possibilities of the logical sequence.

Question: Again, does it exist?

Reply: No. It has no essential substance.

Question: Again, does it not exist?

Reply: No. Because it can cloud true thusness. Make this the standard for the other logical possibilities.

b. Showing the Errors of Attachment

Second is showing the errors of attachment.[25]

b1. Fully Perfected Nature

If one were to posit that true thusness always exists, there are two mistakes. The first is the error of permanence; that is, if one has the idea that true thusness does not accord with conditions, that it exists in impurity and yet is not occluded, and that it is not attendant on the awareness-cause, then one falls into the error of eternalism.

Question: Within all the sacred teachings, true thusness is explained to be a reified permanence that does not accord with conditions. How could this possibly be an error?

Reply: When the sacred teachings explain true thusness to be reified, this is describing the time at which it has formed impurity and purity in accordance with conditions. It is eternally creating impurity and purity and does not lose its own essence. This, then, is the permanence that is not different from impermanence; it is called "the inconceivable permanence." This does not refer to not creating the myriad dharmas, as in the reification posited by deluded sentience. If it referred to it not creating the myriad dharmas and yet being reified, this would be the projection of deluded sentience; it misses the true permanence because that true permanence is not different from the permanence of impermanence. The permanence that is not different from impermanence emerges from beyond sentience, so it is called true permanence. For this reason, the *Sutra* [*of Queen Śrīmālā*] states:

> What is not impurity and is yet impure illuminates that permanence creates impermanence. What is impurity and is yet not impure illuminates that when it creates impermanence, it does not lose its permanence.

Question: Then the teachings affirm the permanence that is not different from
500b impermanence, so they explain true thusness to be a reified permanence. Why do they not affirm the impermanence that is not different from permanence, to explain true thusness as impermanence?

Reply: The teachings have indeed already taught this significance. The [*Laṅkāvatāra*]-*sūtra* states, "The *tathāgatagarbha* receives suffering and pleasure. It is produced and extinguished together with the causes." A treatise (*The Awakening of Faith*) states, "The immaculate mind of self-nature, moved by the winds of ignorance, forms the impure mind," and so on. You should understand by the principle of this teaching that true thusness is not different from the impermanence of permanence. It accords with conditions, concealing its essential substance; it is not existent.

Question: True thusness is a dharma that is not produced or extinguished. It does not differ from the permanence of impermanence, so it is explained to be permanent; it does not differ from the impermanence of permanence, so it is explained to be impermanent. Given that, can you also maintain that other-dependency is a dharma that is produced and extinguished, and must also have the significance of not differing from the impermanence of permanence and not differing from the permanence of impermanence?

Reply: It does indeed have that significance. Why? Because the myriad interdependently arising impermanent dharmas are without self-nature, and by this they form interdependent arising. For this reason, they do not differ from the nature of permanence, and yet they attain impermanence. Thus the [*Vimalakīrti*]-*sūtra* states, "Neither being produced nor being extinguished is the significance of impermanence." As to this other-dependency, it is no different from permanence forming impermanence. And because all interdependently arisen phenomena are precisely without self-nature, it is not the case that interdependent arising is extinguished and only then are phenomena said to be natureless. So, it does not differ from the permanence of impermanence. Thus the [*Vimalakīrti*]-*sūtra* states, "Form is precisely emptiness; it is not that form extinguished is emptiness." It also states, "Living beings are precisely nirvana. There is nothing further to be extinguished," and so on.

You can understand that these two significances (i.e., permanence and impermanence) and the two significances of true thusness are complementary. This is the true and the worldly interfusing as two and yet without duality. Thus the [*Commentary on the*] *Summary of the Great Vehicle* states, "The extreme blindness of cognitive hindrance refers to attachment to a distinction between the true and the worldly." It is this to which it refers. Thus, if one were attached to true thusness, as if it were the same as whatever sentience posits, it would become reified permanence; it would not accord with conditions, conceal its own essential substance, and not be subject to the awareness-cause. This would be to sink into the error of eternalism. Moreover, if true thusness did not accord with conditions and form impurity and purity, then the impure and pure dharmas would have nothing upon which to depend. To think dharmas exist with nothing upon which to depend is also to sink into the error of eternalism, because impure and pure dharmas all lack self-essence and are established in dependence on true thusness.

The second [mistake] is the error of annihilationism. If what exists to sentient beings did not truly exist, then because it did not truly exist, this would be to annihilate existence. Moreover, if what exists to sentient beings were to truly exist, then it would not accord with impurity and purity. But the myriad dharmas of impurity and purity lack their own essence. If true thusness did not accord with conditions, those dharmas would not exist. This is annihilationism.

There are also two errors in attachment to the nonexistence of true thusness. There is the error of eternalism; that is, without true thusness, samsara would have nothing upon which to depend. To maintain that dharmas exist without dependence on other factors would be the error of eternalism. Also, without
500c true thusness, sacred wisdom would have no cause; this is also eternalism. Furthermore, with nothing upon which to rely, dharmas cannot exist; this is annihilationism. Attachment to the idea that true thusness is nonexistent is also annihilationism.

Attachment to both existence and nonexistence of true thusness includes all of the errors above. That is, true thusness being nondual, if both existence and nonexistence are projected, then because they are mental projections of existence and nonexistence they do not match the truth. This misses that true principle of thusness, thus it is annihilationism. If it is meant that what is projected is to be taken as true thusness, taking what lacks true principle to have real existence, this would be eternalism.

Last is attachment to neither existence nor nonexistence of true thusness. Engaging in frivolous discourse about true thusness is deluded thinking, so it misses the true principle. This is annihilationism. To engage in frivolous discourse claiming that there is true thusness and taking that to be the truth—this maintains the existence of true thusness without true principle, so it is eternalism.

b2. Other-dependent Nature

Next are the errors of attachment with regard to the other-dependent nature. If one is attached to its existence, there are again two errors. The first is the error of eternalism, which refers to the other-dependent nature already having its own essence and not being bound to conditions. To maintain an existent dharma without conditions is eternalism. Moreover, due to attachment to its existence it would not be bound to conditions; because it is not bound to conditions, the dharma does not exist. This is annihilationism.

Question: If you say the doctrine that the other-dependent nature exists is mistaken, then why do the *Summary of the Great Vehicle* and other such texts teach that the other-dependent nature does exist?

Reply: As to sages teaching that the other-dependent nature does exist, this is no different from the existence of emptiness. How so? It is so because the myriad conditions (i.e., the "other" upon which any given dharma depends) have no essential self-nature. Because every one of the conditions has no subject to effect causation, the conditions are not effective; hence the other-dependent nature is interdependently arisen. For this reason, it is not the existence of posited "existence"; it is called "other-dependent existence." This, then, is how sages do not move from the parameters of the true and establish myriad dharmas. If you mean that other-dependent nature "exists" as it does in words, then interdependently arisen phenomena would have self-nature. If interdependently arisen phenomena had self-nature, then they would not rely on each other. If they did not rely on each other, then that would be to destroy the other-dependent nature. Destruction of the other-dependent nature is certainly due to attachment to existence. Thus, being afraid of sinking into empty annihilationism, you established existence by the power of mental striving. You did not recognize that because you have not even reached the point of understanding that interdependently arisen dharmas have no self-nature, you destroyed interdependent arising and sank into the view of reified emptiness, annihilating the other-dependent nature.

As to the error of annihilationism, if one is attached to nonexistence, there are also two errors. If it were the case that the other-dependent nature was a nonexistent dharma, then there would be nothing to which conditions could give rise. Because they would give rise to nothing, dharmas would not exist. 501a
This is annihilationism.

Question: If, due to teaching that conditioned production is empty and nonexistent, one falls into the error of annihilationism, then why does the *Treatise on the Middle Way* extensively explain conditioned production to be ultimately empty?

Reply: As to sages teaching conditioned production to be empty, this is no different from the emptiness of existence. How so? Because dharmas follow from conditioned production, so they are explained to have no self-nature. For this reason, the existence of conditioned production is explained to be empty. If it were not like this, the cause of conditioned production would not exist; then how could it be described by the word "emptiness"? For this reason, it does not differ from the emptiness of existence, and it is called "the emptiness of conditioned production." This, then, is the sages not moving from the teaching of conditioned production while teaching the Dharma of the characteristics of reality. If you mean that conditioned production is "empty" as it is in words, then there is no conditioned production. If there is no conditioned production, there is no true principle of emptiness. To have no true principle of emptiness is certainly due to attachment to emptiness. Thus, being afraid of sinking into the erroneous view of [reified] existence, you established emptiness by forceful mental striving. You do not realize that because you do not even reach the point of understanding natureless conditioned production, you err as to the emptiness of self-nature. Because you err regarding the emptiness of self-nature, you even sink into maintaining the [false] emptiness of the evil tendencies within your deluded sentience.

Question: If due to the other-dependent nature having two significances, the scriptural masters of earlier ages each expound one of the significances while fusing and encompassing the whole other-dependent nature without contradiction, then why do the scriptural masters of later ages, such as Bhāviveka, each attach to only one of the significances, refuting the others' interpretations?

Reply: This is actually mutual completion, not mutual refutation. How? For the sake of the sentient beings of later ages, whose spiritual roots are shallow and whose capacities are dull, masters are heard to explain the doctrine of the existence of other-dependency. Because they do not reach the point of understanding that it is no different from the existence of emptiness, they are attached to its existence as what it is posited to be. Thus, those such as

Bhāviveka refute the existence of other-dependency to cause our understanding to arrive at the position of nonexistence. Arriving at ultimate nonexistence, they thereby actually attain that position of the existence of other-dependency. If it didn't arrive at this point of the total thoroughness of the emptiness of nature, then it would not be able to complete the existence of the other-dependent nature. For these reasons, in order to complete the teaching of existence, they refute it on the basis of existence. Furthermore, when those sentient beings of later ages heard the teaching of the ultimate emptiness of the other-dependent nature, they did not reach the point of understanding that it is no different from the emptiness of existence. This is attachment to emptiness as whatever it is posited to be. For these reasons, Dharmapāla and others refuted that posited emptiness to preserve its illusory existence. Because illusory existence was established, this teaching attains the understanding that other-dependency is no different from the emptiness of existence, because if it existed, its extinction is not true emptiness. For these reasons, in order to complete the teaching of emptiness, they refute it on the basis of emptiness. By means of "form is precisely emptiness," Bhāviveka's doctrine was established; by means of "emptiness is precisely form," Dharmapāla's doctrine was preserved. These two doctrines are interfused and totally mutually inclusive. If the scriptural masters of later ages had not rebutted each other on the basis of the total interpenetration of these two principles, we would not have thereby attained the manifestation of the profundity of the dharma of the interdependent arising of the other-dependent nature. For these reasons, their mutual refutation conversely results in mutual completion. 501b

For these reasons, to be attached to nonexistence as it appears to deluded sentience is precisely the error of annihilationism. Furthermore, if one were to explain nonexistent dharmas to be other-dependent, then because nonexistent dharmas are not conditioned, this would be to maintain the existence of dharmas that are not conditioned, which is to fall into the error of eternalism.

As to the position that the other-dependent nature both exists and does not exist, all the above errors can be made a standard for analyzing this position.

Question: On the basis of the above explanations, if we were to take only one side to be valid—either the existence or the nonexistence of the nature of other-dependent arising—such a conclusion would not be allowable.

Taking both existence and nonexistence together to be valid should tally with the true principles. How could such a position in fact have all the above errors?

Reply: Within the nature of other-dependent arising, although those principles of existence and nonexistence are each included, they are both totally interfused as the thorough interpenetration of emptiness and existence. As to both existence and nonexistence being entirely imagined, that position would entail a mutual contradiction including all the above errors.

Last is the position that the other-dependent nature neither exists nor does not exist. Indeed, the interdependent arising posited by frivolous discourse is not the true principle. Why? Because this view is attached to untenable projections about existence and nonexistence. It takes whatever sentience posits as neither existence nor nonexistence to be true principle. This is not true principle; it indeed includes the above errors. Reflect on it by this standard.

b3. Imagined Nature

Next is the nature of attachment to what is entirely imagined. If one takes attachment to imagination to be existent, there are two mistakes. If one takes that to which one is attached to really exist, then the true principle illuminated by the wisdom of the sages would not be emptiness; this is the error of eternalism. Or, if the pervasive projections of deluded attachment are taken to really exist with regard to true principle, this errs in regarding existence as grasped by sentience; this is the mistake of annihilationism.

If one takes attachment to what is entirely imagined to be nonexistence as grasped by deluded sentience, this is to think that the confusion of ordinary people is no different from the wisdom of sages—this is eternalism. Furthermore, because in the resulting view there are no ordinary people, it is annihilationism. Moreover, if there is no confusion, there is no enlightenment, and if there is no enlightenment then there are no sages—this is annihilationism.

There is also the view of both existence and nonexistence of the imagined nature. The imagined nature is nondual; to nevertheless posit its existence and its nonexistence is a contradiction, so it includes the above errors.

Last is the view of neither existence nor nonexistence of the imagined nature. The attachment to imagination posited by frivolous discourse also includes the above errors. Understand it by this standard.

This is the end of the second section on the formation of errors through attachments.

c. Demonstration of Significance

The third section shows their significances.

One: True thusness (i.e., the fully perfected nature) does have the significance of existence, because it is this upon which confusion and enlightenment depend. It also has the significance of not being empty, because it cannot be destroyed. The rest is as explained above. Also, true thusness does have the significance of emptiness, because it is beyond characteristics, because it accords with conditions, and because it is the opposite of impurity. The rest is also as above. Also, true thusness does have the significance of both existence and nonexistence, because it is replete with virtues, because it is autonomous in opposition and compliance, and because of the melding and fusion of both possibilities. Also, it does have the significance of neither existence nor nonexistence, because it is two and not two, and because it can't be grasped in a fixed state. You can understand the rest of the explanation by the standard of the above.

Two: Other-dependent nature does have the significance of existence. It is formed by conditions so it is self-natureless. The rest can be understood by the standard of the previous discussion. Other-dependent nature does have the significance of nonexistence, because it is formed by conditions, so it is natureless. This can also be understood by the standard of the previous discussion. Other-dependent nature does have the significance of both existence and nonexistence,
because it is formed by conditions and is natureless. The previous is the standard. 501c
Other-dependent nature does have the significance of neither existence nor nonexistence, because it is two but not two, and therefore cannot be grasped as one or the other. The previous is the standard.

Three: Attachment to what is entirely imagined does exist, from the perspective of sentient beings. Attachment to imagination is nonexistent from the perspective of true principle. Attachment to imagination is both existent and nonexistent, because it is the object of attachment. Attachment to imagination is neither existent nor nonexistent, because it is the object of attachment. Reflect on the rest according to the standard of the previous discussion.

This is the end of the above separate clarification of the three natures.

2. General Explanation

The second section [of the similarities and differences in the three natures] is the general explanation. The three natures are of one domain, such that to uphold one is to include all; the true and the illusory are mutually fused. The natures are unobstructed. As it is said in the [*Commentary on the*] *Summary of the Great Vehicle,* where it cites the *Sutra of the Questions of the Brāhmins:*

> World-honored One, on the basis of what principle do you teach with such words as "the Tathāgata does not see samsara and does not see nirvana"? Discriminated (i.e., imagined) nature and true thusness nature are within other-dependent nature, and samsara and nirvana depend on the principle of their nondifferentiation. Why is that? Of this other-dependent nature, samsara is formed through the one part of discriminated nature, and nirvana is formed through the one part of true thusness.

Exegesis: The other-dependent nature is not samsara. Because of this nature, true thusness forms nirvana. But the other-dependent nature is not nirvana. Why not? This nature, because of the one part of it that is discriminated nature, is identified with samsara. For this reason, one cannot definitely explain it to be only one of its parts. If one sees one part, the nature of the other part would not be different. For this reason, the Tathāgata does not see samsara and does not see nirvana. Having this intention, the Tathāgata replied to the brahmans in this way.

[The *Commentary on the Summary of the Great Vehicle*] also states:

> In the *Abhidharma Sutra,* the World-honored One teaches that there are three aspects of dharmas. One is the impure part, two is the pure part, and three is the impure and pure part. On the basis of what principle are these three parts taught? Within the other-dependent nature, discriminated nature is the impure part and true thusness nature is the pure part, while other-dependent nature is the impure and pure part. Depending on this principle, the three divisions are taught.

Exegesis: The *Abhidharma Sutra* teaches that the discriminated nature has affliction as nature, the true thusness nature has the pure aspect as nature, and the other-dependent nature includes both parts, having both natures as its nature. Thus, the scripture explains that there are three kinds of dharma: one has the part of affliction, two has the part of purity, and three has the part of both dharmas. This teaching is made on the basis of this doctrine.

The above passages from the treatise also clarify that the true comprehends the ramifications of the false; everything is taken into account. The true and the illusory thoroughly pervade the essence of the wellspring of the true; everything is quiescent. The true and the illusory thoroughly interpenetrate, the two parts fused without obstruction, completely inclusive. Reflect on this and you can see.

B. The Six Significances of the Causal Aspect of Interdependent Arising

Second is the teaching of the six significances of the doctrine of the causal aspect of interdependent arising.[26] I will analyze this doctrine by dividing it in six gates: one, exposition of characteristics; two, establishment [of the doctrine]; three, enumeration of logical possibilities; four, analysis and syn- 502a
thesis; five, fusion and inclusion; six, the perspectives of the teachings.

1. Exposition of Characteristics

Within the first gate there are two sections: the listing of names of the characteristics of interdependent arising of causes, and the exposition of their characteristics.

First, the listing of names. That is, all causes have six significances:

1. They are empty, empowered, and not subject to conditions.
2. They are empty, empowered, and subject to conditions.
3. They are empty, not empowered, and subject to conditions.
4. They are existent, empowered, and not subject to conditions.
5. They are existent, empowered, and subject to conditions.
6. They are existent, not empowered, and subject to conditions.

Next is the exposition of their characteristics. The first characteristic is the significance of extinction of causes in each moment. Why? Through their extinction in each moment, their absence of self-nature is manifested. This is emptiness. Because of this extinction, the resultant dharmas are produced. The causes are empowered. However, this extinction does not come about through the power of conditions, so the causes are not subject to conditions.

The second [characteristic] is the significance of simultaneous existence of the cause and the result. Why? Because they exist simultaneously, it is momentary existence, manifesting the significance of the causes not existing and being empty. Because of simultaneity, they can form existence. The causes are empowered. Because of simultaneity, they are not solitary, so they are subject to conditions.

The third is the significance of being subject to myriad conditions. Why? Because causes have no self-nature, they are empty. Because causes [alone] do not produce results, but conditions produce results, so causes are not empowered. Because of this significance, they are subject to conditions.

The fourth is the significance of moral determination. Why? Because causes are of their own moral type; they do not change, so they have this significance. Able to produce results without changing themselves, they have the significance of empowerment. However, this not changing is not due to the power of conditions, so they do not have the significance of being subject to conditions.

The fifth is the significance of causes producing only their own results. Why? Because they bring about the manifestation of their own results, they have the significance of existence. Although they produce results in being subject to conditions, they do not produce the results of those conditions. This is the significance of being empowered, and because of this they have the significance of being subject to conditions.

The sixth is the significance of continuous evolution in consciousness. Why? Because causes accord with other conditions, they cannot be nonexistent; and, they cannot oppose their conditions, so they have no functional empowerment. Therefore, they are subject to conditions.

For these reasons the *Summary of the Great Vehicle,* in order to demonstrate these six significances, explains it in verse as follows:

> Extinction in each moment, simultaneous existence of cause and result, continuous evolution;
> You should understand moral determination, being subject to myriad conditions, and only bringing about their own results.

2. Establishment of the Doctrine

The second gate is establishment [of the doctrine of interdependent arising of causes].

Question: For what reason is the explanation settled at six significances, not increased up to seven nor reduced down to five?

Reply: In matching direct causes to conditions, there are only three significances: (1) The cause is empowered and not subject to conditions; it completely produces the result by itself, so it does not depend on the power of various other conditions. (2) The cause is empowered and subject to conditions; cause and conditions mutually support the expression of the result. (3) The cause is not empowered and is subject to conditions; it is completely ineffective and causation returns to the conditions. And as the above three significances each have two significances within them: the significance of emptiness and the significance of existence; these two combine with each of the three, making six. There are only six significances and they do not increase or decrease.

Question: Why don't you establish a fourth logical possibility, which would 502b
be the significance of not being empowered and not being subject to conditions?

Reply: Because that possibility would not in fact be causation, it is not established. Reflect on this and you can see.

Question: As to being subject to conditions, to what kind of conditions is it subject?

Reply: It is subject to three kinds of causal conditions—auxiliary conditions and so on—that are outside of the immediate causal situation. These are not taken from among its own six significances, which are mutually subject to each other.

Question: We view causes in terms of conditions to attain the six significances. I don't yet understand whether or not conditions are likewise matched with causes to also have these six significances.

Reply: There are two significances to this. When we view an auxiliary condition in terms of its own auxiliary result we attain the six significances, because it is encompassed among the proximate causes of that result. In terms of the other results, the auxiliary conditions form remote conditions, and so the six are not complete. When we view the proximate causes in terms of other results, it's also like this.

Question: Do results have these six significances, or not?

Reply: Results only have the two significances of existence and emptiness. That is, as they follow from others' production they have no essential self-nature, so they have the significance of emptiness. As they exist in response to causes, they have the significance of existence. If this is explained from the perspective of the doctrine of the mutual becoming of cause and result, then this one dharma, when it is the cause of another result, includes all these six significances. When it is acting as the result of another cause, then it has only the two significances. For this reason, the six significances are only found within causes.

Question: If so, when latent seeds actively occur, they would become the causes of seeds. Shouldn't they have the six significances?

Reply: They accord with predominating conditions and do not include the six. As the *Treatise* [*on the Theory of Consciousness Only*] explains, seeds have the six significances. This is from the perspective of the initial teaching. But according to the esoteric doctrine of interdependent arising, they all include these six significances. This is from the perspective of the Final Teaching. Because in this Final Teaching the sixth and seventh consciousnesses, being the significance of the *tathāgatagarbha*'s accordance with conditions, have no distinct self-natures, so the sixth and seventh consciousnesses include the six significances that are found within original consciousness. Reflect on it and you can see.

3. Enumeration of Logical Possibilities

The third gate is the examination of the logical possibilities of the doctrine of the interdependent arising of causes. There are two kinds: from the perspective of essence and from the perspective of function.

From the perspective of the existence and nonexistence of the essence of causes, there are four logical possibilities: (1) It exists. This refers to the significance of moral determination. (2) It does not exist. This refers to the significance of extinction in each moment. (3) It both exists and does not exist. This refers to the nondual combination of those significances of bringing about its own result and the simultaneous existence of cause and result. (4) It neither exists nor does not exist. This refers to the nondual combination of those significances of continuous evolution in consciousness and being subject to myriad conditions.

As to the four logical possibilities of the function of causes, they are: (1) Because causes combine, without duality, those significances of continuous evolution and being subject to myriad conditions, their function is not self-produced. (2) Because causes combine, without duality, those significances of extinction in each moment and moral determination, it is not other-produced. (3) Because causes combine, without duality, those significances of simultaneous existence of cause and result and bringing about their own results, it is not produced together by both self and other. (4) Because the existence and nonexistence aspects of causes each include the three possibilities just listed, combining as six significances, the significances of causation are complete; so, the function is not produced without cause.

This, then, is how, through these six significances, causes and conditions are completely seized to show the superior virtue of this teaching of interdependent arising. Thus the *Treatise on the Ten Stages* states:

> Causes do not produce the result, because conditions produce it. Conditions do not produce it, because its own cause produces it. Both do not produce it, because there is no cognition [of causes and conditions together], and 502c
> because when [causes and conditions] are active they do not abide [as causes and conditions]. It is not without cause, because its production complies with existence.

Moreover, the *Treatise on the Collected Abhidharma* states:

> Its own seed exists, so it is not produced following from other factors. It is subject to myriad conditions, so it is not self-produced. It has no effective function, so it is not produced by both self and others. It has capabilities, so it is not produced without cause.

Question: What would you say are the differences between these six significances and the eight negations [of Nāgārjuna]?

Reply: The eight negations are based on blocking false views; the six significances take the approach of affirmative representation. Moreover, the eight negations take the perspective of opposing deluded sentience so that true principle shows itself. The six significances, on the other hand, are based on showing true principles, so that deluded sentience perishes of itself. We have these as the left and right hands of the teaching (i.e., they are complementary).

4. Analysis and Synthesis

The fourth gate is analysis and synthesis. With regard to essential substance, there is only one, because causes do not have two essences. With regard to significance, causes are divided into two, referring to emptiness and existence, because they have no self-nature, and because interdependent arising has made them appear. With regard to function, causes are divided into three: (1) The cause is empowered and is not subject to conditions, (2) the cause is empowered and is subject to conditions, (3) the cause is not empowered and is subject to conditions. The first is total empowerment, the last is total powerlessness, and the middle is both empowered and not empowered. Because the fourth logical possibility, not empowered and not subject to conditions, is not any kind of causation, it is not discussed. Thus, there are only three possibilities.

Or, causes are divided into six, referring to the analysis into three logical possibilities and inserting the two gates of emptiness and existence into each of the three, as in the foregoing discussion. Or, they are divided into nine, referring to the above three significances, with each including those three. How so? If a cause is not empowered, then it has no non-empowerment [and so on]. Thus, each one includes three, so there are nine. Or they are divided into twelve. This refers to the above six significances. The two gates of emptiness and existence are inseparable, so that pursuing the gate of emptiness yields the significance of existence and pursuing the gate of existence yields the significance of emptiness. The emptiness of existence has six, and the existence of emptiness has six, so there are twelve. Sometimes causes are divided into eighteen, referring to each one among the above six significances having three significances: (1) the existence or nonexistence of essence; (2) the existence or nonexistence of power; (3) being subject to conditions or not subject to conditions. Three times six makes eighteen. Sometimes they are divided into thirty-six, referring to the above six significances, each of which includes six. Why? Because if one were lacking, all the others would be lacking. Reflect on the other gates by this standard.

5. Fusion and Inclusion

The fifth gate is fusion and inclusion. Now these six significances will be grasped by the fusion and inclusion of their six characteristics. This refers to:

1. Fusing the six significances as one cause; this is the characteristic of totality.

2. Analyzing the one cause as six significances; this is the characteristic of 503a
distinction.

3. The six significances equally having the name of cause is the characteristic of commonality.

4. The six significances being unrecognizable among one another is the characteristic of differentiation.

5. Through these six significances, causes attain formation; this is the characteristic of formation.

6. The six significances each have the significance of abiding in its own rank; this is the characteristic of disintegration.

Question: What is the distinction between the six significances and the six characteristics?

Reply: The six significances are based on the essential substance of interdependent arising itself. The six characteristics are based on the doctrinal gate of interdependent arising. As the essence of a dharma enters the doctrinal gate, differences are subsequently formed. For example, putting the six significances into the framework of the four logical possibilities shows what is correct by negating what is wrong, thus complying with the three vehicles. Putting them into the framework of the six characteristics shows their own virtues, thus complying with the One Vehicle. Thus, the four logical possibilities and the six characteristics are both meant to be skillful means for entering the Dharma.

6. Perspectives of the Teachings

The sixth gate is discernment from the perspective of the teachings. Within the Lesser Vehicle we find the teaching of the characteristics of the causes of attachment to dharmas. With respect to these six significances the Lesser Vehicle has neither the names nor the doctrine. Within the three vehicles teachings on storehouse consciousness, *tathāgatagarbha,* and the causes of the selflessness of dharmas, the six significances exist in name and doctrine, but the teaching of principal and attendants is not yet complete.

Within the One Vehicle teaching of the perfect causation of Samantabhadra, the fully complete teaching of the infinitely interdependent arising of principal and attendants is finally realized. Moreover, due to the doctrine of emptiness and existence, it has the gate of mutual identity; due to the doctrine of empowerment and non-empowerment, it has the gate of mutual intersection; due to the doctrine of being subject to conditions and not subject to conditions, it has the gates of common essence and differentiated essence. Because it has these doctrinal gates, it attains the status of "a single pore accommodating lands and seas." Reflect upon this and you can understand.

C. The Ten Mysterious Dharma Gates of Unobstructed Interdependent Arising

Third is the doctrine of the ten mysterious Dharma gates of unobstructed interdependent arising. Now, the interdependent arising of the Dharma realm is autonomous and inexhaustible, but I will summarize it in two sections via its most important entry points. These are, one, the significance of verifying the ultimate result [of buddhahood] as the realms of the ten buddhas themselves; and two, the discernment of the doctrine from the perspective of causes according with conditions, which is the realm of Samantabhadra.

1. Verification of the Ultimate Result

As to the former significance, in the teaching of the perfect interfusion and autonomous identification of one with all and all with one, we cannot speak of characteristic marks. This is the matter described in the *Flower Garland Sutra:* the interfused significance of the oceans of lands of the ultimate result aspect (i.e., buddhahood), on the one hand, and the essence of the ten buddhas themselves on the other—not to mention Indra's net and the accommodation of subtle particulars; this is indeed an inexpressible doctrine. Why? It does not correspond to the teachings. The *Treatise on the Ten Stages* states, "The causal aspect can be explained; the result aspect cannot be explained." This is its meaning.

Question: If the significance is thus, then why does scripture teach such results as that found in "The Inconceivable Dharma of Buddhas" chapter [of the *Flower Garland*]?

Reply: This doctrine of result is taught as a representation based in conditionality, for the purpose of forming a teaching of causation. These results are not that ultimate autonomous result (i.e., true buddhahood itself). It is like that in the scripture you cite in order to be taught together with the ranks of causation [prior to buddhahood]. Thus you should understand that it is merely representation.

2. Discernment in the Causal State

As to discernment of the doctrine, in this there are two parts: presenting it briefly through analogy, and discerning it extensively from the perspective 503b of doctrine.

i. The Analogy of Counting Coins

As to the former, showing by analogy, I will use the example of methods of counting ten coins.[27] The reason I say "ten" is because I want this analogy to correspond with the perfect number that manifests infinity. Within this there are two parts: differentiated essence and common essence. The reason there are these two gates is because within the myriad gates of interdependent arising there are two significances. One is the significance of nonmutual causation, referring to dharmas being replete with virtues in themselves, such as the cause not being subject to conditions and so on. The other is the significance of mutual causation, such as [the cause] being subject to conditions and so on. The former is common essence; the latter is differentiated essence.

a. Differentiated Essence

Within differentiated essence there are two gates: mutual identification and mutual intersection. The reason why there are these two gates is because all interdependently arisen phenomena have two significances. First is the significance of emptiness and existence; this is from the point of view of its own essence. Second is the significance of empowerment and nonempowerment; this is from the point of view of its functional power. From the former significance we get mutual identification, and from the latter significance we get mutual intersection.

Within the former gate of emptiness and existence, when a "self" (i.e., a single cause) exists, the others (i.e., the conditions) must be nonexistent. Thus, the others are identified with self. How is this so? Due to the others having no self-nature, this "self" creates the result. Moreover, when the "self" is empty, the others must exist as themselves. Thus, self is identified with others.

How so? Due to the self's lack of self-nature, it uses the others to create the result. Because if both existed or both were empty, then each would be incomplete; without that respective other they are not mutually identified. The existence of nonexistence and the nonexistence of existence are nondual, so they are always mutually identifiable. If it were not so, interdependent arising would not be complete and we would have the errors of maintaining reified self-nature and so on. Reflect on this and you will see.

Second is the clarification of empowerment. Within its functioning a self has complete power, so it can by this encompass the others. Because the others completely lack power, they can be intersected by the self. When the others have power, the self lacks power (contrast this with the above and you can understand). This is not based on their self-essences, so they are not mutually identified. Their functional powers pervade each other, so they form mutual intersection. Again, because if both were empowered or both were nonempowered, each would be incomplete; without each other they are not mutually intersected. The nonempowerment of empowerment and the empowerment of nonempowerment are nondual, so they are always mutually intersecting. Moreover, because function encompasses essence, there is no separate essence, so there is only mutual intersection. Because essence encompasses function, there is no separate function, so there is only mutual identification. This is based on the standards within the six significances of causation.

Among these two gates of differentiated essence, I will first clarify mutual intersection. First are the ten gates of upward counting. The first [coin] is one, which is the root number. How so? Because it is formed by conditions. As far as ten, it is ten within the one. Why? If there were no one, then ten would not be formed. One is therefore completely empowered, so it encompasses the ten. Thus it is ten, not one. The other nine gates are also like this. Each and every one is ten. You can understand them according to this example.

In counting downward there are also ten gates. The first is ten, which encompasses the one. How so? Because it is formed by conditions. That is,
503c if there were no ten, then one would not be formed, so the one completely
lacks power and returns to the ten. Thus, it is one, not ten. The rest of the ten are as in this example. In this way, each of the two gates of root and ramifications is replete with ten gates. Reflect on each one of the rest of the coins

by this standard. This is explained with regard to the characteristics of the gate of differentiation.

Question: You spoke about one. How do you get one to have ten within it?

Reply: The Dharma of the great *dhāraṇī* of interdependent arising is that without one, all things do not form. You must know without a doubt that it is like this. What does this doctrine mean? The "one" it speaks of is not the one of self-nature, because it is formed by conditions. For this reason, the one containing ten within it is the conditionally formed one. If this were not so, it would have self-nature without interdependent arising, and could not be called by the name "one." As far as the ten, none of them are the "ten" of self-nature, because they are formed by conditions. For this reason, the ten containing one within them are the conditionally formed, self-natureless ten. If it were not so, they would have self-nature without interdependent arising, and could not be called "ten." For this reason, all things are interdependently arisen and none are self-natured. How so? If one condition is removed, then all of the things are not completely formed. Thus, the one containing many within it is named the interdependently arisen one.

Question: If by removing one condition causation is not complete, then it has no self-nature. How can something without nature form the interdependent arising of one and many?

Reply: It is only through lacking self-nature that it forms the interdependent arising of one and many. How so? Because this interdependent arising is the real virtue of the family of the Dharma realm; because the realm of Samantabhadra is replete with virtues, autonomous and unobstructed. The *Flower Garland Sutra* states:

> Bodhisattvas, contemplate well the dharmas of interdependent arising. Within one dharma, understand that there are multitudes of dharmas; within multitudes of dharmas, understand that there is one dharma.

For this reason, you should understand that ten are within one and one is within ten, mutually accommodating without obstruction, and still each is not the other. Because within one gate, the ten significances are already complete, you should clearly understand that within one gate each has infinite significance. The other gates are also like this.

Question: Within one gate, are the ten totally encompassed, or not?

Reply: Totally, and not totally. How so? Within one is ten, so the ten are totally encompassed. Within ten is one, so the ten are not totally encompassed. The four logical possibilities guard against errors, remove wrong ideas, manifest the virtues of the teachings, and so on. Take this as a standard and you can understand. Within each and every distinct gate, the standard exemplified is also like this.

The marvelous principle of interdependent arising should be understood like this. This is the end of the first part (i.e., on mutual intersection).

Within the first gate of differentiated essence, the second part is the doctrine of mutual identification. Within this, there are two gates: counting upward and counting downward. Within the former, there are ten gates. The first is one. Why? Because it is formed by conditions. One is identified with ten. How so? Because if there were no one, then there would be no ten. Due to the existence of the essence of one, the rest are all empty. For this reason,
504a this one is identified with the ten. In this way, count upward until the tenth. They can each be understood according to the previous standard.

As to counting downward, it also has ten gates. The first is ten. Why? Because of conditional formation. Ten is one. How so? Because if there were no ten, then there would be no one. Due to one having no essence, the rest all exist. Thus, these ten are identified with one. In this way, count downward until reaching one. They all can each be understood according to this standard. Because of this doctrine, you should understand that every single coin is identified with many coins.

Question: If I think one is not identified with ten, what mistake am I making?

Reply: If you think one is not identified with ten, there are two errors. The first is the mistake of not completing ten coins. Why? If one is not identified with ten, many ones will still not complete ten. How so? Because all the single ones are not the ten. Now they have formed ten, so you should clearly understand that one is identified with the ten. The second mistake is not forming one. Why? If one is not identified with ten, ten does not attain formation.

Because it does not complete ten, the significance of one is also not complete. How so? If there are not ten, what one is this? Now since there is already one, you should clearly understand that one is identified with ten. Moreover, if they are not mutually identified, then the two significances of emptiness and existence within the gate of interdependent arising would not appear, and that would be an even greater mistake. This refers to [the error of attachment to the existence of] self-nature, and so on. Reflect on this and you can understand.

Below, the gates of common essence are understood by this standard. The other gates can likewise be understood.

Question: If one is identified with ten, then it should not be one. If ten is identified with one, then it should not be ten.

Reply: It is only because one is identified with ten that it is named one. How so? The one I speak of is not the posited "one," but is a conditionally-formed self-natureless one. Because of this one being identified with many, it is named "one." If this were not so, it would not be named "one." How so? Because it has no self-nature. Without conditions, it would not be formed as one. The teaching that ten is identified with one follows the standard of the previous. Do not be blindly attached to your views! You should understand by means of this standard.

Question: Regarding the above gate of the significance of one and many, are both one and many alike at the same time, or are they different and sequential?

Reply: They are the same, and they are sequential. How so? Due to this interdependent arising of Dharma-nature, they are replete in progression and retrogression, they do not contradict their common essence, they are autonomous in functioning of virtues, they are unobstructed; they are all like this.

Question: What would you say about the characteristics of the significance of upward and downward counting, as taught above?

Reply: The coins do not move from their own ranks, yet they are always going up and down. How so? Because in going up and down and not moving, they are in [still] fact the same things. It is only in order to produce knowledge and demonstrate the true principle that I explain such significances as upward and downward counting. If you cast aside knowledge, then all things are inexpressible. This matter is just as in the above discussion of the result aspect (i.e., the state of buddhahood).

504b Question: If this teaching exists because of knowledge, then it is not something that existed before knowledge. How can you teach that it has always been like this?

Reply: If you were to cast aside knowledge, then there would be no discussion of interdependent arising. It is through taking the perspective of knowledge that I explain that it has always been like this. How so? The unformed is identified with the already-formed, so they are beyond beginning and end; knowledge as well as dharmas have always been formed like this.

Question: Is this teaching created because of knowledge, or is the Dharma truly thus?

Reply: It is created because of knowledge, and the Dharma is truly thus. How so? They simultaneously complete each other. Reflect on the further significance by this standard.

The first major section, the gate of differentiated essence, is concluded.

b. Common Essence

Second is the gate of common essence, which also has two significances. The first is many within one and one within many. The second is one identified with many and many identified with one.

The first gate also contains two: many within one and one within many. As to the former, many within one, there are ten gates that are not the same. The first is one. Why? Because of conditional formation. It is the root number. Within one, then, ten are included. How so? Because this one coin's self-nature is one. Furthermore, it makes a one for the second, so it is a one of the two, and so on until it makes a one for the tenth and is then a one of the ten. Thus, this one includes within itself ten ones. Therefore it is one, not ten—because this is not yet the gate of identification. This first single coin was like this, and the other two, three, four, five, and above nine gates are all each like this. They can be understood by the standard of this example.

As to the second, one within many, it also has ten gates. The first is ten. Why? Because of conditional formation. Within ten is one. How so? Because this one makes one for the ten, so that first one exists among the ones of ten. If it were beyond the ones of ten, there would be no first one. Thus, this one is one within ten. Therefore it is ten, not one. The other nine, eight, seven, and so on down to one are all each like this. Reflect on it by this standard.

Question: What is the difference between this and the previous explanation of differentiated essence?

Reply: In the previous section, on differentiated essence, the first one views the latter nine, and the different gates mutually intersect. Now, with this common essence, ten are already naturally included within one. It is not explained by taking the point of view of the former and latter different gates. This significance you should also consider as a standard.

Second, one is identified with ten, and ten is identified with one. This also has two gates. The first is the identification of one with ten, which also has ten different gates. The first is one. Why? Because it is formed by conditions. One is identified with ten. How so? Because this one of the ten is precisely the first one. Because it has no distinct self-essence, so the ten are identified with one. The other nine gates are all also like this. By this standard you can understand it.

The second, ten is identified with one, also has ten different gates. The first is ten. Why? Because of conditional formation. Ten is identified with
one. Why? That first one is identified with ten, and furthermore there is no 504c
self-same one. Thus, the first one is identified with ten. The other nine gates can be understood by the standard of this example.

Question: Within this gate of common essence, does this teaching of one being identified with ten and so on only encompass these ten coins? Or does it encompass infinite things?

Reply: These are both formed according to knowledge. When it should be ten it is ten, when it should be infinite it is infinite. Such increase and decrease accords with what knowledge can grasp. Identification with ten is as stated in the previous explication. As to the infinite, within one gate there are already ten, and as these ten are again multiplied by themselves in mutual identification and mutual intersection, they are doubled and redoubled to form infinity.

And yet all this infinite redoubling is entirely encompassed within the first gate.

Question: Does this explanation only encompass infinite redoubling within this one gate? Or does it also encompass infinity within the rest of the different gates?

Reply: It may encompass all, or it may encompass only its own infinity. How is this so? If there were no infinity within the one gate itself, the infinities within all the rest of the gates would not form. For this reason, the first gate of common essence then encompasses infinity, infinity, infinity, infinity, infinity, infinity, infinity, infinity, infinity, and infinity (i.e., ten infinities) within the two gates of common and differentiated essence. Exhaustively encompassing the ultimate perfection of the Dharma realm, nothing is left out. Or, it may be that it only encompasses the infinity of its own one gate of common essence. How so? Because the other different gates are like empty space and they do not know of one another. It is complete of itself, and there is nothing more to encompass. This is only what is graspable according to knowledge; not one thing is out of place. In this way, one gate is already replete with inexhaustible numbers of infinities. And mutual identification and mutual intersection and so on form infinities: within each and every other gate, all are like this; each is forming infinite infinities. You should understand it according to this standard.

We have taken, for a moment, the perspective of showing true principle and phenomena within coins. It is even more so within the One Vehicle Dharma of the *dhāraṇī* of the infinity of interdependent arising. It doesn't mean that only these phenomena—the coins—are like this. You should discard deluded sentience and reflect on this in accordance with true principles.

ii. Discernment from the Perspective of Dharma

Second is discerning the doctrine of infinite interdependent arising extensively from the perspective of Dharma. In summary there are two parts: the gate of establishing the doctrine and the gate of interpretation.

In the former, the gate of establishing the doctrine, the ten Dharma gates of significance are summarily established, in order to show the infinite. What
505a are these ten?

1. The doctrine that encompasses all the doctrines of the One Vehicle, the three vehicles, and so on up to the five vehicles. This is the standard of the rest, below.

2. The doctrine of true principle and phenomena that encompasses all principles and all phenomena.

3. The doctrine of understanding and practice that encompasses all understandings and practices.

4. The doctrine of causation and result that encompasses all causation and results.

5. The doctrine of persons and dharmas that encompasses all persons and dharmas.

6. The doctrine of distinctions in ranks and objects of mind that encompasses all distinctions in ranks and objects of mind.

7. The doctrine of master and disciple and Dharma and wisdom that encompasses all masters and disciples and all Dharma and wisdom.

8. The doctrine of principal and attendants and ancillary and primary [karmic recompense] that encompasses all principals and attendants and all ancillary and primary [karmic recompenses].

9. The doctrine of manifesting the teachings in accordance with the spiritual roots and desires of living beings that encompasses all manifestations in accordance with the roots and desires of living beings.

10. The doctrine of the autonomy of progression and retrogression in essence and function that encompasses all autonomies of progression and retrogression in essence and function.

These ten are the head gates; they all each totally encompass all dharmas, forming the infinite.

Second is the gate of interpretation in words. It explicates the previous ten doctrines by means of the ten gates, in order to manifest the infinite [nature of this Distinct Teaching].

Question: How do you understand the number ten to be the manifestation of the infinite?

Reply: In the *Flower Garland Sutra,* the number ten is established as a norm in order to manifest infinite significances.

a. Simultaneous Repletion and Mutual Correspondence

First is the gate of simultaneous repletion and mutual correspondence. These above ten significances are simultaneous and mutually correspondent, forming a single teaching of interdependent arising. There are no distinctions of before and after, beginning and end, and so on. They are replete with all things, autonomously progressing and retrogressing, mixing without chaos, to form the parameters of interdependent arising. This relies on the ocean-seal *samādhi* that brilliantly and simultaneously reveals the formation of all things.

b. Mutual Accommodation of Difference

Second is the gate of one and many being different but mutually accommodating. All these doctrines above, when pursued within one gate, completely encompass all the previous causes and results and principles and phenomena of all Dharma gates. Like that first coin that within it encompasses infinite significances—this is also like that. But within this one, although it includes the existence of many, one is not identified with the combined many. Within many there is one, and so on according to the standards reflected upon above. Within each and every one of the other gates, they are all completely like this, doubled and redoubled infinitely. Thus, a verse of this [*Flower Garland*] *Sutra* states:

> The ten directions are filled by one buddha land. The ten directions enter the one, and there is no remainder, and the original characteristics of the worlds are not destroyed. This is possible because of incomparable virtues.

However, although this one and many may accommodate each other autonomously and without obstruction, their essences are not the same. Just as it is explained above regarding the significances of the coins, this has the aspects of common essence and differentiated essence. You can understand this by reflecting on the standard of the preceding.

c. Autonomous Mutual Identification

Third is the gate of autonomous mutual identification of the myriad dharmas. With regard to the various significances above, this is one identified with all and all are identified with one; they are formed in perfect interfusion, autonomously

and without obstruction. When considered from the perspective of the gate of common essence, this self-identified phenomenon is complete and encompasses all dharmas. However, all the dharmas of this self-identified phenomenon are themselves mutually intersecting, because their interrelationships are doubled and redoubled infinitely. But these infinite interrelationships are all completely 505b
within the initial gate. Thus the [*Flower Garland*] *Sutra* states:

> When bodhisattvas first aspire to enlightenment, the virtue of that one thought is deep, broad, and boundless. The Tathāgata may expound it, exhausting *kalpa*s, but the Tathāgata cannot reach the end of the virtue of this first thought. How much more so is the Tathāgata unable to exhaustively describe the boundless, innumerable, immeasurable *kalpa*s replete with the cultivation of myriad *pāramitā*s and myriad stages, merits, virtues, and practices!

This means that one thought of enlightenment is deep, broad, and boundless; it is certainly so due to the identification of one with all things in the interdependent arising of the Dharma realm. Like that one coin within the gate of common essence attaining infinitely doubled and redoubled significances—this is what it means. How much more so is this true of boundless *kalpa*s! Within each and every other gate, each dharma manifests infinite significances, like this. As to the reason why it is like this, this sutra also states, "The bodhisattva who first aspires to enlightenment is already a buddha." Because of this marvelous principle of interdependent arising, the beginning and the end are equal. Attaining the beginning is attaining the end. Exhausting the end is at once to begin at the origin. As in the above, they are simultaneously replete, so they are attained like so. It also states, "Within one bodhisattva stage, one universally encompasses the merits of all the various stages." For this reason, attaining one is attaining all. It also states, "Understand that one is many and many are one." This is the matter of realizing buddhahood in the final mind of the ten stages of faith.

Question: If the one gate of common essence encompasses all things within it infinitely, do all things manifest together at once, or do they manifest in sequence?

Reply: The brilliant manifestation of all things within one gate, at one time, belongs to the aspect of the accommodation of subtle particulars. The hidden and revealed manifesting each other in infinite interrelationship belongs to the aspect of Indra's net. The rest of the significances are identified with the same and identified with the different, identified with many and identified with few, identified with existence and identified with nonexistence, identified with the beginning and identified with the end; such is the infinite Dharma gate's autonomous repletion with all things. Yet by raising one as the chief, the rest are identified as the attendants. In truth, not one is out of place, and it has been like this since the beginning. Within this one gate of discerning the common essence is found the repletion of autonomous inexhaustible virtues. Reflect accordingly on the rest of the gates of differentiated essence and so on.

Question: If one gate is replete with all things in infinite autonomy, what is the purpose of the other gates?

Reply: The other gates are like empty space. Why? Because the one gate of common essence encompasses all things together and nothing remains unfinished by its scope.

Question: As to all the things encompassed within this gate of common essence, it must only encompass all the things within its own gate; how could it possibly encompass all the things within the other gates?

Reply: It already encompasses its own everything; it further encompasses the infinite everythings within each and every other gate. Such are the doubled and redoubled interrelationships that exhaustively pervade the Dharma realm. How so? In the infinite interdependent arising of the Dharma realm of perfect interfusion, if one is lacking, then all things together do not form. The school
505c of Dharma-nature argues that this is a real virtue, but its scope is inexpressible. Thus a verse of the [*Flower Garland*] *Sutra* states:

> When all of the inexpressible teachings are expounded within
> inexpressible myriads of *kalpa*s,
> The inexpressible *kalpa*s may be finished, but the expression of the
> inexpressible can never be finished.

Another verse states:

> The minds of all living beings can be analyzed and understood.
> The fine dust of all the lands can be counted and calculated.

> The worlds of empty space in the ten directions can be measured
> with a single hair.
> But a bodhisattva's first aspiration to enlightenment can never be
> ultimately fathomed.

This is certainly because in the Dharma gate of the One Vehicle's perfect utmost freedom and unobstructedness, attaining one is attaining everything. Cause and result are both equal, without distinction of before and after. Thus, the *Treatise on the Ten Stages* states:

> Because bodhisattvas at the stage of faith and even the inconceivable dharma of buddhahood are one in interdependent arising, the significance of the six characteristics of conditioned phenomena—totality, separateness, and so on—can be taken to enclose them.

Understand clearly: cause and result are simultaneously present, mutually inclusive, and mutually identifiable. Each encompasses all things, becoming each other's principal and attendants. You must reflect on this matter deeply; do not doubt. This sutra also states:

> How is it that with this first aspiration to enlightenment, the bodhisattva is indeed a buddha? They are completely equal to the various tathāgatas of the three times, and they are equal to the buddha realms of the three times. They are completely equal to the correct Dharma of the buddhas of the three times. They attain the one body and the immeasurable bodies of the Tathāgata, and wisdom equal to that of the myriad buddhas of the three times. The living beings transformed by their teaching are also all completely equal.

It also states, "At the time of the first aspiration to enlightenment, they immediately complete correct awakening. Being endowed with the wisdom body, they are not enlightened by others." Such statements as these are countless, as extensively found in the scriptures.

Question: These statements praise the virtues within the causal state. How could they possibly be the same virtues of the fulfilled result?

Reply: In this One Vehicle doctrine, cause and result are of common essence and formed in one interdependent arising; attaining this is attaining that.

Because of the mutual identification of this and that, if one does not attain the result, then the cause is an unformed cause. How so? If its result is not attained, it is not a cause.

Question: Above you said that the result aspect (i.e., buddhahood) is beyond conditionality and its characteristics are inexpressible, so you would only discuss the causal aspect. Why then do you assert that the final mind of the ten stages of faith is realizing buddhahood and attaining the resultant dharma?

Reply: What I mean when I speak of becoming a buddha is only that following from the first seeing and hearing of the teachings and onward up to the second rebirth, one completes understanding and practice; one exhaustively fulfills the causal ranks in the final mind of understanding and practice, and then in the third rebirth attains that final result of autonomous perfect harmony. Because this essence of the causal state depends on the completion of the result, it is only by fulfilling the causal ranks that one is then submerged into the ocean of the result. As to this realm of realization, it is inexpressible. This is like the dragon's daughter, Prince Universal Adornment, Prince Sudhana, the Prince of Tuṣita, and so on—in three rebirths they were able to gain that result (i.e., buddhahood). This is as extensively discussed in the scriptures; reflect on it accordingly.

506a Question: Above you said that in a single thought one already realizes buddhahood. In the three vehicles this doctrine already exists. What is the difference between this and that?

Reply: The three vehicles take the point of view of true principle and consider one thought to be attaining realization of buddhahood. Now, in this One Vehicle, one thought is attainment of the completion of all teachings and doctrines—principle and phenomena, causation and result, and so on, as in all the Dharma gates above—and is attainment together with all living beings, completely, simultaneously realizing buddhahood. After, all beings renew the severing of delusions; they do not abide in the stage of learning but form correct awakening and completely realize the ten buddhas, because they manifest infinite virtues in both progression and retrogression. Furthermore, Indra's net and the simultaneous accommodation of subtle particulars, and the nine time periods and the ten aspects of time and so on, are all-pervasive in the various ranks. In reference to the final mind of the ten stages of faith and onward, the ten understandings, the ten practices, the ten conversions of merit, the ten bodhisattva stages, and the buddha stage are simultaneously pervasive, formed without the existence of before or after, replete with all things. So, between this one thought and one hundred thousand *kalpa*s, no difference exists. You must reflect on this accordingly.

This is the end of the third gate of the autonomy of mutual identification of the characteristics of myriad dharmas.

d. The Realm of Indra's Net

Fourth is the gate of the realm of Indra's net. This section only takes up an analogy, which is different from the preceding. The essence and characteristics of the various significances above all autonomously conceal and reveal each other, manifesting manifold infinitude. Thus, this [*Flower Garland*] *Sutra* states:

> Within one mote of dust is shown billions of innumerable hundreds
> of millions of myriad buddhas explaining the Dharma.
> Within one mote of dust is manifested immeasurable buddha lands,
> with adamantine mountains encircling their Mount Sumerus, and
> the worlds are not constrained.
> Within one mote of dust is manifest the three evil destinies, the
> heavenly beings and humans, and the *asura*s, each among them
> receiving their karmic recompense.

These three verses are identified with the three temporal worlds. [The sutra] also states:

> Buddhas as countless as the motes of dust in all the buddha lands sit in a single pore [of your skin]. They all have assemblies of innumerable bodhisattvas, and each is fully explaining the practices of Samantabhadra. Innumerable lands and seas are located in a single pore. Every time a buddha sits on the lotus throne of *bodhi,* that buddha fully pervades all Dharma realms. Every pore freely manifests this.

It also states, "As it is shown in a single mote of dust, all of the motes of dust are also like this." Other statements such as these are innumerable, as extensively discussed in the scriptures. These are all truly real, and are not formed through miraculous transformations. This is the object realm of discriminating wisdom seen through the wisdom attuned with true principle. Those other miraculous transformations are not included among these examples. Why? These are the real virtues of Dharma-nature; they are just like this as dharmas. They are not of the realm posited by discriminatory, impassioned consciousness. You can reflect on this when you discard deluded sentience.

Question: As to the above single mote of dust manifesting within it innumerable buddha lands, and so on—this is merely onefold manifestation. Why
506b do you then state that the manifestations are "manifold"?

Reply: At the time when this *Flower Garland Sutra* was taught, it was said that within all motes of dust it was also being taught like so. When the *Flower Garland Sutra* is taught within those motes of dust, it is likewise said that within all motes of dust it is also being taught like so. In this way it expands and evolves as manifold infinitude. Reflect on this accordingly.

Question: Based on these passages, the teaching is indeed a manifold infinity. What do they say about its distinctions, or in discussion of its beginning and end?

Reply: It is grasped according to wisdom. Raising one to be the chief, the rest then become the attendants. By making this chief the center, the rest then become the retinue that surrounds it. As in the doctrine above, they are all autonomously formed like this. Again, as previously, they are mutually identified and mutually intersecting with absolute autonomy. They all in this way completely encompass all dharmas and the inexhaustible Dharma realm, all together forming Indra's net.

e. Mutual Accommodation of Subtle Particulars

Fifth is the gate of securely establishing the teaching of the mutual accommodation of subtle particulars. The various significances above this, within a single thought, are replete with all Dharma gates, such as beginnings and endings, simultaneity and temporal separateness, before and after, progression and retrogression. Within a single thought they manifest brilliantly, simultaneously and all at once, so that nothing is not illuminated, like the simultaneous appearance of arrow tips when they are neatly bundled up. Thus, this [*Flower Garland*] *Sutra* states:

> Within one thought, the bodhisattva's spirit descends from Tuṣita Heaven into the mother's womb, and so on even to the distribution of the relics throughout the world to prolong the time that the Dharma abides in the world, and the myriad living beings that have been so benefited—within a single thought all these are completely manifested.

This is as extensively found in the texts of the scriptures. It also states, "Within one pore immeasurable buddha lands, resplendent and immaculate, expansively and peacefully abide." It also states, "Inside one mote of dust are the lands of minute kingdoms; they dwell within all motes of dust." You should reflect on this according to true principles.

Question: How is this doctrine distinct from that of Indra's net, above?

Reply: The mutual manifestation of manifold concealment and revelation is what the teaching of Indra's net encompasses. The brilliant manifestation of equality and simultaneity is what the teaching of the accommodation of subtle particulars encompasses. These various significances are distinct and not the same. This deserves careful reflection.

f. Esoteric Concurrent Formation

Sixth is the gate of the esoteric concurrent formation of concealment and manifestation. The above various significances are occluded or revealed, but at all times complete. So the [*Flower Garland*] *Sutra* states:

> One enters into unified concentration here, and arises from *samādhi* there. One enters into unified concentration by the subjective faculty of the eye, and arises from *samādhi* by the objective field of visible forms.

And so on. It also states, "One enters into unified concentration in the body of a son, and arises from *samādhi* in the body of a daughter," and so on; also, "Within one tiny mote of dust one enters into unified concentration, and one arises from *samādhi* on the tip of a single hair." In this way freely concealed here and revealed there, entering concentration and arising from concentration are esoterically completed at the same time. Moreover, this sutra states:

> Bodhisattvas have conditions of karmic connection in the worlds of the ten directions, so they go and return, leave and enter, to deliver living beings.

> Sometimes living beings see a bodhisattva enter into unified concentration.
> 506c Sometimes they see a bodhisattva arise from concentration.

It also states:

> Within those worlds of the ten directions, with every thought they show complete correct awakening, the turning of the true Dharma wheel, and entry into nirvana; they reveal the dividing of the relics, and deliver living beings.

Teachings such as these are innumerable, as extensively discussed in the scriptures. It is also like when the Buddha causes various bodhisattvas to receive their predictions of future buddhahood: some receive their predictions right before our eyes, and some receive their predictions not before our eyes but esoterically. This is as above: the ten coins within the first coin are said to be revealed, while the second coin, in view of the ten within the first, is esoterically hidden. Why? Because to see this is to not see that; because they do not know of each other. Although they do not know or see each other, yet it follows that by forming this, that is formed. This is called "concurrent formation." You should reflect on this according to this standard.

g. Endowment with all Pure and Mixed Virtues

Seventh is the gate of endowment with all pure and mixed virtues. The various significances above are either pure or mixed. As in the previous discussion of the dharmas of a person: if one grasps them through the gate of personhood, then all of the dharmas are of personhood, so they are called "pure." This gate of personhood also contains all the differentiated dharmas of true principle and particular phenomena, so it is called "mixed." It is also like the bodhisattva entering one *samādhi* and only practicing generosity; it is immeasurable, boundless, and there are no other practices, so it is called "pure." But entering into one *samādhi* is also generosity, precepts, delivering living beings, and so on; it is immeasurable, boundless, and includes all the other "mixed" practices. Both are simultaneously accomplished. Proliferating in this way, the pure and mixed exist autonomously in the Dharma realm, and there is nothing they do not include. Reflect on this accordingly.

h. Unique Formations of the Ten Temporal Worlds

Eighth is the gate of the unique formations of the dharmas of ten temporal worlds. The various significances above pervade the ten times, completely manifesting simultaneously and distinctly, because time and dharmas are not mutually exclusive. I speak of ten times, which are the three times of past, future, and present, within each of which there is also its own past, future, and present, making [altogether] nine times. As these nine times are repeatedly mutually identified and intersected, they constitute one comprehensive unit. The comprehensive and the separate times together form ten times. These ten times are replete with distinctions but manifest simultaneously, forming interdependent arising, so they are mutually identified and intersected. Thus, this [*Flower Garland*] *Sutra* states:

> Sometimes a long *kalpa* intersects a short *kalpa*, or a short *kalpa* intersects a long *kalpa*. Sometimes a hundred thousand great *kalpa*s become a single thought, or a single thought is identified with a hundred thousand great *kalpa*s. Sometimes a *kalpa* of the past intersects a future *kalpa*, or a future 507a
> *kalpa* intersects a past *kalpa*.

Such is the autonomy of times and *kalpa*s, mutually identifying and mutually intersecting without obstruction, formed by merging. This sutra also states, "Within a single mote of dust the three times and all buddha lands are universally manifested." It also states, "Within a single mote of dust all the living beings of the three times are universally manifested." It also states, "Within a single mote of dust the works of all the buddhas of the three times are universally manifested." It also states, "Within a single mote of dust all of the buddhas' turnings of the wheels of the Dharma of the three times are established." Such statements are innumerable, as extensively found in the texts of the scriptures. This universally encompasses the above various doctrinal gates. All are autonomously manifested within the ten temporal worlds. You can reflect on this accordingly.

i. Formation by Evolutions of Mind-only

Ninth is the gate of formation by the evolutions of mind-only. All the above significances are only the turning of the mind of immaculate self-nature of this one *tathāgatagarbha*. But this is the inherent virtue of arising from original nature, so it is different from the teachings of the three vehicles. Now, the one mind is moreover replete with ten kinds of virtues, as explained in the doctrine of the ten minds in the "Arising from Original Nature" chapter [of the *Flower Garland Sutra*] and so on—this is the matter with which it is concerned. As to there being ten of them in the explanation, by this the sutra intends to show the infinite; in this way it shows that the one mind is autonomously replete with inexhaustible varieties of virtues. These various gates of significance above are all the autonomous functioning of this mind. There is no other thing [besides this mind], so it is called "formation by the evolutions of mind-only." Consider this accordingly.

j. Phenomenal Manifestation of the Dharma

Tenth is the gate of producing understanding by example of any phenomenon's manifestation of the Dharma. The phenomena taken as examples for the various significances above are used to distinctly show distinct dharmas, which are true principle and phenomena, and all the rest of the Dharma gates. For example, in the [*Flower Garland*] *Sutra,* where it teaches the characteristics of ten kinds of things, such as jewels, kings, clouds, and so on, these are identified with the various Dharma gates. It shows that all the above significances are precious, so it uses jewels to represent them. It shows that all the above significances are autonomous (i.e., sovereign), so it uses kings to represent them. It shows that all the above significances are beneficial, sustaining, and thunderous, so it uses clouds to represent them. Statements regarding such phenomena as these are innumerable. Reflect on this by the scripture.

Question: This doctrine exists in the three vehicles. How is that different from this?

Reply: The three vehicles take up the characteristics of different phenomena to represent different principles. Now, the characteristics of phenomena taken up by this One Vehicle are themselves just those true principles being manifested; there is no difference. Replete with all the principles and phenomena, teachings and significances, and so on of all the above Dharma gates, there is nothing it does not completely encompass. You can reflect on this appropriately by the true principles.

The analyses of these above ten gates, and the above ten doctrines of the original text, are all at the same time completely interfused to form the gate of the interdependent arising of one Dharma realm, replete with virtues.

When from the truth of the realm of the universal eye one contemplates the other gates, they are only within the mind of great understanding, great practice, and great seeing and hearing. Then these ten gates are pursued through 507b
one gate, which encompasses the other gates without anything unfinished. You should comprehend this by considering the skillful means of the six characteristics of existence as the standard.

iii. Summary

The teachings illuminated above are together a summary demonstration of the doctrine of interdependent arising in the Distinct Teaching of One Vehicle. Moreover, the various other characteristics of dharmas, questions-and-answers, and methods of removing doubts that are within it are sometimes the same and sometimes different from those of the three vehicles. What those teachings intend and what they design are the skillful means of the One Vehicle, as is extensively attested in the interpretations of them in the *Flower Garland Sutra* and its treatises, commentaries, and subcommentaries, in the *Essays on the Contents of the Flower Garland Sutra,* and in the *Fifty Essentials of Huayan by Question and Answer.* These teachings are completely distinct and dissimilar from those of the three vehicles. You should reflect on this appropriately, as it is extensively based on the realm of the universal vision of the *Flower Garland Sutra.*

Question: I can trust that the above principles are distinct and dissimilar from the doctrines of the three vehicles. But by what textual proofs do we know that the One Vehicle exists distinctly outside of the three vehicles?

Reply: This sutra itself has evidential passages. So a verse states:

> Of the many kinds of living beings in all the worlds,
> Few are those who desire to pursue the way of the *śrāvaka;*
> Those who pursue the way of the *pratyekabuddha* are even fewer;
> Those who pursue the Great Vehicle are few indeed.
> Those who pursue the Great Vehicle may find it easy,
> To be able to trust in this Dharma is extremely difficult.

Certainly this Dharma exceeds deluded sentience and is difficult to trust. For this reason the sage resolved the issue by comparison with the three vehicles. Another verse states:

If there are living beings
Who are inferior, their minds submerged [in samsara],
Show them the way of the *śrāvaka,*
To cause them to depart from myriad sufferings.
This is the Lesser Vehicle.
If there are also living beings
Whose spiritual capacities are a little brighter and keener,
Who take pleasure in the dharma of causes and conditions,
Teach them the way of the *pratyekabuddha.*
This is the Middle Vehicle.
If there are people
Whose capacities are bright and keen,
Having minds of great compassion,
Bountiful in their benefit to living beings,
Teach them the way of the bodhisattva.
This is the Great Vehicle.
If there are those of unsurpassed mind,
Determined in their desire to pursue the Great Matter,
Show them the bodies of Buddha,
And teach the infinite Buddha-Dharma.
This is the One Vehicle.

Because of this, you know that the One Vehicle is not something those of lower capacity can fully receive. Thus, it is the wonderful skill of the Great Sage to reduce the explanation for those of the ranks of the three vehicles according to their capacities and desires, as skillful means. Because it does not in this way exhaust the source of the Dharma realm, the Sage only provisionally manifests the two bodies or three bodies of Buddha. Now, for those of unsurpassed mind and capacities, who take pleasure in the Great Matter, for them the realms of the ten bodies of Buddha are first manifested and the infinite Buddha-Dharma is explained. This is called "showing them the bodies of Buddha and teaching the infinite Buddha-Dharma." The three vehicles merely accord with the capacities of practitioners; they do not yet reveal all ten bodies of the Buddha's own realms, so theirs are not the true manifestations of the bodies of Buddha. Moreover, they reduce the explanation

according to the capacities of practitioners, teaching the principles of one characteristic, one quiescence, one flavor, and so on; so theirs is not the completely exhaustive explanation. How is this so? Because those of the three vehicles take the inexhaustibility [of the Buddha-Dharma] to be an error. However, this One Vehicle takes inexhaustibility to be the real virtue [of the Buddha-Dharma]. The sutra also states, "Within one world, you may hear of One Vehicle, or of two, three, four, five, or even innumerable vehicles." 507c
This is taught on the basis of the distinctions of root and ramifications. The doctrine of the sacred teachings is evident. Do not be shocked or skeptical because of attachment to deluded sentience.

D. Perfect Interfusion of the Six Characteristics of Conditioned Phenomena

Fourth is the doctrine of the perfect interfusion of the six characteristics of conditioned phenomena. The interdependent arising of the six characteristics is divided into three gates: the list of their names and summary explanations; the clarification of the idea inspiring this teaching; and interpretation through question and answer.

1. List of Names and a Brief Explanation

First is the list of names: the characteristic of totality, the characteristic of distinctness, the characteristic of commonality, the characteristic of difference, the characteristic of formation, and the characteristic of disintegration. Conditioned phenomena have the characteristic of totality, because one contains the virtues of the many. They have the characteristic of distinctness, because the many virtues are not one. Distinctness, being based on totality, fulfills that totality. They have the characteristic of commonality, because the many significances do not contradict each other, forming one totality in common. They have the characteristic of difference, because when the many significances view each other, each and every one is different. They have the characteristic of formation, because through these various significances, interdependent arising is formed. They have the characteristic of disintegration, because each of the various significances abides in its own dharma, and does not move from itself.

2. Purpose of this Teaching

Second is the idea inspiring this teaching of the perfect interfusion of the six characteristics of conditioned phenomena. This teaching is meant to show that in the Perfect Teaching of the One Vehicle, the interdependent arising of the Dharma realm is infinite, perfectly interfused, autonomous, mutually identifying, unobstructed, and so on, even to the inexhaustible principles and phenomena of Indra's net. These significances directly reveal all delusive hindrances, such that when one is severed all are severed, and the extinction of the delusions of the nine times and the ten times is attained. The practice of virtues is such that one completed is all completed. The nature of true principles is that one manifested is all manifested. Moreover, universality and distinctness are complete; beginnings and endings are all equal. The time of the first aspiration to enlightenment is the completion of correct awakening. Certainly because the interdependent arising of the Dharma realm is thus, the six characteristics are interfused, causes and results are simultaneous, mutual identification and so on occurs autonomously, and progression and retrogression are complete. Causation is indeed the understanding and practice of Samantabhadra, and by verifying it one enters into the result that is the realms of the ten buddhas. What it manifests is inexhaustible. This is as extensively taught in the *Flower Garland Sutra.*

3. Interpretation through the Analogy of a House

Third is interpretation through question and answer. As the dharma of interdependent arising pervades all places, I will now summarize this teaching through the discussion of how conditions form a house.[28]

[One: the characteristic of totality.]

Question: What is its characteristic of totality?

Reply: It is the house.

Question: This is only the various conditions of rafters and so on. What is the house?

Reply: The rafters are the house. How is this so? By the rafters being entirely themselves alone, we can make a house. If we remove the rafters, the house is not complete; but when we have the rafters, we have a house.

Question: If it is by the rafters being entirely themselves alone that we can make a house, then if we don't yet have roof tiles and so on, it should still

508a make a house.

Reply: When we don't yet have roof tiles, it is not because of the rafters that the house isn't made. It is not that we can't make it because of the rafters. Now, what I mean by saying that we can make a house is only to demonstrate that rafters can make it. I am not explaining making it with things that are not rafters. Why? The rafters are its causes and conditions. When we have not yet formed the house it has no causes and conditions, so they are not its rafters. If they were its rafters, it would already be completely formed. If it were not completely formed, they could not be called its rafters.

Question: If the rafters are the various conditions, each one exerts a small part of its strength[29] and they combine to make the house—each one does not entirely make it. What is the error in this view?

Reply: This errs in annihilationism and in eternalism. If each single rafter did not entirely form the house and were only a part of its strength, all of the various conditions would each only be a part of its strength. This would only be many units of partial strength. They would not form one entire house, so this is annihilationism. If the various conditions were all small parts of its strength and there was no entire formation, but you were still attached to the existence of the entire house, this would be existence without cause; this is the eternalism of your view. If the house were not entirely formed, then if we took out one rafter, the house would still exist. But in that case the house would not be entirely formed, so we know that it is formed not by parts of its strength, but entirely.

Question: If it lacks but a single rafter, how could it possibly not be a house?

Reply: It is only a broken house, not a good house. So we know that a good house is entirely inherent in the one rafter. As it is already inherent in the one rafter, we know the rafter is the house.

Question: If the house is already identified with the rafters, then shouldn't the other planks, roof tiles, and so on be identified with the rafters?

Reply: As a totality they all are the rafters. How so? Take out the rafters, and there is no house. The reason it is like this is because without rafters, the house collapses. If the house has collapsed, they are not called planks, roof tiles, and so on. Thus, the planks, roof tiles, and so on are identified with the rafters. If they were not identified with the rafters, the house would not be formed, and the rafters, roof tiles, and so on also would not be formed. Now, they are already formed together, so we know they are mutually identified. One rafter is already so; the other rafters are likewise. Thus, all interdependently arisen phenomena, when they are not formed, cease to exist; when they are formed, they are mutually identified. The ultimate perfection of interfused unobstructed autonomy is extremely difficult to ponder, far beyond the capacity of sentience. You should accordingly understand that the interdependent arising of the nature of dharmas pervades all places.

Two: the characteristic of distinction. The rafters and such conditions are distinct from the totality. If they were not distinct, the significance of totality would not form, because when there are no distinctions then there is no totality. What does this mean? Basically, totality is formed by distinctions. Due to lacking distinctions, the totality is not formed. Thus, the distinctions are formed as distinctions by means of totality.

Question: If the totality is identified with distinctions, shouldn't it not form a totality?

Reply: Because totality is identified with distinctions, it is thus that it attains the status of totality. It is like the rafters. When they are being identified with the house, we call that the characteristic of totality, and when they are being identified as rafters, we call that the characteristic of distinction. If they are not identified with the house, they are not rafters. If they are not identified as rafters, it is not a house. Totality and distinction are mutually identifiable;
508b you can reflect on it by this.

Question: If they are mutually identified, what does it mean to teach that they are distinct?

Reply: It is only because of this mutual identification that they form distinctions. If they were not mutually identified, the totality would exist outside of the distinctions, so it would not be their totality, and the distinctions would exist outside of the totality, so they would not be its distinctions. Reflect on it and you can understand.

Question: If they were not considered to be distinct, what would be the mistake?

Reply: This view has the errors of annihilationism and eternalism. If there were no distinctions, there would be no distinct rafters and roof tiles. If there were no distinct rafters and roof tiles, then they would not form a total house. This is annihilationism. If there were no distinct rafters, roof tiles, and so on, and yet there was a total house, this would be a house that exists without causes. This is the error of eternalism.

Three: the characteristic of commonality. The rafters and other such conditions join together in common to make the house. They do not contradict each other, so they are all called the conditions of the house. They do not make other things, so this is called the characteristic of commonality.

Question: How is this different from the characteristic of totality?

Reply: The characteristic of totality is only taught from the point of view of the one house. Now, this characteristic of commonality is taught from the perspective of the various conditions of the rafters and so on. Although their essences are each distinct, in terms of the significance of their formative strengths they are equal; so it is called the characteristic of commonality.

Question: If they did not have commonality, what would be the mistake?

Reply: If they are not viewed as having commonality, there are the errors of annihilationism and eternalism. Why? If they do not have commonality, the various conditions such as the rafters would be mutually contradictory and would not make a house in common. The house would not attain the status of existence; this view is annihilationism. If they contradicted each other and did not make a house, and yet you are attached to the existence of the house, this would be a house that exists without causes; this is eternalism.

Four: the characteristic of difference. The various conditions such as the rafters accord with their own forms and types, so they have differences from each other.

Question: If they are different, shouldn't they not have commonality?

Reply: It is only because of their difference that they have commonality. If they were not different, then since the rafters are twenty feet long, the roof tiles would also be twenty feet long. This would destroy the basic conditional dharmas. Thus, they would lose the previous significance, that of the equality needed to become, in common, a house. Now, the house is already formed. As to what are called conditions in common, you should understand that they are different.

Question: How is this different from the characteristic of distinction?

Reply: The previously discussed characteristic of distinction only explains how the various conditions, such as rafters, are distinct from the one house, so it is taught as the characteristic of distinction. Now, with the characteristic of difference, we are considering the various conditions in turn, such as rafters and so on, from each other's point of view. Each and every one has different characteristics.

Question: If they were not considered to be different, what would be the mistake?

Reply: There would be the errors of annihilationism and eternalism. Why? If they were not different, roof tiles would be the same as rafters—twenty feet long. This would destroy the basic conditional dharmas, and they would not form a house together; this is annihilationism. If it were destroyed and the conditions did not form a house, and yet you are attached to the existence of the house, this would be a house that exists without causes; this is eternalism.

Five: the characteristic of formation. Because of these various conditions, the significance of the house is formed. Because they form the house, the rafters and so on are called conditions. If it were not so, neither of the two would be formed. Now, since the house is actually formed, we know that the characteristic of formation is their mutual formation.

508c Question: I clearly see the rafters and such conditions. Each abides in its own dharma, and originally does not make a house. By what cause is the existence of the significance of the house formed?

Reply: It is only because the various conditions, such as the rafters, do not make the house that the significance of the house attains formation. It is like this because if the rafters made the dharma of the house, then they would lose their original dharma of being rafters, so the significance of the house would not attain formation. Now, because they do not make it, the various conditions such as rafters appear. Because of this appearance, the significance of the house attains formation. Moreover, if they did not make a house, the rafters would not be called the various conditions [of the house]. Now, as they have already attained the name of "conditions," you should clearly understand that they will definitely make a house.

Question: If they are not formative, what is the error?

Reply: There are the errors of annihilationism and eternalism. Why? The formation of the house originally depends on rafters and other such conditions. Now, if the conditions actually don't make the house, then no house comes into existence. This is annihilationism. We take the original conditions of the formation of the house to be called rafters. Now, as they did not make the house, there would be no rafters; this is annihilationism. If they were not formative, the house would exist without a cause; this is eternalism. Moreover, the rafters would not make the house and would yet attain the name "rafters"—this is also eternalism.

Six: the characteristic of disintegration. The various conditions such as rafters each abide in their own dharmas, and originally do not make [a house].

Question: I can clearly see that the various conditions such as rafters have actually made a house. Why do you still say that they originally don't make it?

Reply: Only by their not making it does the dharma of the house attain formation. If they made the house, they would not abide in their own dharmas, and the significance of the existence of the house would then not be formed. How so? If they made the house they would err as dharmas, so the house would not be formed. Now, as the house is already formed, we can clearly understand that they are not making it.

Question: If we discard the idea of their making it, what is the error?

Reply: There are the two errors of annihilationism and eternalism. If we said the rafters make the dharma of the house, then they would err in terms of the dharma of being rafters. Because they would err in the dharma of being rafters, then the house would have no rafters and it would not attain existence.

This is annihilationism. If they were to err in the dharma of being rafters and yet there was a house, then we would have a house that existed without conditions. This is eternalism.

So, totality is the one house. Distinction is the various conditions. Commonality is the conditions working with each other and not contradicting each other. Difference is the various conditions each being distinct. Formation is the various conditions accomplishing the result. Disintegration is each abiding in its own dharma.

4. Concluding Verse

Let me state it again in a hymn:

One is what includes many: this is called the characteristic of totality.
The many are not the one: this is the characteristic of distinction.
509a The many kinds having commonality, they form the totality;
Each in essence different, they manifest commonality.
One and many arise interdependently, their principle is marvelous formation;
Disintegration is each abiding in its own dharma, never making [a thing].
This is only the realm of wisdom; it is not phenomenal consciousness.
By these skillful means, you encounter the One Vehicle.

Notes

1 The *Treatise* is also known simply as the *Treatise on the Five Ranks, Wu jiao zhang* 五教章. Fazang's title of *śramaṇa* may be conventional; for a thorough discussion of Fazang's monastic status, see Chapter 4 of Jinhua Chen's biography, *Philosopher, Practitioner, Politician: The Many Lives of Fazang (643–712)* (Leiden: Brill, 2007).

2 This refers to the *Avataṃsaka-sūtra,* or *Flower Garland Sutra,* which expounds the Dharma from the perspective of the Buddha's ocean-seal *samādhi.* The *Flower Garland Sutra* in Chinese is known as the *Huayan jing,* lending its name to the school of Buddhism known in China as Huayan, in Korea as Hwaeom, in Vietnam as Hoa Nghiêm, and in Japan as Kegon. In this translation, Huayan refers to the school, as in the title, while *Flower Garland* refers to the scripture.

3 "Distinct" and "Common" indicate that the Buddha delivered the true Dharma in two ways, either apart from other teachings or in common with other teachings, as illustrated below in the parable of the burning house in this section and again in section VI, "The Sequence of the Emergence of the Teachings."

4 The word most frequently used in this text for the concept of *pratītyasamutpāda* (dependent origination) is *yuanqi* 緣起, which we have translated as "interdependent arising" in order to convey the Huayan emphasis on the simultaneity and omnidirectionality of the arising of the *dharmadhātu* (Dharma realm), as distinct from the linear process of dependence expressed in the teaching of the twelvefold chain.

5 Sanskrit scriptures are often composed of prose narrative or exposition interspersed with metrical verse sections that recapitulate or praise the ideas of the text. This format is convenient for memory and was often applied in Chinese compositions as well—including this treatise, which ends with an original verse by Fazang. Fazang often specifies when he is citing a verse passage.

6 The word *zang* 藏, translated here as "matrix," is used to render the Sanskrit terms *garbha* ("womb") in *tathāgatagarbha* and *garbha* ("treasury") in *padmagarbha lokadhātu* (lotus flower treasury world), and is also the *ālaya* ("storehouse") in *ālayavijñāna* (storehouse consciousness). The word "matrix" is meant to convey both senses.

7 In early Chinese history, turtle plastrons—the flat, ventral piece of a tortoise shell—were used as tools of divination in the royal court, while mirrors were precious objects with a unique ability to accurately reveal forms. Thus, turtle shells and mirrors serve as stock metaphors for discerning the truth.

8 The four logical possibilities, also called the tetralemma, are a philosophical framework for analyzing propositions and dharmas in terms of emptiness: a thing may be empty, not empty, both empty and not empty, and/or neither empty nor not empty. When this

framework is employed in the text, the possibilities are marked with numbers in parentheses.

9 The *Fifty Essentials of Huayan by Question and Answer* and the *Essays on the Contents of the Flower Garland Sutra,* which is mentioned in the next paragraph, were written by Fazang's Dharma teacher Zhiyan 智儼 (602–668), the second patriarch of Huayan.

10 The organization offered for the end of this section (section I, part B, 1, iii) in the translation is tentative, as the Taishō text is ambiguous. There are at least two possible interpretations of the groupings of the vehicles, depending in part on the use of textual variants. For an alternative organization, see the *Huayan yisheng fenqi zhang fugu ji* 華嚴一乘分齊章復古記, *juan* 1, p. 207 recto, in the *Xuzangjing* 續藏經, vol. 103.

11 The compound word translated as "doctrines," *jiaoyi* 教義, is made up of the words for "teaching" and "significance." In this section Fazang breaks the compound apart to discuss the combinations of teaching and significance that make up the relative provisionality of the doctrines of various vehicles.

12 This note provides some additional information about these ten masters.

A. Bodhiruci 菩提流支 (?–527) was an Indian monk, scholar, and translator.

B. Hu 護 (or in a variant of the text, Dan 誕), is identified in some commentaries as the monk and exegete Tanyan 曇延 (516–588), but it is possible that commentators made this identification only because they could find no information about a person named Hu who specialized in the *Laṅkāvatāra-sūtra.* Yuan 遠 is probably Huiyuan 慧遠 (523–593) of Jingying Temple.

C. Guangtong 光統, also known as Huiguang 慧光 (468–537), was the patriarch of the *Four-part Vinaya* school. Zuntong, also known as Tanzun 曇遵 (480–564?), was one of Huiguang's disciples.

D. Master Dayan 大衍 is Tanyin 曇隱 (503–581), of Dayan Temple, and also one of Huiguang's disciples.

E. Master Hushen 護身 is Zigui 自軌 (d.u.) of Hushen Temple.

F. Qishe 耆闍 ("vulture," a Chinese transliteration of the Sanskrit *gṛdhra*), also known as Anlin 安凜 or 安廩 (507–583), was also in Huiguang's lineage.

G. Si of Nanyue 南岳思 (515–577) and Zhizhe of Tiantai 天台智者 (538–597), also known as Huisi 慧思 and Zhiyi 智顗, respectively, were the second and third patriarchs of Tiantai Buddhism.

H. Min of Jiangnan 江南愍, also known as Famin 法敏 (579–645) was a scholar and the master of Jinglin Temple.

I. Yun of Guangzhai Temple光宅寺雲, also known as Fayun 法雲 (437–529), wrote a commentary on the *Lotus Sutra.* Xinxing 信行 (540–594) founded the Three Levels teachings (*sanjie jiao* 三階教).

J. Tripiṭaka Master Xuanzang 玄奘三藏 (ca. 600–664), was a monk, traveler, translator, scholar, and founder of the Consciousness Only (Faxiang) school of Buddhism in China.

13 The number of grains of sand of the Ganges River is a stock metaphor for innumerability; "Ganges River" is rendered in Chinese as "Eternal River."

14 The three natures are three modes of cognition as described in Yogācāra. Fazang discusses the three natures thoroughly in section X, part A, of the *Treatise*.

15 The image is of handling a scroll, the format in which most sutras and other manuscripts were written during Fazang's time. During this time block printing was also just beginning to develop. The mention of printed Dharma in this paragraph probably refers to small printed Buddhist charm texts, as full sutras in book form are not known to have been printed at that time.

16 The connection between *tathāgatagarbha* and *ālayavijñāna* is made extremely clear in Chinese translations of the *Laṅkāvatāra* and other texts by including the word *zang* 藏 ("treasury," "womb," "matrix," or "storehouse") in both terms: *tathāgatagarbha* is *rulaizang* 如來藏 ("womb of the Tathāgata"), and *ālayavijñāna* is *zangshi* 藏識 ("storehouse consciousness"); see especially the translation of the *Laṅkāvatāra* by Fazang's contemporary Śikṣānanda (T. 672). Thus, the connection between these concepts is made explicit in Chinese in a way that it is not in either Sanskrit or in English.

17 In this section, the terms seed-nature, buddha-nature, self-nature, and original nature are somewhat conflated. Seed-nature is a metaphor used to describe an aspect of causation in terms of consciousness only, whereas buddha-nature and so on are metaphysical qualities. Buddha-nature is also one kind of seed-nature; i.e., the seed that grows to produce the fruit of buddhahood. Other seed-natures produce other results, such as arhatship and so on.

18 The text of the *Sutra on the Accumulations of the Six Senses* is no longer extant, although references to it appear in other texts.

19 For an explanation of the hindrances, see part IX, section F.

20 I believe the four kinds indicated here are the four ranks explained in part IX, section F, 2ii, in the discussion of the eighth gate (p. 130).

21 In this section Fazang frequently refers to the Early Teaching as the two vehicles, in this case meaning the first two of the three vehicles; the Final Teaching, below, is the third of the three.

22 *Zhiduan jing* 指端經 (*Fingertip Sutra*), is the title of an unknown scripture.

23 This paragraph is a good example of why *xin* 心 is sometimes translated as "heart-mind." The anatomical metaphor indicates the heart as an organ and as an essential core, but the same *xin* also indicates the thinking mind and the mind that aspires to *bodhi*.

24 In this discussion Fazang uses "true thusness" (*zhenru* 真如) interchangeably with the "fully perfected nature" (*yuanchengshi xing* 圓成實性) of the three natures.

25 Through section X, part A, 1, iib Fazang examines the logical errors of maintaining attachment to each of the three natures using the four-part scheme of the tetralemma (existent, nonexistent, both existent and nonexistent, neither existent nor nonexistent), further dividing each of these four possibilities into the two erroneous views of eternalism and annihilationism. The numbering of these divisions in the original text is

dense and somewhat inconsistent, so in the translation many of the numbers have been omitted for clarity.

26 What Fazang calls "causes" (*yin* 因) in this section are the karmic seeds (*zhongzi* 種子) of the storehouse consciousness discussed above; the six significances here attributed to causation are explicitly attributed to seeds in other texts.

27 The ten coins are the context of the discussion through the end of part X, section C, 2, although the language becomes extremely abstract at times.

28 Although there are many words in Chinese that could be used to signify a type of building that would have rafters, the word "house" (*she* 舍) here is the same word used in the *Lotus Sutra* parable of the burning house, discussed at length at the beginning of the *Treatise*. In addition, the word for "rafter" (*chuan* 椽) is graphically similar to, and rhymes with, the word for "conditions" (*yuan* 緣).

29 This structural "strength" is *li* 力, the same character that was rendered as "power" in the section on empowerment in part X, section B, 1.

Glossary

Abhidharma: A collection of texts that interpret Buddhist teachings in technical, scholarly terms, and the scholarly approach demonstrated in those texts.

anuttarā samyaksaṃbodhi: Complete perfect enlightenment, unsurpassed enlightenment; specifically, this refers to the compassionate, salvific enlightenment ideal of the bodhisattva in Mahayana Buddhism.

arhat: "Honored One." In this text, this refers to practitioners who have achieved nirvana in terms of "Lesser Vehicle" doctrine, but have not attained buddhahood in terms of Mahayana doctrine; i.e., they have liberated themselves from suffering, but do not liberate all beings.

asura: A demigod, and also the characteristic class of beings of one of the six realms of rebirth. Sometimes translated as "titans," *asura*s are seen as wrathful beings that wage war against the gods.

bodhi: True awakening; the wisdom of the Buddha; Fazang often uses *bodhi* in an aspirational context: the mind that thinks of, or intends to achieve, the true enlightenment of buddhahood, as in *bodhicitta,* the mind of aspiration for awakening.

dhāraṇī: A type of incantation, a mnemonic code or chant, included in many Buddhist texts and rituals; a powerful invocation that produces merit and transmits the Buddhist teachings.

dharma/Dharma: When capitalized, Dharma means the truth, the laws of reality, or a teaching of the Buddha; the lower-case form is a common noun meaning any phenomenon, thing, concept, or object of mind. However, both are translations of the Chinese word *fa* 法, and there is no capitalization in Chinese. In fact the *Treatise* sometimes deliberately collapses the distinction between ordinary dharmas and the sacred Dharma as part of its overall philosophical purpose. Thus, many of the capitalizations or non-capitalizations of the term in this translation are unavoidably provisional.

icchantika: A being that is said (in other texts) to be doomed to transmigrate through samsara endlessly without the possibility of attaining nirvana, due to lack of buddhanature.

Indra's net: An image from the *Flower Garland Sutra* that is frequently discussed in Huayan Buddhism to explain the infinite interrelationship of all phenomena. The net is infinitely vast, and in each intersection of its strands hangs a perfect multifaceted jewel. The facets of any single jewel reflect all the other jewels in the net, and all of the reflections in their facets, infinitely.

kalpa: A unit of time in Buddhist cosmology; generally an extremely long period of time, and specifically the temporal duration of a world.

nonreturner (*anāgāmin*): One who will no longer be reborn into the desire realm; one who will become an arhat in their next lifetime.

pāramitā: A practice of bodhisattvas; one of the six perfections of bodhisattva practice, which are *dāna* (generosity), *śīla* (discipline, morality), *kṣānti* (patience), *vīrya* (zeal), *dhyāna* (concentration), and *prajñā* (wisdom).

prajñāpāramitā: The practice or teaching of the perfection of wisdom, which is the perception of the true nature of reality.

pratyekabuddha: One who attains enlightenment alone, without the aid of a buddha. One of the two kinds of enlightened practitioners in early Buddhism, along with the *śrāvaka.*

samādhi: A cultivated state of consciousness in which the mind is concentrated or unified.

seed (Skt. *bīja*): In one metaphor of causation, karmic potentialities are stored in consciousness as seeds, where they may be fertilized and germinate into karmic activities.

śramaṇa: A Buddhist mendicant or monk.

śrāvaka: Rendered in Chinese as "voice-hearer," one who attains enlightenment by hearing the teachings of the Buddha. One of the two kinds of enlightened practitioners in early Buddhism, along with the *pratyekabuddha.*

storehouse consciousness (Skt. *ālayavijñāna*): The consciousness that stores the latent seeds of karma. In Yogācāra and Huayan, the eighth of the eight consciousnesses. *See also* seed.

stream-enterer (Skt. *śrotaāpanna*): One who has entered the stream of the Dharma on the path to liberation; the first stage of spiritual attainment in Buddhism.

tathāgata/Tathāgata: "Thus-come One," an honorific title for a buddha, one who has come from and realized thusness; the embodiment of true reality as it is; also rendered "Thus Gone One," one who has passed into nirvana.

tathāgatagarbha: The embryo or womb of a tathāgata that exists in all sentient beings, providing the basis for buddha-nature and universal awakening. This concept is articulated in the *Tathāgatagarbha-sūtra.*

ten stages (Skt. *bhūmi*): The spiritual stages undertaken by bodhisattvas in order to progress toward buddhahood are presented in various texts as summarized in this *Treatise,* but according to Fazang they are most fully and correctly articulated in the *Flower Garland Sutra* chapter (and sometimes independent scripture) known as "The Ten Stages" (*Daśabhūmika*).

three worthy sets of practices: Various ranks and practices that follow the ten stages of faith and precede the ten bodhisattva stages, according to Huayan. The three sets are the ten abodes (or the ten understandings), the ten practices, and the ten conversions of merit.

thusness (Skt. *tathatā*): Reality as it truly is, i.e., interdependently arisen; the absolute reality of phenomena, encompassing both conventional, phenomenal existence and ultimate emptiness. Also translated as "suchness."

Yogācāra: A branch of Buddhism that emphasized the absolute interdependence of mind and objects of mind; hence, it is also known as the school of Consciousness Only or Mind Only.

Bibliography

Fazang's References

Abhidharmakośa-bhāṣya: Jushe 俱舍 (俱舍論), T. 1558.

Abhidharma Sutra: Damo jing 達磨經 (阿毘達磨大乘經). Extant only in fragments, as quotations within other texts.

Accumulation of Jewels Sutra: Baoji jing 寶積經 (大寶積經), T. 310.

Benevolent King Sutra: Renwang jing 仁王經 (仁王般若波羅蜜經), T. 245.

Bodhisattva Stages Sutra: Dichi jing 地持經, also called *Pusa dichi jing* 菩薩地持經 or *Dichi lun* 地持論, T. 1581.

Brahmā's Net Sutra: Brahmajāla-sūtra; Fanwang jing 梵網經, T. 1484.

Commentary on The Awakening of Faith: Qixinlun yiji 起信論義記, T. 1846. A commentary by Fazang.

Commentary on the Summary of the Great Vehicle: She dasheng lunshi 攝大乘論釋. Two commentaries have this title, by Vasubandhu (T. 1595, T. 1596, T. 1597) and by Asvabhāva (T. 1598).

Dharma Drum Sutra: Fagu jing 法鼓經 (大法鼓經), T. 270.

Diamond Sutra: Jingang bore 金剛般若 (金剛經, 金剛般若波羅蜜經), T. 235, T. 236, T. 237.

"Essay on Consciousness Only": *Weishi zhang* 唯識章, a chapter in Zhiyan's *Essays on the Contents of the Flower Garland Sutra* (T.1870:543a13).

Essays on the Contents of the Flower Garland Sutra: Kongmu zhang 孔目章 (華嚴經內章門等雜孔目章), T. 1870. Written by Zhiyan, Fazang's teacher.

Fifty Essentials by Question and Answer: Wushi yao wenda 五十要問答 (華嚴五十要問答), T. 1869. Written by Zhiyan, Fazang's teacher.

Flower Garland Sutra: Avataṃsaka-sūtra; Huayan jing 華嚴經 (大方廣佛華嚴經), T. 278, T. 279, T. 293. Fazang refers to the sixty-fascicle version (T. 278).

Four Agama Sutras: Si ahan jing 四阿含經, a collection consisting of the *Chang ahan jing* 長阿含經 (*Dīrghāgama*), T. 1; the *Zengyi ahan jing* 增一阿含經 (*Ekottarikāgama*), T. 125; the *Za ahan jing* 雜阿含經 (*Samyuktāgama*), T. 99, T. 100, T. 101; and the *Zhong ahan jing* 中阿含經 (*Madhyamāgama*), T. 26.

Four-part Vinaya: Sifen lü 四分律, T. 1428.

Incremental Āgama Sutra: Zengyi jing 增一經 (增一阿含經), T. 125.

Jewel Cloud Sutra: Baoyun jing 寶雲經, T. 658, T. 659.

Laṅkāvatāra-sūtra: Lengqie jing 楞伽經 (入楞伽經, 楞伽阿跋多羅寶經), T. 670, T. 671, T. 672.

Larger Prajñāpāramitā Sutra: Dapin 大品, *Dapin jing* 大品經, or *Da bore jing* 大品般若經 (大般若波羅蜜多經), T. 220, T. 221, T. 222, T. 223. The full edition of the *Perfection of Wisdom Sutra.*

Lotus Sutra: Fahua jing 法華經 (妙法蓮華經), T. 262, T. 263, T. 264.

Mahāvibhāṣā-śāstra: Da piposha lun 大毘婆沙論, abbreviated to *Posha* 婆沙, T. 1545, T. 1546.

Mahīśāsaka-vinaya: Mishasai lü 彌沙塞律 (彌沙塞五分戒本), T. 1421, T. 1422.

Mañjuśrī's Sutra on Prajñāpāramitā: Wenshu bore jing 文殊般若經, T. 232, T. 233.

Nirvana Sutra: Niepan jing 涅槃經, T. 374.

Sarvāstivāda-vinaya-vibhāṣā: Sapoduo lun 薩婆多論 (薩婆多毘尼毘婆沙), T. 1440.

Summary of the Great Vehicle: She lun 攝論, a translation of the *Mahāyānasaṃgraha, She dasheng lun* 攝大乘論, T. 1592, T. 1593, T. 1594. The Liang *Summary* refers specifically Paramārtha's Liang dynasty translation (T. 1593); Xuanzang also translated this text (T. 1594).

Sutra of Golden Light: Jinguangming jing 金光明經, T. 663, T. 664, T. 665.

Sutra of King Pravaradeva: Shengtianwang jing 勝天王經 (勝天王般若波羅蜜經), T. 231.

Sutra of Queen Śrīmālā of the Lion's Roar: Shengman jing 勝鬘經 (勝鬘師子吼一乘大方便方廣經), T. 353.

Sutra of the Buddha's First Twelve Years: Shier you jing 十二遊經, T. 195.

Sutra of the Questions of the Brāhmins: Boluomen wen jing 婆羅門問經. No longer extant; quoted in the *Summary of the Great Vehicle* (T.1593:120c28, T.1595:193a7).

Sutra of the Warrior with the Hidden Tracks: Miji lishi jing 密迹力士經. This refers to a section of the *Accumulation of Jewels Sutra* (T.310:42b7).

Sutra on Awakening of Practice: Xingqi xing jing 興起行經, T. 197.

Sutra on Basic Activities: Benye jing 本業經 (菩薩瓔珞本業經), T. 281, T. 282.

Sutra on Mañjuśrī's Transcendental Samādhi: Puchao sanmei jing 普超三昧經 (文殊師利普超三昧經), T. 627.

Sutra on No Increase and No Decrease: Buzeng bujian jing 不增不減經, T. 668.

Sutra on the Accumulations of the Six Senses: Liu genju jing 六根聚經. No longer extant.

Sutra on the Buddha Stage: Fodi jing 佛地經, T. 680.

Sutra on the Common Nature of the Great Vehicle: Dasheng tongxing jing 大乘同性經, T. 673.

Sutra on the Emptiness of All Dharmas: Zhufa wuxing jing 諸法無行經, T. 650.

Sutra on the Essential Nature of Entering the Dharma Realm: Fajie tixing jing 法界體性經 (入法界體性經), T. 355.

Sutra on the Expedient Means of the Great Vehicle: Dasheng fangbian jing 大乘方便經. This refers to a section of the *Accumulation of Jewels Sutra* (T.310:594c2).

Sutra on the Explication of Underlying Meaning: Shenjiemi jing 解深密經, T. 676.

Sutra on the Good Moral Discipline of Bodhisattvas: Shanjie jing 善戒經 (菩薩善戒經), T. 1582.

Sutra on the Questions of Viśeṣacinti Brahmā: Siyi jing 思益經 (思益梵天所問經), T. 585, T. 586, T. 587.

Sutra on the Samadhi of Contemplating Buddha: Guanfo sanmei jing 觀佛三昧經, T. 643.

Sutra on Universal Brilliance: Puyao jing 普曜經, T. 186.

Sutra on Unsurpassed Refuge: Wushangyi jing 無上依經, T. 669.

Sutra on Upāsaka Precepts: Youposai jie jing 優婆塞戒經, T. 1488.

Ten Stages Sutra: Shi di jing 十地經, T. 286. Also called *Shi zhu jing* 十住經, T. 287. It also exists in the *Flower Garland Sutra,* chapter titled "The Ten Stages," *Shi di pin* 十地品 (T.278:542a5).

The Awakening of Faith: full title *Treatise on the Awakening of Faith in the Great Vehicle, Dasheng qixin lun* 大乘起信論, abbreviated to *Qixin lun* 起信論, T. 1666, T. 1667.

Treatise on Buddha-nature: Foxing lun 佛性論, T. 1610.

Treatise on Entering the Great Vehicle: Ru dasheng lun 入大乘論, T. 1634. By Sāramati.

Treatise on Praise of the Sacred Teachings: Xianyang lun 顯揚論 (顯揚聖教論), T. 1602.

Treatise on the Adornment of the Great Vehicle: Zhuangyan lun 莊嚴論 (大乘莊嚴論), T. 1604.

Treatise on the Collected Abhidharma: Zaji 雜集 or Duifa lun 對法論 (大乘阿毘達磨雜集論), T. 1606.

Treatise on the Jewel-nature: Baoxing lun 寶性論 (究竟一乘寶性論), T. 1611.

Treatise on the Larger Prajñāpāramitā Sutra: Zhilun 智論 or *Dazhidu lun* 大智度論 (摩訶般若波羅蜜), T. 1509. A commentary attributed to Nāgārjuna.

Treatise on the Middle Way: Zhong lun 中論, T. 1564. By Nāgārjuna.

Treatise on the Nonexistence of Characteristics: Wuxiang lun 無相論, extant as fragments. By Paramārtha.

Treatise on the Sutra of the Questions of Maitreya: Mile pusa suowen jinglun 彌勒菩薩所問經論, T. 1525.

Treatise on the Sutra on the Buddha Stage: Fodi lun 佛地論 (佛地經論), T. 1530.

Treatise on the Ten Stages: Di lun 地論 (十地經綸), T. 1522. This treatise expounds the *Ten Stages Sutra,* which also exists as "The Ten Stages" chapter in the *Flower Garland Sutra* (see *Ten Stages Sutra,* above).

Treatise on the Theory of Consciousness Only: Cheng weishi lun 成唯識論, T. 1585.

Treatise on the Three Kinds of Naturelessness: San wuxing lun 三無性論, T. 1617.

Treatise on True Attainment: Chengshi lun 成實論, T. 1646.

Treatise on Yogācāra Stages: Yuqie lun 瑜伽論 or *Yuqieshidi lun* 瑜伽師地論, T. 1579.

Vimalakīrti Sutra: Weimo jing 維摩經 (維摩詰所說經), T. 474, T. 475, T. 476.

Vinaya in Ten Recitations: Shi song lü 十誦律; also called *Sarvāstivāda-vinaya,* T. 1435.

Selected Bibliography

Chen, Jinhua. *Philosopher, Practitioner, Politician: The Many Lives of Fazang (643–712).* Leiden: Brill, 2007.

Cleary, Thomas. *Entry into the Inconceivable.* Honolulu: University of Hawai'i Press, 1983.

Cook, Francis H. "Causation in the Chinese Hua-Yen Tradition," *Journal of Chinese Philosophy* 6/4 (1979): 367–385.

—."Fa-tsang's Treatise on the Five Doctrines: An Annotated Translation." Ph.D dissertation, University of Wisconsin, 1970.

—.*Hua-Yen Buddhism: the Jewel Net of Indra.* Institute for Advanced Studies of World Religions Series. University Park, PA: Pennsylvania State University Press, 1977.

Elstein, David, trans. Fazang, "The Rafter Dialogue," in Justin Tiwald and Bryan W. Van Norden, eds., *Readings in Later Chinese Philosophy,* pp. 80–86. Indianapolis: Hackett Publishing, 2014.

Gimello, Robert M., Frédéric Girard, and Imre Hamar, eds. *Avataṃsaka Buddhism in East Asia: Huayan, Kegon, Flower Ornament Buddhism: Origins and Adaptation of a Visual Culture.* Wiesbaden: Harrassowitz Verlag, 2012.

Hamar, Imre, ed. *Reflecting Mirrors: Perspectives on Huayan Buddhism.* Wiesbaden: Harrassowitz Verlag, 2007.

Jones, Nicholaos. "Huayan Numismatics as Metaphysics: Explicating Fazang's Coin-Counting Metaphor," *Philosophy East and West* 68/4 (October 2018): 1155–1177.

Li, Zijie. "Fazang's theory of zhenru 真如 (Skt. tathatā) and zhongxing 種姓 (Skt. gotra): with a focus on the influence of the Ratnagotravibhāga," *Studies in Chinese Religions* 6/1 (2020): 31–48.

Liu, Ming-Wood. "The Pan-chiao System of the Hua-yen School in Chinese Buddhism," *T'oung Pao* 67/1–2 (1981): 10–47.

Ryan, James A., trans. "Fazang, 'Coins' and 'Rafter and Building,'" in James A. Ryan, ed., *Chinese Philosophy: A Reader,* pp. 401–416. Self-published, 2017.

Satō, Kaion. "The Theory of Kleśa in Fazang's Huayan Wujiao Zhang," *Indogaku Bukkyō-gaku Kenkyū* 65/1 (2016): 190–193.

Weinstein, Stanley. "Imperial Patronage in the Formation of T'ang Buddhism," in Arthur F. Wright and Denis Twitchett, eds., *Perspectives on the T'ang,* pp. 265–306. New Haven, CT: Yale University Press, 1973.

Wright, Dale S. "The Significance of Paradoxical Language in Hua-Yen Buddhism," *Philosophy East and West* 32/3 (1982): 325–338.

KEY TO THE SECRET OF THE HEART SUTRA

Translator's Introduction

Matthew D. McMullen

The *Key to the Secret of the Heart Sutra* (*Hannya shingyō hiken*) is a commentary on the *Heart Sutra,* the commonly abbreviated title for the *Heart Sutra of the Great Perfection of Wisdom* (*Mahāprajñāpāramitā-hṛdaya-sūtra*). Composed by Kūkai (774–835), the revered founder of the Japanese Shingon school and patriarch of Japanese esoteric Buddhism, this commentary purports to reveal the underlying secret meaning to the *Heart Sutra,* which according to Kūkai had yet to be explicated by previous commentators. Like the *Heart Sutra,* Kūkai's secret commentary is a brief work, constituting less than two pages of the Taishō canon. However, despite its brevity, it functions as an introduction to Kūkai's view of mantra as well as a polemical comparison of his Shingon school with the dominant Buddhist schools in Japan at the time.

A central theme throughout Kūkai's writings is the claim that mantra, short incantations often derived from Sanskrit phrases, contain the entirety of the Buddha's teachings, and by properly reciting them one can immediately harness their power and benefits. The *Heart Sutra* exemplifies this claim. As a summary of the Prajñāpāramitā sutras, the *Heart Sutra* was thought to embody the wisdom of this enormous corpus of texts. The closing mantra of the *Heart Sutra* even further abbreviated these teachings. For Kūkai, this condensing of the unabridged teaching of the Buddha into a few lines, or even a single phrase, could be applied to all Buddhist sutras. Moreover, to realize the teachings of a sutra, one only needed to master the associated mantra. Such mantras were usually linked to buddhas and bodhisattvas in the text. Therefore, Kūkai was fixated on identifying buddhas, bodhisattvas, and deities with their proper mantra, or, even more succinctly, with their seed syllables (*bīja*).

The *Key to the Secret of the Heart Sutra* is traditionally read as a taxonomy of teachings (*kyōsō hanjaku*). Kūkai alludes to two taxonomical paradigms in the text, the "seven schools" and the "five vehicles." The seven schools presumably refer to the six Buddhist schools established in the Nara capital, Ritsu,

Kusha, Jōjitsu, Hossō, Sanron, and Kegon, plus the Tendai school founded on Mount Hiei by Saichō (766–822). The term "five vehicles" typically denotes the teachings intended for humans, *devas*, *śrāvakas*, *pratyekabuddhas*, and bodhisattvas. However, the commentaries on Kūkai's text, most of which are published in the *Shingonshū zensho,* vol. 6, and the *Zoku Shingonshū zensho,* vol. 20, attempt to combine these two paradigms into a single sectarian polemic that positions the Shingon school as superior to other traditions in Japan. Thus, the five vehicles signify the Kegon school (represented by Samantabhadra Bodhisattva), the Sanron school (Mañjuśrī), the Hossō school (Maitreya), the Tendai school (Avalokiteśvara), *pratyekabuddhas* (signified by the doctrine of *pratītyasamutpāda*) and *śrāvakas* (the doctrine of the four noble truths), respectively. Consequently, the "seven schools" are then interpreted through this framework and are given as (1) Kegon, (2) Sanron, (3) Hossō, (4–5) the two vehicles of *śrāvakas* and *pratyekabuddhas*, (6) Tendai, and (7) Shingon as the "secret" meaning of the sutra.[1]

Although the commentaries clearly interpret Kūkai's *Key to the Secret of the Heart Sutra* through a sectarian polemical lens, the text itself is not explicit about this purpose. The earliest commentaries by Saisen (1025–1115), the *Hannya shingyō hiken kaimon ketsu* (T. 2204), and Kakuban (1095–1143), the *Hannya shingyō hiken ryakuchū* (T. 2203B), were written almost three centuries after Kūkai's death, at a time when the doctrinal and institutional boundaries between the Buddhist schools were in the process of being delineated by sectarian partisans. Kūkai's reason for composing the essay may have been more functional than polemical. Prior to and during Kūkai's lifetime, the *Heart Sutra* was frequently used by Sanron and Hossō scholiasts as an abbreviated form of the Prajñāpāramitā sutras, citing its list of doctrinal concepts as a digest of Mahayana teachings. Kūkai, however, found the short text of the sutra to be a useful example of his broader project of integrating Mahayana doctrine with ritual practice. By providing a metaphorical reading of the text, Kūkai situated the doctrinal content within a liturgical framework of mantra recitation. In other words, if the concluding mantra is taken to be the core of the text rather than an appended incantation, as interpreted by his predecessors and contemporaries, then, as Kūkai suggests in his commentary, the *Heart Sutra* also has a ritual function in addition to doctrinal meaning.[2]

The authorship of the *Key to the Secret of the Heart Sutra* has never been in dispute; however, when exactly Kūkai wrote it has long been a matter of debate.

The colophon states that Kūkai wrote it in spring 818 and purports to be the words of Kūkai himself. According to the colophon, Emperor Saga (r. 809–823) had fallen ill. To aid the emperor in his recovery, Kūkai composed this commentary on the *Heart Sutra* as a key to unlocking the secrets to the sutra so that the emperor might benefit from this wisdom. However, scholars have long doubted the authenticity of the colophon, which was probably added to the text sometime in the thirteenth or fourteenth centuries.[3]

Although the evidence is inconclusive, most scholars agree that the more probable date of its composition is 834. This agreement is primarily based on comparisons with other Kūkai writings. If read as a taxonomy of Buddhist schools, the *Key to the Secret of the Heart Sutra* includes expressions found in Kūkai's magnum opus, the *Treatise on the Secret Mandala of the Ten Abiding Minds* (*Himitsu mandara jūjūshinron*), and its companion text, the *Precious Key to the Secret Treasury* (*Hizō hōyaku*). Modern scholars consider both of these works to have been written after 830 and before Kūkai's death in 835. Thus, the consensus among Shingon scholars is that Kūkai must have composed his commentary on the *Heart Sutra* around the same time.[4]

Historical documents also support a later date of composition. In his subcommentary, Saisen notes that according to oral tradition, Kūkai wrote the text at Tōdaiji. He then presented it to the Sanron monk Dōshō (798–875), who, in turn, lectured on the contents of Kūkai's essay (T.2204:20a24–28). Saisen does not provide a date for this exchange. However, a corresponding record can be found in the *Tōdaiji yōraku,* a twelfth-century history of events at Tōdaiji in Nara, which documents a lecture by Dōshō in the second month of 834 regarding the *Key to the Secret of the Heart Sutra.*[5] Saisen's reference to an "oral account" could denote this lecture at Tōdaiji. Whether or not the two sources allude to the same event, the historical record suggests that Kūkai's commentary must have been circulating in some form prior to Dōshō's lecture in 834.

The following translation of Kūkai's *Key to the Secret of the Heart Sutra* is based on the version in volume fifty-seven of the Taishō canon (T.2203A:11a1–12c25), which was taken from the previously published *Kōbō Daishi zenshū.* I have consulted the critical edition in *Teihon Kōbō Daishi zenshū,* vol. 3, as well as previous translations and scholarship listed in the references. For a more extensive example of Kūkai's taxonomy of teachings, readers should see Rolf W. Giebel's translation of *The Precious Key to the Secret Treasury.*[6]

The Great Incantation Sutra of the Mahāprajñāpāramitā

(T.250:847c7–29)

Translated by the Indian Tripiṭaka Master Kumārajīva
during the Late Qin Dynasty

When cultivating the profound perfection of wisdom, Avalokiteśvara Bodhisattva realized that the five aggregates are empty, [a realization that] saves all beings from suffering and calamity.

Śāriputra, because form is empty, there is no characteristic of decay. Because feeling is empty, there is no characteristic of feeling. Because perception is empty, there is no characteristic of perception. Because intention is empty, there is no characteristic of creating. Because consciousness is empty, there is no characteristic of awareness. Why? Śarīputra, because form is not different than emptiness, emptiness is not different than form; form is thus empty, and emptiness is thus form. Feeling, perception, intention, and consciousness are also like this.

Śāriputra, the dharmas with the characteristic of emptiness neither rise nor cease, are neither unsoiled nor impure, neither increase nor decrease. Empty dharmas do not exist in the past, future, or present. Therefore, in emptiness there is no form, feeling, perception, intention, or consciousness; there are no eyes, ears, nose, tongue, body, or mind; there are no images, sounds, smells, tastes, touch, or perceived objects; there are no visible realms up to and including the realm without consciousness; there is no ignorance nor is there the elimination of ignorance up to and including no old age and death, nor the elimination of old age and death; there is no suffering, accumulation, extinction, or path; there is no wisdom and no attainment, because there is nothing to attain. The bodhisattva relies on the perfection of wisdom, and, thus, a mind without impediments. Because there are no impediments, there is no fear; one is free from this dream-state of incorrect views and ultimately reaches nirvana.

Because the buddhas of the three times rely on the perfection of wisdom, they attain *anuttarā samyaksaṃbodhi.* Thus, know that the perfection of wisdom is the great incantation, the unsurpassable incantation, the unparalleled incantation that can eradicate all suffering. It is true and not false. Thus, expounding the incantation for the perfection of wisdom, one says: *gate gate pāragate pārasaṃgate bodhi svāhā.* (Gone, gone, gone beyond, awaken thusly!)

[End of] *The Great Incantation Sutra of the Mahāprajñāpāramitā*

The Key to the Secret of the Heart Sutra

Preface by Henjō Kongō

The sharp sword of Mañjuśrī severs mental proliferations, 11a
And the Sanskrit text of the mother of awakening[7] is the Supreme Tamer.
The mantras *dhiḥ* and *maṃ* are their seed syllables,
Which are *dhāraṇī* that contain all teachings.[8]
How is it possible to end the limitless cycle of birth and death?
Only with meditation and correct thought.[9]
Out of respect for the *samādhi* of the Venerable One,
I will not resign [myself to the traditional interpretation of the text].
Rather, I now reverently explicate [its meaning].
May compassion be bestowed upon me.

The Buddha-Dharma is not distant but is near in one's own mind. Suchness is not external. If one abandons the body, how can it be sought? Delusion and awakening both reside within oneself. As soon as one has given rise to the intention [to attain awakening], it has already been attained. Knowledge and ignorance are indistinct. If one faithfully practices, they will suddenly realize awakening.

Pitiful, pitiful, is the child who has long slumbered. Suffering and in pain is the person who is wildly intoxicated. Afflicted, they mock the sober and in a drunken haze insult the Awakened One. Having never sought the medicine of the Physician King, when would they gaze upon the radiance of the Great Sun?[10] Similar to the clarity of vision or the speed of reaching awakening, the spiritual capabilities [of individuals] are not the same and their intentions differ.

Accordingly, the two teachings, running along different tracks, are split between the platforms of the *vajra,* on the one hand, and the lotus, on the other. The five vehicles align their bits and prance about in front of an illusionary wall.[11] Antidotes are administered according to the poison. These are the guidelines by which a compassionate father instructs his son.

[On the Meaning of the Sutra]

The *Mahāprajñāpāramitā-hṛdaya-sūtra* is a teaching of *samādhi* and the central mantra of the great Prajñā Bodhisattva. The text is less than a page and is only fourteen lines.[12] One could say that although brief, it is fundamental; although concise, it is profound. Although the *prajñā* of the five collections[13] is contained in a single text, they do not satisfy. Although the fruits of practice in the seven schools[14] are subsumed within a single line, they are not enough [to fill it].

"Avalokiteśvara Bodhisattva" represents the practitioners of the various vehicles. "Crossing from suffering into nirvana" expresses the joy attained through the teachings. "The five aggregates" refers to all confused beings. "The buddhas [of the three times of past, present, and future]" denotes the awakened minds of those who have progressively achieved the goal. Referring to the "emptiness of form," Samantabhadra cracks a smile at the meaning of complete interfusion. Discussing "nonarising," Mañjuśrī's face beams at the view of severed mental proliferations. Maitreya applauds the explanation of the "realm of consciousness." When "objects" and the "cognition of objects" merge, Avalokiteśvara rejoices. The twelve links of conditioned existence point to the arising and ceasing of the *pratyekabuddha.* The Dharma wheel of the four noble truths makes the *śrāvaka* aware of the emptiness of suffering.

Moreover, the two syllables *gate* engulf the fruits of practice in the various collections of texts. The two words *pāra* and *saṃ* are pregnant with the exoteric
11b and esoteric teachings. [The meaning of] each and every sound and syllable, even if explained over the course of an eon, is inexhaustible. Each and every name and its ultimate reality, like the buddhas who are [as numerous as] specks of dust or drops of water, are without limit. Therefore, reciting, possessing, expounding, and worshiping the sutra alleviates suffering and provides bliss. Cultivating and contemplating [the meaning of the sutra], one reaches the path and advances along it. The label "extremely profound" is truly appropriate.

[Questions and Answers about the Text]

When I teach students, I begin by picking out the essentials of the sutra and explain them in five sections. Although there have been many commentators, they have yet to uncover the secret of the text. The differences among the translations and distinctions between the exoteric and esoteric [meanings of the sutra] will be elucidated below.

Question: The Prajñā[pāramitā] belongs to the second category of incomplete teachings. How is it possible that it is included among the sutras revealed in the third [turning of the wheel of the Dharma]?[15]

[Response:] A single syllable of the Tathāgata's preaching encompasses the meaning of the five vehicles. In a single moment of thought, he preaches the teachings of the Tripiṭaka. How then could a single section or chapter [of the Tripiṭaka] be insufficient or incomplete? Even the readings of the lines on tortoise shells and in hexagrams encompass the myriad phenomena and are inexhaustible. Indra's net and his grammar[16] comprise a multitude of meanings and are unlimited.

Follow-up question: If this is the case, why have previous scholars not stated such?

Response: A sage prescribes medicine as it is needed. A wise person speaks or remains silent, waiting for the appropriate time and individual [who can understand such words]. I do not know whether [previous scholars] did not speak when they should have, or if they did not speak because they should not have. Perhaps I should not speak on these matters either. Only a wise person can determine whether this is a mistake.[17]

[On the Title of the Sutra]

There are two distinct titles for the *Buddha's Preaching of the Heart Sutra for the Great Perfection of Wisdom,* one in Sanskrit and the other in Chinese. The so-called *Foshuo mohe bore boluomiduo xinjing* is a mix of Central Asian and Chinese terms. The three characters *shuo* ("preach"), *xin* ("heart"), and *jing* ("sutra") are Chinese terms, and the other nine characters are Central Asian.

The complete Sanskrit title is *Buddha-bhāṣā-mahā-prajñā-pāramitā-hṛdaya-sūtraṃ.* The first two syllables (*buddha*) are the name of the Fully Awakened One. The next two syllables (*bhāṣā*) are a reference to realizing the secret treasury and administering the nectar. The next two syllables (*mahā*) carry the meaning of great, many, or supreme. The next two syllables (*prajñā*) are the term for establishing meditation and wisdom. The next three (*pāramitā*) are the designation for completed actions [that lead to enlightenment]. The next two (*hṛdaya*) express the meaning of being central. The final two (*sūtraṃ*) are syllables expressing the meaning of suturing together.

Explaining the general meaning of sutras, each possesses an individual, teaching, and metaphor.[18] In this case, the name of the great Prajñāpāramitā Bodhisattva is the individual. This bodhisattva is equipped with the *samādhi* teaching of the Dharma mandala and mantra. Each of these syllables are a teaching. Each and every word, through the superficial language of the profane world, express the profound designation of Dharma-nature. These [words] are metaphors.

This *samādhi* teaching was preached by the Buddha on Vulture Peak for the sake of Śāriputra and others. The sutra has several translations. The first was Tripiṭaka Master Kumārajīva's translation, [the *Mohe bore boluomi daming zhoujing* (T. 250)], which is the basis for this discussion. The next is a translation by Tripiṭaka Master Xuanzang of Tang, [the *Bore boluomiduo xinjing* (T. 251)]. The title lacks the four characters *foshuo mohe* ("Buddha's preaching," "great"). Following the "five aggregates," it adds the character *deng* ("and so on") and omits the characters *yiqie* ("all") after *yuanli* ("distant from"). Following the *dhāraṇī,* there is not [an exhortation of the sutra's]
11c efficacy. Next, there is a version by Tripiṭaka Master Yijing of Dazhou.[19] The title is missing the characters *mohe* ("great"), but it adds [an exhortation of the sutra's] efficacy after the mantra. Furthermore, the translations by Tripiṭaka Masters Dharmacandra, [the *Pubian zhizang bore boluomiduo xinjing* (T. 252]), and Prajñā, [the *Bore boluomiduo xinjing* (T. 253)], both have prefaces and concluding exhortations. Finally, in the third fascicle of the *Dhāraṇī Collection Sutra* (T.901:804c) explaining mantra rites, the title of the sutra is the same as Kumārajīva's translation.

The "heart of *prajñā*" is the *dhāraṇī* of the body, mind, etc. possessed by the bodhisattva [Prajñā]. The mantra of this sutra is the great heart incantation [of Prajñā].[20] In accordance with this heart mantra, it is called the "heart of Prajñā." Some also say that [the sutra] is called "heart" because it abbreviates the essentials of the *Mahāprajñāpāramitā-sūtra,* and that [the Buddha] did not preach it for another audience. This is like saying a dragon has the scales of a snake.[21]

[On the Structure and Content of the Sutra]

This sutra has five sections in total. The first is a general introduction to the interlocutor and the teaching, which extends from "Avalokiteśvara" to "saves all beings from suffering and calamity." The second is a section distinguishing the various vehicles, which extends from "form is not different than emptiness" to "because there is nothing to attain." The third is a section on the benefits obtained by the practitioner, which extends from "bodhisattva" to "*anuttarā samyaksaṃbodhi.*" The fourth is a general conclusion, which extends from "thus know that wisdom" to "true and not false." The fifth is the mantra of the secret treasury, which extends from "*gate gate*" to "*svāhā.*"

The first section, a general introduction to the interlocutor and the teaching, has five parts: cause, cultivation, realization, entering [nirvana], and time. The reference to Avalokiteśvara denotes the dedicated practitioner, that is, the individual who takes originally awakened *bodhi* as their cause. "Profound *prajñā,*" which is both that which contemplates and the teaching that is contemplated, is the cultivation. "Recognizing emptiness" is to realize wisdom. "Saves [all beings] from suffering" is the fruit that is obtained. The "fruit" is the entering [into nirvana]. In accordance with the teaching and the [abilities] of the individual, [the difference between their levels of] wisdom is limitless. Based on these distinctions [in levels of] wisdom, the time [required to enter nirvana] varies. Whether [it takes] three lifetimes, three, sixty, or a hundred eons[22] due to false views, is called "time."

Stated in verse:

The contemplator, by cultivating wisdom,
Acutely recognizes the emptiness of the five aggregates.
Cultivating his thoughts over the course of eons,
He is liberated from the afflictions and realizes the singular mind.[23]

The second section on distinguishing the various vehicles also has five parts: establish, sever, characteristic, two, and singular. First, "establish" means to establish the Tathāgata's *samādhi* teaching, which extends from "form is not different from emptiness" to "also like this." "Establishing the Tathāgata" is the secret title for Samantabhadra Bodhisattva.[24] The perfect cause of Samantabhadra's [awakening] takes the three teachings of complete infusion as its purport. Therefore, I have labeled [this part of the commentary] in such a way. Furthermore, Samantabhadra is the bodily form of the vows and practices that give rise to the *bodhi*-mind of all tathāgatas.

Stated in verse:

Form and emptiness are originally nondual.
Phenomena and principle are identical from the beginning.
Unhindered and fused in three types,
Their purpose is similar to gold and water.[25]

Second, "sever" denotes the Tathāgata's *samādhi* teaching that is without
mental proliferations, which extends from "dharmas with the characteristic of
12a emptiness" to "neither increases nor decreases." The so-called "Tathāgata without
mental proliferations" is the esoteric title of Mañjuśrī Bodhisattva. The sharp
blade of Mañjuśrī wields the eight negations[26] and severs deluded thoughts.
Therefore, I have labeled [this part of the commentary] in such a way.

Stated in verse:

The eight negations sever mental proliferations;
Mañjuśrī is the one [who wields them].
Emptiness alone is ultimately the principle;
Its meaning and function are the most profound reality.

Third, the "characteristic" alludes to the *samādhi* teaching of Mahā Maitreya Bodhisattva, which extends from "therefore in emptiness there is no form" to "realm without consciousness." His *samādhi* of great compassion takes the bestowing of joy as its purport and demonstrates cause and effect as guidance. Regarding theories on the differences between the characteristics and nature [of dharmas], the Consciousness Only [school] refutes that perceptional objects [really exist]; only consciousness exists.

Stated in verse:

When will the two views of self[27] be extinguished?
In three incalculable eons upon realizing the body of the Dharma.
The *ādāna* is the essence of consciousness;
It is an illusion or a mirage; it is just a label or a visitor.

Fourth, the "two" are thinking that only the aggregates exist and that the self does not, and the elimination of karmic causes and seeds. These [two] are the *samādhi* teaching of the two vehicles. From "there is no ignorance" to "nor the elimination of old age and death" is the *samādhi* of the *pratyekabuddhas*.

Stated in verse:

Seeing the windblown leaves, they know the causes and conditions;
How many rebirths does it take to awaken?
Viewing the dew-soaked flowers, removes the seeds.
The designations of goat and deer are yoked together.[28]

The five-syllable phrase "There is no suffering, accumulation, extinction, or path" refers to the *samādhi* of the *śrāvakas*.

Stated in verse:

Other than white bones, what of the self is there?
Just a mottled corpse, a person never really exists.
Their master is the four bases of mindfulness.[29]
How halcyon is the arhat?

Fifth, the "singular" is the *samādhi* teaching of Ārya Avalokiteśvara Bodhisattva, which extends from "there is no wisdom" to "there is nothing to attain." Through the purity of the singular path and the untainted wondrous lotus, the "Tathāgata whose nature is pure"[30] opens and reveals [his teaching] to sentient beings and alleviates their suffering. "Wisdom" is that which attains, and "attainment" is that which is realized. If one has already merged principle and wisdom, then this in essence is called "singular." The teachings in the *Lotus* and *Nirvana* sutras, which assimilate the branches into the source,[31] are contained in only ten syllables [of the *Heart Sutra*]. A wise person considers this when differentiating between the various vehicles.

Stated in verse:

Contemplating the lotus, one knows their own pure [mind].
Seeing the fruits, one realizes the virtues in their mind.
On the singular path, subject and object merge.
The three carts return in silence.

The third section on the benefits obtained by the practitioner has two parts:
12b practitioner and teaching. First, there are seven [types of] practitioners: the previous six and one [discussed] below. Because beings all have unique differences, the vehicles differ accordingly. Moreover, there are four [types] of beings: dimwitted, knowledgeable, adamantine, and wise. The teachings have four [components]: cause, cultivation, realization, and entering into nirvana. "[Relies on the perfection of] wisdom" is the cause and cultivation. "There are no impediments . . . free from incorrect views" is entering nirvana, and the realization of the wisdom of awakening is the result that is realized. Reflect on these passages.

Stated in verse:

The number of [types of] practitioners is seven,
And there are two sets of teachings.
Complete extinction follows from *bodhi,*
How could this be anything other than the direct and circumstantial [results of practice]?

The fourth section, the general conclusion, also has three parts: category, essence, and function. The four types of incantation provide terminology [for the categories]. "Is true and not false" points to the essence. "Cures all suffering" expresses the function. Among the terms provided, the first "supremely divine incantation" is the mantra of the *śrāvaka*s; the second is the mantra of the *pratyekabuddha*s; the third is the mantra of Mahayana; and the fourth is the mantra of the secret treasury. If we consider the universal meaning [of the four types of incantation], then every mantra is endowed with these four types. I have briefly demonstrated one corner.[32] For the person who has perfected wisdom, the [prior] three rely on the [latter] one.

Stated in verse:

Incantations consist of words and meaning.
[The perfection of] patience and spells are all incantations.[33]
Sound and syllables, practitioners and teachings:
These terms are imbued with ultimate reality.

The fifth section on the mantra of the secret treasury has five [words]. First, *gate* reveals the fruits of *śrāvaka* practice. Second, *gate* yields the fruits of *pratyekabuddha* practice. Third, *pāragate* points to the fruits of the supreme practices of Mahayana. Fourth, *pārasaṃgate* illuminates the fruits of the complete and perfect practices of mantra and mandala. Fifth, *bodhi svāhā* explains how one ultimately attains *bodhi* and enters nirvana through the vehicles explained above. Such is the meaning of this phrase. If we were to interpret this [phrase] in terms of the ultimate meaning of the syllables, then it would have as many meanings as there are beings and teachings; they would be difficult to exhaust even in the course of eons. Those who wish to know more about these matters should inquire according to protocol.[34]

Stated in verse:

The mantra is inconceivable.
Contemplating and reciting it will eradicate ignorance.
A single syllable contains a thousand meanings.
In this very body, one realizes the suchness of the Dharma.
Advance, advance to reach complete extinction.
Go, go beyond to enter the source.
The three realms are like a guesthouse,
But the singular mind is the real home.

[On the Esoteric Reading of the Sutra]

Question: *Dhāraṇīs* are the secret language of the Tathāgata. Therefore, previous commentators on the Tripiṭaka kept silent and did not write about them. Why are you now writing a commentary that contradicts the intentions of the Venerable One?

[Response:] The preaching of the Tathāgata has two types: one is exoteric and the other is esoteric. For those with exoteric abilities, he preached the many words and phrases [of the sutras]. For those with esoteric capabilities,
he preached the syllables of incantations. Hence, the Tathāgata himself 12c
preached the meaning of the syllables *a, oṃ,* and so on, which he expounded for those with esoteric abilities. Nāgārjuna, Śubhākarasiṃha, and Amoghavajra also explain the meaning of [these syllables]. Whether a teaching is available or not merely depends on one's capacity [to hear it]. Both preaching and remaining silent [on these matters] conform to the Buddha's intent.

Question: The two teachings of the exoteric and esoteric and their purport vastly differ. How is it possible to preach the esoteric based on the content of this exoteric sutra?

[Response:] The eyes of a master physician[35] spot along the wayside all [plants] that are medicines. The jeweler sees the gems in the ore and rocks. There are those who know [these matters] and those who do not. Who is to blame?

Furthermore, the mantra rites and contemplation practices of this Honorable One (Prajñā Bodhisattva) are explained by the Buddha in the *Admantine Pinnacle.*[36] Among the esoteric [teachings], this is the most esoteric. As the manifested body [of the Buddha], Śākyamuni resided in the grove of Anāthapiṇḍada, where he preached the drawn images, mandala rites, mantras, and *mudrās* to bodhisattvas, deities, and humans. These [teachings] are also esoteric and are in the third fascicle of the *Dhāraṇī Collection Sutra* (T.901:804c). Whether [a teaching] is exoteric or esoteric refers to the individual [who receives it]; the sounds and syllables [of the sutra] are irrelevant. Nevertheless, within the exoteric is the esoteric, and within the esoteric is the extremely esoteric. It is just that there are varying degrees of simplicity and profundity.

In accordance with the meaning of the secret mantra,
I have briefly commented on the five sections of the *Heart Sutra.*
Each syllable and phrase pervades the Dharma realm;
They are without end or beginning and within one's own mind.
Cataracts blind sentient beings;
Mañjuśrī and Prajñā can remove the opacity.
The sprinkling of sweet nectar refreshes the deluded.
May this likewise eradicate ignorance and subdue the armies of Māra.

[End of] *The Key to the Secret of the Heart Sutra*

Notes

1 Yūkei Matsunaga, *Yakuchū: Hannya shingyō hiken* 訳注一般若心経秘鍵 (Tokyo: Shunjūsha, 2018), p. 23; Thomas Eijō Dreitlein, "An Annotated Translation of Kūkai's Secret Key to the Heart Sūtra," *Kōyasan Daigaku mikkyō bunka kenkyūjo kiyō* 高野山大学密教文化研究所紀要 24 (2011): 16.

2 Ryūichi Abé, "Scholasticism, Exegesis, and Ritual Practice: On Renovation in the History of Buddhist Writing in the Early Heian Period," in Mikael Adolphson, Edward Kamens, and Stacie Matsumoto, eds., *Heian Japan: Centers and Peripheries* (Honolulu: University of Hawai'i Press, 2007), pp. 179–211.

3 Matsunaga, *Yakuchū: Hannya shingyō hiken,* pp. 74–77.

4 Matsunaga, *Yakuchū: Hannya shingyō hiken,* pp. 70–73.

5 Abé, "Scholasticism, Exegesis, and Ritual Practice," p. 195.

6 Rolf W. Giebel, *The Precious Key to the Secret Treasury,* in *Shingon Texts* (Moraga, CA: BDK America, 2018), pp. 113–184.

7 Although "mother of awakening" could refer to various bodhisattvas or deities, in this case it is most likely a reference to Prajñā Bodhisattva, the manifestation of the teachings in the *Mahāprajñāpāramitā-sūtra.*

8 Readers should note that the Siddham scripts included in the Taishō version of the text do not always match the grammatically correct Sanskrit reading of the terms.

9 Later commentaries interpret the terms "meditation" (Skt. *dhyāna*) and "correct thought" (Skt. *samyaksaṃkalpa*) as references to the bodhisattvas Mañjuśrī and Prajñā, respectively; Dreitlein, "An Annotated Translation of Kūkai's Secret Key to the Heart Sūtra," p. 11, n. 33.

10 "Great Sun" functions metaphorically as a reference to Mahāvairocana Tathāgata, which literally means "Great Luminous Tathāgata."

11 The *vajra* and lotus mentioned here could refer to the Vajra and Lotus divisions of deities in the mandala, the *Adamantine Pinnacle* and *Lotus Sutra,* or the esoteric and singular vehicle teachings of the *Lotus Sutra,* alluding to the difference between the esoteric teachings and the Tendai school. Interpreting this line depends on how one understands the five vehicles. The five vehicles are typically the vehicles for humans, *deva*s (gods), *śrāvaka*s (disciples), *pratyekabuddha*s (self-enlightened buddhas), and bodhisattvas. However, later in this text, Kūkai applies this term to Buddhist schools in Japan.

12 Although the modern version of the *Heart Sutra* is typically written with seventeen characters per line, resulting in seventeen and a half lines, commentators suggest that

it was originally composed in fourteen lines; Dreitlein, "An Annotated Translation of Kūkai's Secret Key to the Heart Sūtra," p. 15, n. 46; Motohiro Yoritomi, *Hannya shingyō hiken* 般若心経秘鍵, in *Kūkai korekushon* 空海コレクション (Tokyo: Chikuma Shobō, 2004), vol. 2, p. 325.

13 The five collections, or baskets, is an alternative rendering of the term Tripiṭaka. Kūkai adopted this paradigm from Prajñā's translation of the *Dasheng liqu liu boluomiduo jing* (T.261:868b29–c19).

14 The commentaries offer two theories regarding these seven schools. One theory presumes that the term refers to the six Nara schools, Ritsu, Kusha, Jōjitsu, Hossō, Sanron, Kegon, plus Tendai, which seems to be favored in earlier commentaries. The second theory is that the seven schools are the ones discussed later in the text: 建 (Kegon), 絶 (Sanron), 相 (Hossō), 二 (*śrāvaka, pratyekabuddha*), 一 (Tendai), 祕藏 (Shingon). The latter theory is favored by modern scholars; see Matsunaga, *Yakuchū: Hannya shingyō hiken,* p. 23; Dreitlein, "An Annotated Translation of Kūkai's Secret Key to the Heart Sūtra," p. 16.

15 This question alludes to a three-part taxonomy of the Buddha's teachings in the *Saṃdhinirmocana-sūtra* (T.676:697a23–b4), in which the Buddha preaches first in the Deer Park for the sake of the *śrāvaka*s, then for those of the Mahayana, and finally preaches to beings belonging to all vehicles. As a Mahayana sutra, the *Prajñapāramitā* should be included in the second turning of the Dharma. However, Kūkai's previous statement suggests that it is all-inclusive and should belong to the final category.

16 "Indra's grammar" refers to the notion that the Sanskrit language was originally created by Brahmā and later abridged for practical use by Indra. Kūkai refers to this notion in his works on language; Shingen Takagi and Thomas Eijō Dreitlein, *Kūkai on the Philosophy of Language* (Tokyo: Keio University Press, 2010), pp. 90, 175, 285.

17 The rhetoric in this line is possibly an allusion to Confucius's *Analects,* Dialogue 15.8: "When a person should be spoken with, and you don't speak with them, you lose them. When a person shouldn't be spoken with and you speak to them, you waste your words. The wise do not lose people, nor do they waste their words"; see translation by A. Charles Muller, http://www.acmuller.net/con-dao/analects.html#div-16, accessed April 26, 2021.

18 This three-part hermeneutic for titles of sutras was a common method for elucidating the meaning of a title; see, for example, the preface to the *Commentary on the Sutra of the Meditation on the Buddha of Immeasurable Life* (T.1750:186c).

19 Yijing's translation is almost identical to Xuanzang's, and for that reason it was not included in the Taishō canon; Matsunaga, *Yakuchū: Hannya shingyō hiken,* pp. 56, 126.

20 The third fascicle of the *Dhāraṇī Collection Sutra* consists of a list of *mudrā*s and mantras used in rites involving Prajñā Bodhisattva. *Dhāraṇī* number sixteen in the list is almost identical to the mantra at the end of the *Heart Sutra,* which is glossed as the "the great heart incantation" (T.901:807c22).

21 This comparison of the dragon and snake scales is an allusion to a passage in the *Liuzi:* "The dragon has a scale of the snake, but cannot be called a snake"; Dreitlein, "An Annotated Translation of Kūkai's Secret Key to the Heart Sūtra," p. 22, n. 81. In other words, it is said that the *Heart Sutra* is just an abbreviated version of the *Mahāprajñāpāramitā-sūtra* and was not preached at a different time and place. Kūkai seems to reject this claim, or at least dismiss it, by suggesting that just because two texts are similar does not mean they are the same.

22 Three eons are the standard amount of time required for sentient beings to achieve enlightenment, but for *śrāvaka*s it takes sixty and for *pratyekabuddha*s it takes one hundred; Matsunaga, *Yakuchū: Hannya shingyō hiken,* pp. 140–141.

23 The meaning of the term "singular mind" in this verse is unclear, and the scholarship differs on how to interpret it; see Matsunaga, *Yakuchū: Hannya shingyō hiken,* p. 141; Yoritomi, *Hannya shingyō hiken,* p. 347. These various interpretations stem from Kakuban's explanation in his commentary, in which he offers three possible meanings: (1) the wisdom necessary to cross over from samsara to nirvana, (2) perfection in "perfection of wisdom," and (3) the combination of these two meanings (T.2203B:16a14–22). In other words, "realizing the singular mind" alludes to the process of attaining enlightenment.

24 The association of "establish" with Samantabhadra comes from Amoghavajra's translation of the *Prajñāpāramitā-naya-sūtra,* in which he identifies the preacher of the sutra as the "Tathāgata who established the equality of all dharmas" (T.243:785c1–3). In his commentary to this sutra Amoghavajra asserts, without explanation, that this tathāgata is Samantabhadra Bodhisattva (T.1003:615b6).

25 The phrase "gold and water" is a combination of two metaphors: that of the golden lion and that of water and waves. Fazang uses the golden lion metaphor to explain Huayan notions of essence and function (T.1880:663c20) and the water and waves analogy in his commentary on the *Avataṃsaka-sūtra* (T.1733:119a20–21). Both metaphors emphasize the inseparability of essence (gold/water) and function (golden lion/waves). Based on this allusion to these metaphors found in Huayan commentaries, the first of the distinct vehicles has traditionally been associated with the Kegon school.

26 The eight negations doctrine is attributed to Nāgārjuna and associated with Madhyamaka. Therefore, the second vehicle is traditionally considered to be a reference to the Sanron school.

27 These "two views of self" probably refer to the notions of a permanently existing self (*ātman*) and that dharmas have a permanent existence. Along with the reference to "consciousness only" (*ādāna*) in the next line, this phrase is the basis for associating the third vehicle with the Hossō school.

28 "The designations of the goat and deer" refer to the three-carts metaphor in the *Lotus Sutra* (T.262:12c). In this parable of skillful means, a father entices his three children to flee a burning house by offering them carts pulled by a goat, deer, and ox. In Kūkai's use of this metaphor, the goat cart refers to the vehicle of the *śrāvaka*s and the deer cart denotes the vehicle of the *pratyekabuddha*s.

29 The four bases of mindfulness are the first of the thirty-seven factors of enlightenment. In this passage Kūkai associates this practice with the *śrāvaka*s and dismisses it as simplistic.

30 Like the association of Samantabhadra with the preacher of the sutra in the first vehicle, this definition of Avalokiteśvara as the "tathāgata whose nature is pure" is from Amoghavajra's commentary (T.1003:612a).

31 In his commentaries on the *Lotus Sutra,* Jizang uses the phrase "assimilate the branches into the source" to explain how the singular vehicle of the *Lotus Sutra* encompasses the teachings of other sutras (see, for example, T.1721:469a). Because this concept of a singular vehicle is fundamental to Tiantai doctrine, this passage is traditionally associated with the Tendai school.

32 The reference to "one corner" is another allusion to Confucius's *Analects,* Dialogue 7.8: "If a student is not eager, I won't teach him; if he is not struggling with the truth, I won't reveal it to him. If I lift up one corner and he can't come back with the other three, I won't do it again"; see translation by A. Charles Muller, http://www.acmuller.net/con-dao/analects.html#div-8, accessed April 27, 2021.

33 This four-part taxonomy of incantations comes from the *Yogācārabhūmi* (T.1579:542c16–19). Kūkai discusses this taxonomy extensively in his essay on Sanskrit letters and their pronunciation; Takagi and Dreitlein, *Kūkai on the Philosophy of Language,* pp. 280–285.

34 This passage requesting that readers interested in the esoteric meaning of the mantra follow the proper protocols probably refers to consecration rites required for further study of the esoteric teachings; Dreitlein, "An Annotated Translation of Kūkai's Secret Key to the Heart Sūtra," p. 38, n. 132.

35 Although previously in the commentary Kūkai uses the term "Physician King" as an epithet for the Buddha, in this case it probably alludes to a metaphor in the *Commentary on the Mahāvairocana-sūtra,* which compares the skillful means required of an *ācārya* to a skilled physician who can easily recognize plants with medicinal properties (T.1796:636b2–5). The jeweler metaphor can be found in the same commentary (604b9–10).

36 Kūkai is probably referring here to a ritual text, *Recitation Rites for Cultivating the Contemplation of Prajñāpāramitā Bodhisattva* (T. 1151).

Glossary

Admantine Pinnacle (Skt. *Vajraśekhara;* Jp. *Kongōchō*): The Chinese translation of the *Sarvatathāgatatattvasaṃgraha* and its related ritual texts.

ādāna ("appropriating consciousness"): The aspect of consciousness that holds together the seeds of the storehouse consciousness (Skt. *ālayavijñāna*).

Amoghavajra (705–774): A propagator of esoteric Buddhism in China and patriarch of the Japanese Shingon school. He translated numerous esoteric texts including ritual manuals.

Anāthapiṇḍada: A wealthy patron of the Buddha from Śrāvastī; also called Sudatta.

complete infusion (Jp. *ennyū*): The harmony between opposites or differences. In Tiantai and Huayan thought, the term is used to describe ultimate reality.

dhāraṇī: An incantation, spell, vow, or long mantra that is usually chanted and believed to possess religious efficacy.

Dhāraṇī Collection Sūtra (Skt. *Dhāraṇī-samuccaya-sūtra;* Jp. *Daranijikkyō*): A collection of esoteric rites and incantations published in Taishō vol. 18, no. 901.

Dharmacandra (653–743): Originally from India, he translated a version of the *Heart Sutra* into Chinese.

eight negations (Jp. *hachifu*): A doctrine attributed to Nāgārjuna and associated with Madhyamaka. The eight negations are: neither rising nor ceasing, neither permanent nor impermanent, neither the same nor different, neither going nor coming.

five collections (Skt. *pañcapiṭaka;* Jp. *gozō*): The Tripiṭaka (Sutra, Vinaya, Abhidharma) plus the categories of the Prajñāpāramitā and *dhāraṇī* teachings.

five vehicles (Skt. *pañcayāna;* Jp. *gojō*): The means for teaching to humans, *deva*s (gods), *śrāvaka*s, *pratyekabuddha*s, and bodhisattvas.

Henjō Kongō ("Universally Radiant Vajra"): The ordination name of Kūkai (774–835).

Kumārajīva (344–413): A famous translator of sutras and commentaries in China. His idiomatic translations accelerated the spread of Buddhism in East Asia.

mental proliferations (Skt. *prapañca;* Jp. *keron*): In a general sense, this term refers to frivolous speech that perpetuates ignorance in sentient beings. As a technical term, it denotes the proliferation of thoughts that lead to such speech.

Nāgārjuna (second–third centuries C.E.): A well-known Indian intellectual who influenced Mahayana Buddhist thought. He is revered as the third (first human) patriarch in the Japanese Shingon school.

nectar (Skt. *amṛta;* Jp. *kanro*): A substance that is consumed by the gods as a source of immortality. In Buddhism, the term is used as a metaphor for the teachings of the Buddha or nirvana.

Prajñā (744–ca. 810): A translator of Buddhist texts into Chinese, notably a version of the *Avataṃsaka-sūtra* and the *Dasheng liqu liu boluomiduo jing.*

Prajñā Bodhisattva: A bodhisattva who is the personification of the perfection of wisdom and the *Mahāprajñāpāramitā-sūtra.* This bodhisattva is often the object of worship in esoteric rites.

seed syllables (Skt. *bīja;* Jp. *shuji*): A syllable in Sanskrit that signifies a buddha, bodhisattva, deity, etc. and symbolizes their teachings.

seven schools (Jp. *shichishū*): The schools in Japanese Buddhism in the early ninth century: Ritsu, Kusha, Jōjitsu, Hossō, Sanron, Kegon, and Tendai.

Śubhākarasiṃha (637–735): An Indian translator of many Buddhist texts into Chinese, most notably the *Mahāvairocana-sūtra.*

Supreme Tamer: Someone with the ability to save sentient beings from their own negative activity; one of the ten epithets of the Buddha.

three carts (Jp. *sansha*): In the metaphor of the burning house in the skillful means chapter of the *Lotus Sutra,* the goat, deer, and ox carts denote the varying sets of teachings and efficacy for reaching awakening.

Vulture Peak (Skt. Gṛdhrakūṭa-parvata; Jp. Juhōsan or Ryōjusen): A mountain in ancient India frequently visited by the Buddha.

Xuanzang (602–664): The most famous translator of sutras and commentaries after Kumārajīva. He retranslated numerous sutras and propagated Yogācāra in China.

Yijing (635–713): A translator of Buddhist texts into Chinese, most notably the *Sutra of Golden Light.*

Bibliography

Abé, Ryūichi. "Scholasticism, Exegesis, and Ritual Practice: On Renovation in the History of Buddhist Writing in the Early Heian Period," in Mikael Adolphson, Edward Kamens, and Stacie Matsumoto, eds., *Heian Japan: Centers and Peripheries,* pp. 179–211. Honolulu: University of Hawai'i Press, 2007.

Buswell, Robert E., Jr., and David S. Lopez Jr., eds. "Hannya shingyō hiken," in *The Princeton Dictionary of Buddhism,* pp. 343–344. Princeton, NJ: Princeton University Press, 2017.

Dreitlein, Thomas Eijō. "An Annotated Translation of Kūkai's *Secret Key to the Heart Sūtra,*" *Kōyasan Daigaku mikkyō bunka kenkyūjo kiyō* 高野山大学密教文化研究所紀要 24 (2011): 216–170 (1–48).

Kawahara, Eihō, and C. Yūhō Jobst. *Ausgewahlte Schriften: Sokushin jōbutsu-gi Shōji-jissō-gi, Unji-gi, Hannya-shingyō-hiken.* München: Iudicium, 1992.

Hakeda, Yoshito S. *Kūkai Works: Translated with an Account of His Life and Study of His Thought.* New York: Columbia University Press, 1972.

Matsunaga, Yūkei 松長有慶. *Yakuchū: Hannya shingyō hiken* 訳注一般若心経秘鍵. Tokyo: Shunjūsha, 2018.

Takagi, Shingen, and Thomas Eijō Dreitlein. *Kūkai on the Philosophy of Language.* Tokyo: Keio University Press, 2010.

Yamamoto, Chikyō. *Works of St. Kōbō Daishi.* Kōya, Japan: Kōyasan University, 1993.

Yoritomi, Motohiro 頼富本宏. *Hannya shingyō hiken* 般若心経秘鍵, in *Kūkai korekushon* 空海コレクション, vol. 2, pp. 311–384. Tokyo: Chikuma Shobō, 2004.

Index

G

H

I

M

T

Z

BDK English Tripiṭaka
(First Series)

Abbreviations

Ch.: Chinese
Skt.: Sanskrit
Jp.: Japanese
Eng.: Published title

Title		Taishō No.
Ch.	Chang ahan jing (長阿含經)	1
Skt.	Dīrghāgama	
Eng.	*The Canonical Book of the Buddha's Lengthy Discourses* (Volume I, 2015) *The Canonical Book of the Buddha's Lengthy Discourses* (Volume II, 2017) *The Canonical Book of the Buddha's Lengthy Discourses* (Volume III, 2018)	
Ch.	Zhong ahan jing (中阿含經)	26
Skt.	Madhyamāgama	
Eng.	*The Madhyama Āgama (Middle-length Discourses)* (Volume I, 2013) *The Madhyama Āgama (Middle-length Discourses)* (Volume II, 2020) *The Madhyama Āgama (Middle-length Discourses)* (Volume III, 2022)	
Ch.	Dasheng bensheng xindi guan jing (大乘本生心地觀經)	159
Eng.	*The Mahayana Sutra of Previous Lives and Contemplation of the Mind-ground* (2021)	
Ch.	Fo suoxing zan (佛所行讚)	192
Skt.	Buddhacarita	
Eng.	*Buddhacarita: In Praise of Buddha's Acts* (2009)	

Title		Taishō No.
Ch.	Zabao zang jing (雜寶藏經)	203
Eng.	*The Storehouse of Sundry Valuables* (1994)	
Ch.	Faju piyu jing (法句譬喻經)	211
Eng.	*The Scriptural Text: Verses of the Doctrine, with Parables* (1999)	
Ch.	Xiaopin banruo boluomi jing (小品般若波羅蜜經)	227
Skt.	Aṣṭasāhasrikā-prajñāpāramitā-sūtra	
Ch.	Jingang banruo boluomi jing (金剛般若波羅蜜經)	235
Skt.	Vajracchedikā-prajñāpāramitā-sūtra	
Ch.	Daluo jingang bukong zhenshi sanmoye jing (大樂金剛不空眞實三麼耶經)	243
Skt.	Adhyardhaśatikā-prajñāpāramitā-sūtra	
Eng.	*The Sutra of the Vow of Fulfilling the Great Perpetual Enjoyment and Benefiting All Sentient Beings Without Exception* (in *Esoteric Texts,* 2015)	
Ch.	Renwang banruo boluomi jing (仁王般若波羅蜜經)	245
Skt.	*Kāruṇikārājā-prajñāpāramitā-sūtra	
Ch.	Banruo boluomiduo xin jing (般若波羅蜜多心經)	251
Skt.	Prajñāpāramitāhṛdaya-sūtra	
Ch.	Miaofa lianhua jing (妙法蓮華經)	262
Skt.	Saddharmapuṇḍarīka-sūtra	
Eng.	*The Lotus Sutra* (Revised Second Edition, 2007)	
Ch.	Wuliangyi jing (無量義經)	276
Eng.	*The Infinite Meanings Sutra* (in *Tiantai Lotus Texts,* 2013)	
Ch.	Guan Puxian pusa xingfa jing (觀普賢菩薩行法經)	277
Eng.	*The Sutra Expounded by the Buddha on Practice of the Way through Contemplation of the Bodhisattva All-embracing Goodness* (in *Tiantai Lotus Texts,* 2013)	
Ch.	Dafangguang fo huayan jing (大方廣佛華嚴經)	279
Skt.	Avataṃsaka-sūtra	
Ch.	Shengman shizihou yisheng defang bianfang guang jing (勝鬘師子吼一乘大方便方廣經)	353
Skt.	Śrīmālādevīsiṃhanāda-sūtra	
Eng.	*The Sutra of Queen Śrīmālā of the Lion's Roar* (2004)	

Title		Taishō No.
Ch.	Wuliangshou jing (無量壽經)	360
Skt.	Sukhāvatīvyūha	
Eng.	*The Larger Sutra on Amitāyus* (in *The Three Pure Land Sutras,* Revised Second Edition, 2003)	
Ch.	Guan wuliangshou fo jing (觀無量壽佛經)	365
Skt.	*Amitāyurdhyāna-sūtra	
Eng.	*The Sutra on Contemplation of Amitāyus* (in *The Three Pure Land Sutras,* Revised Second Edition, 2003)	
Ch.	Amituo jing (阿彌陀經)	366
Skt.	Sukhāvatīvyūha	
Eng.	*The Smaller Sutra on Amitāyus* (in *The Three Pure Land Sutras,* Revised Second Edition, 2003)	
Ch.	Da banniepan jing (大般涅槃經)	374
Skt.	Mahāparinirvāṇa-sūtra	
Eng.	*The Nirvana Sutra* (Volume I, 2013)	
Ch.	Fochuibo niepan lüeshuo jiaojie jing (佛垂般涅槃略說教誡經)	389
Eng.	*The Bequeathed Teaching Sutra* (in *Apocryphal Scriptures,* 2005)	
Ch.	Dizang pusa benyuan jing (地藏菩薩本願經)	412
Skt.	*Kṣitigarbhapraṇidhāna-sūtra	
Ch.	Banzhou sanmei jing (般舟三昧經)	418
Skt.	Pratyutpanna-buddhasammukhāvasthita-samādhi-sūtra	
Eng.	*The Pratyutpanna Samādhi Sutra* (1998)	
Ch.	Yaoshi liuli guang rulai benyuan gongde jing (藥師琉璃光如來本願功德經)	450
Skt.	Bhaiṣajyaguru-vaiḍūrya-prabhāsa-pūrvapraṇidhāna-viśeṣavistara	
Eng.	*The Scripture of Master of Medicine, Beryl Radiance Tathāgata* (2018)	
Ch.	Mile xiasheng chengfo jing (彌勒下生成佛經)	454
Skt.	*Maitreyavyākaraṇa	
Eng.	*The Sutra That Expounds the Descent of Maitreya Buddha and His Enlightenment* (2016)	
Ch.	Wenshushili wen jing (文殊師利問經)	468
Skt.	*Mañjuśrīparipṛcchā	
Eng.	*The Sutra of Mañjuśrī's Questions* (2016)	

Title		Taishō No.
Ch.	Weimojie suoshuo jing (維摩詰所説經)	475
Skt.	Vimalakīrtinirdeśa-sūtra	
Eng.	*The Vimalakīrti Sutra* (2004)	
Ch.	Yueshangnü jing (月上女經)	480
Skt.	Candrottarādārikā-paripṛcchā	
Eng.	*The Sutra of the Girl Candrottarā* (2018)	
Ch.	Zuochan sanmei jing (坐禪三昧經)	614
Eng.	*The Sutra on the Concentration of Sitting Meditation* (2009)	
Ch.	Damoduoluo chan jing (達磨多羅禪經)	618
Ch.	Yuedeng sanmei jing (月燈三昧經)	639
Skt.	Samādhirāja-candrapradīpa-sūtra	
Ch.	Shoulengyan sanmei jing (首楞嚴三昧經)	642
Skt.	Śūraṅgamasamādhi-sūtra	
Eng.	*The Śūraṅgama Samādhi Sutra* (1998)	
Ch.	Jinguang ming zuishengwang jing (金光明最勝王經)	665
Skt.	Suvarṇaprabhāsa-sūtra	
Ch.	Dasheng rulengqie jing (大乘入楞伽經)	672
Skt.	Laṅkāvatāra-sūtra	
Ch.	Jie shenmi jing (解深密經)	676
Skt.	Saṃdhinirmocana-sūtra	
Eng.	*The Scripture on the Explication of Underlying Meaning* (2000)	
Ch.	Yulanpen jing (盂蘭盆經)	685
Skt.	*Ullambana-sūtra	
Eng.	*The Ullambana Sutra* (in *Apocryphal Scriptures,* 2005)	
Ch.	Sishierzhang jing (四十二章經)	784
Eng.	*The Sutra of Forty-two Sections* (in *Apocryphal Scriptures,* 2005)	
Ch.	Dafangguang yuanjue xiuduoluo liaoyi jing (大方廣圓覺修多羅了義經)	842
Eng.	*The Sutra of Perfect Enlightenment* (in *Apocryphal Scriptures,* 2005)	
Ch.	Da Biluzhena chengfo shenbian jiachi jing (大毘盧遮那成佛神變加持經)	848
Skt.	Mahāvairocanābhisambodhi-vikurvitādhiṣṭhāna-vaipulyasūtrendra-rājanāma-dharmaparyāya	
Eng.	*The Vairocanābhisaṃbodhi Sutra* (2005)	

Title		Taishō No.
Ch.	Jinggangding yiqie rulai zhenshi she dasheng xianzheng dajiao wang jing (金剛頂一切如來眞實攝大乘現證大教王經)	865
Skt.	Sarvatathāgata-tattvasaṃgraha-mahāyānābhisamaya-mahākalparāja	
Eng.	*The Adamantine Pinnacle Sutra* (in *Two Esoteric Sutras,* 2001)	
Ch.	Suxidi jieluo jing (蘇悉地羯囉經)	893
Skt.	Susiddhikara-mahātantra-sādhanopāyika-paṭala	
Eng.	*The Susiddhikara Sutra* (in *Two Esoteric Sutras,* 2001)	
Ch.	Modengqie jing (摩登伽經)	1300
Skt.	*Mātaṅgī-sūtra	
Eng.	*The Mātaṅga Sutra* (in *Esoteric Texts,* 2015)	
Ch.	Mohe sengqi lü (摩訶僧祇律)	1425
Skt.	*Mahāsāṃghika-vinaya	
Ch.	Sifen lü (四分律)	1428
Skt.	*Dharmaguptaka-vinaya	
Ch.	Shanjianlü piposha (善見律毘婆沙)	1462
Pāli	Samantapāsādikā	
Ch.	Fanwang jing (梵網經)	1484
Skt.	*Brahmajāla-sūtra	
	The Brahmā's Net Sutra (2017)	
Ch.	Youposaijie jing (優婆塞戒經)	1488
Skt.	Upāsakaśīla-sūtra	
Eng.	*The Sutra on Upāsaka Precepts* (1994)	
Ch.	Miaofa lianhua jing youbotishe (妙法蓮華經憂波提舍)	1519
Skt.	Saddharmapuṇḍarīka-upadeśa	
Eng.	*The Commentary on the Lotus Sutra* (in *Tiantai Lotus Texts,* 2013)	
Ch.	Shizha biposha lun (十住毘婆沙論)	1521
Skt.	*Daśabhūmika-vibhāṣā	
Ch.	Fodijing lun (佛地經論)	1530
Skt.	*Buddhabhūmisūtra-śāstra	
Eng.	*The Interpretation of the Buddha Land* (2002)	
Ch.	Apidamojushe lun (阿毘達磨俱舍論)	1558
Skt.	Abhidharmakośa-bhāṣya	
Ch.	Zhonglun (中論)	1564
Skt.	Madhyamaka-śāstra	

Title		Taishō No.
Ch.	Yüqie shidilun (瑜伽師地論)	1579
Skt.	Yogācārabhūmi-śāstra	
Ch.	Cheng weishi lun (成唯識論)	1585
Eng.	*Demonstration of Consciousness Only* (in *Three Texts on Consciousness Only,* 1999)	
Ch.	Weishi sanshilun song (唯識三十論頌)	1586
Skt.	Triṃśikā	
Eng.	*The Thirty Verses on Consciousness Only* (in *Three Texts on Consciousness Only,* 1999)	
Ch.	Weishi ershi lun (唯識二十論)	1590
Skt.	Viṃśatikā	
Eng.	*The Treatise in Twenty Verses on Consciousness Only* (in *Three Texts on Consciousness Only,* 1999)	
Ch.	She dasheng lun (攝大乘論)	1593
Skt.	Mahāyānasaṃgraha	
Eng.	*The Summary of the Great Vehicle* (Revised Second Edition, 2003)	
Ch.	Bian zhongbian lun (辯中邊論)	1600
Skt.	Madhyāntavibhāga	
Eng.	*Analysis of the Middle and Extremes* (2021)	
Ch.	Dasheng zhuangyanjing lun (大乘莊嚴經論)	1604
Skt.	Mahāyānasūtrālaṃkāra	
Ch.	Dasheng chengye lun (大乘成業論)	1609
Skt.	Karmasiddhiprakaraṇa	
Ch.	Jiujing yisheng baoxing lun (究竟一乘寶性論)	1611
Skt.	Ratnagotravibhāga-mahāyānottaratantra-śāstra	
Ch.	Yinming ruzheng li lun (因明入正理論)	1630
Skt.	Nyāyapraveśa	
Ch.	Dasheng ji pusa xue lun (大乘集菩薩學論)	1636
Skt.	Śikṣāsamuccaya	
Ch.	Jingangzhen lun (金剛針論)	1642
Skt.	Vajrasūcī	
Eng.	*The Diamond Needle* (2023)	
Ch.	Zhang suozhi lun (彰所知論)	1645
Eng.	*The Treatise on the Elucidation of the Knowable* (2004)	

Title		Taishō No.
Ch.	Putixing jing (菩提行經)	1662
Skt.	Bodhicaryāvatāra	
Ch.	Jingangding yuqie zhongfa anouduoluo sanmiao sanputi xin lun (金剛頂瑜伽中發阿耨多羅三藐三菩提心論)	1665
Eng.	*The Bodhicitta Śāstra* (in *Esoteric Texts,* 2015)	
Ch.	Dasheng qixin lun (大乘起信論)	1666
Skt.	*Mahāyānaśraddhotpāda-śāstra	
Eng.	*The Awakening of Faith* (2005)	
Ch.	Shimoheyan lun (釋摩訶衍論)	1668
Ch.	Naxian biqiu jing (那先比丘經)	1670B
Pāli	Milindapañhā	
Eng.	*The Scripture on the Monk Nāgasena* (2021)	
Ch.	Banruo boluomiduo xin jing yuzan (般若波羅蜜多心經幽賛)	1710
Eng.	*A Comprehensive Commentary on the Heart Sutra* (*Prajñāpāramitā-hṛdaya-sūtra*) (2001)	
Ch.	Miaofalianhua jing xuanyi (妙法蓮華經玄義)	1716
Ch.	Guan wuliangshou fo jing shu (觀無量壽佛經疏)	1753
Ch.	Sanlun xuanyi (三論玄義)	1852
Ch.	Dasheng xuan lun (大乘玄論)	1853
Ch.	Zhao lun (肇論)	1858
Ch.	Huayan yisheng jiaoyi fenqi zhang (華嚴一乘教義分齊章)	1866
Eng.	*Treatise on Doctrinal Distinctions of the Huayan One Vehicle* (2023)	
Ch.	Yuanren lun (原人論)	1886
Ch.	Mohe zhiguan (摩訶止觀)	1911
Ch.	Xiuxi zhiguan zuochan fayao (修習止觀坐禪法要)	1915
Ch.	Tiantai sijiao yi (天台四教儀)	1931
Eng.	*A Guide to the Tiantai Fourfold Teachings* (in *Tiantai Lotus Texts,* 2013)	
Ch.	Guoqing bai lu (國清百録)	1934
Eng.	*The Hundred Records of the Temple of National Purity* (2022)	

Title		Taishō No.
Ch.	Zhenzhou Linji Huizhao chanshi wulu (鎮州臨濟慧照禪師語録)	1985
Eng.	*The Recorded Sayings of Linji* (in *Three Chan Classics,* 1999)	
Ch.	Foguo Yuanwu chanshi biyan lu (佛果圜悟禪師碧巖録)	2003
Eng.	*The Blue Cliff Record* (1998)	
Ch.	Wumen guan (無門關)	2005
Eng.	*Wumen's Gate* (in *Three Chan Classics,* 1999)	
Ch.	Liuzu dashi fabao tan jing (六祖大師法寶壇經)	2008
Eng.	*The Platform Sutra of the Sixth Patriarch* (2000)	
Ch.	Xinxin ming (信心銘)	2010
Eng.	*The Faith-Mind Maxim* (in *Three Chan Classics,* 1999)	
Ch.	Huangboshan Duanji chanshi chuanxin fayao (黄檗山斷際禪師傳心法要)	2012A
Eng.	*Essentials of the Transmission of Mind* (in *Zen Texts,* 2005)	
Ch.	Yongjia Zhengdao ge (永嘉證道歌)	2014
Eng.	*Yongjia's Song of Actualizing the Way* (2021)	
Ch.	Chixiu Baizhang qinggui (勅修百丈清規)	2025
Eng.	*The Baizhang Zen Monastic Regulations* (2007)	
Ch.	Yibuzonglun lun (異部宗輪論)	2031
Skt.	Samayabhedoparacanacakra	
Eng.	*The Cycle of the Formation of the Schismatic Doctrines* (2004)	
Ch.	Ayuwang jing (阿育王經)	2043
Skt.	Aśokāvadāna	
Eng.	*The Biographical Scripture of King Aśoka* (1993)	
Ch.	Maming pusa zhuan (馬鳴菩薩傳)	2046
Eng.	*The Life of Aśvaghoṣa Bodhisattva* (in *Lives of Great Monks and Nuns,* 2002)	
Ch.	Longshu pusa zhuan (龍樹菩薩傳)	2047
Eng.	*The Life of Nāgārjuna Bodhisattva* (in *Lives of Great Monks and Nuns,* 2002)	
Ch.	Posoupandou fashi zhuan (婆藪槃豆法師傳)	2049
Eng.	*Biography of Dharma Master Vasubandhu* (in *Lives of Great Monks and Nuns,* 2002)	

Title		Taishō No.
Ch.	Datang Daciensi Zanzang fashi zhuan (大唐大慈恩寺三藏法師傳)	2053
Eng.	*A Biography of the Tripiṭaka Master of the Great Ci'en Monastery of the Great Tang Dynasty* (1995)	
Ch.	Gaoseng zhuan (高僧傳)	2059
Ch.	Biqiuni zhuan (比丘尼傳)	2063
Eng.	*Biographies of Buddhist Nuns* (in *Lives of Great Monks and Nuns,* 2002)	
Ch.	Gaoseng Faxian zhuan (高僧法顯傳)	2085
Eng.	*The Journey of the Eminent Monk Faxian* (in *Lives of Great Monks and Nuns,* 2002)	
Ch.	Datang xiyu ji (大唐西域記)	2087
Eng.	*The Great Tang Dynasty Record of the Western Regions* (1996)	
Ch.	Youfangjichao: Tangdaheshangdongzheng zhuan (遊方記抄: 唐大和上東征傳)	2089-(7)
Ch.	Hongming ji (弘明集)	2102
Eng.	*The Collection for the Propagation and Clarification of Buddhism* (Volume I, 2015)	
	The Collection for the Propagation and Clarification of Buddhism (Volume II, 2017)	
Ch.	Fayuan zhulin (法苑珠林)	2122
Eng.	*A Forest of Pearls from the Dharma Garden* (Volume I, 2019)	
Eng.	*A Forest of Pearls from the Dharma Garden* (Volume II, 2019)	
Eng.	*A Forest of Pearls from the Dharma Garden* (Volume III, 2020)	
Eng.	*A Forest of Pearls from the Dharma Garden* (Volume IV, 2020)	
Eng.	*A Forest of Pearls from the Dharma Garden* (Volume V, 2022)	
Ch.	Nanhai jigui neifa zhuan (南海寄歸内法傳)	2125
Eng.	*Buddhist Monastic Traditions of Southern Asia* (2000)	
Ch.	Fanyu zaming (梵語雜名)	2135
Jp.	Shōmangyō gisho (勝鬘經義疏)	2185
Eng.	*Prince Shōtoku's Commentary on the Śrīmālā Sutra* (2011)	
Jp.	Yuimakyō gisho (維摩經義疏)	2186
Eng.	*The Expository Commentary on the Vimalakīrti Sutra* (2012)	
Jp.	Hokke gisho (法華義疏)	2187

Title		Taishō No.
Jp.	Hannya shingyō hiken (般若心經秘鍵)	2203A
Eng.	*The Key to the Secret of the Heart Sutra* (2023)	
Jp.	Daijō hossō kenjin shō (大乘法相研神章)	2309
Jp.	Kanjin kakumu shō (觀心覺夢鈔)	2312
Eng.	*Oberving the Mind, Awakening from a Dream* (2021)	
Jp.	Risshū kōyō (律宗綱要)	2348
Eng.	*The Essentials of the Vinaya Tradition* (1995)	
Jp.	Tendai hokke shūgi shū (天台法華宗義集)	2366
Eng.	*The Collected Teachings of the Tendai Lotus School* (1995)	
Jp.	Kenkairon (顯戒論)	2376
Jp.	Sange gakushō shiki (山家學生式)	2377
Jp.	Hizōhōyaku (秘藏寶鑰)	2426
Eng.	*The Precious Key to the Secret Treasury* (in *Shingon Texts*, 2004)	
Jp.	Benkenmitsu nikyō ron (辨顯密二教論)	2427
Eng.	*On the Differences between the Exoteric and Esoteric Teachings* (in *Shingon Texts*, 2004)	
Jp.	Sokushin jōbutsu gi (即身成佛義)	2428
Eng.	*The Meaning of Becoming a Buddha in This Very Body* (in *Shingon Texts*, 2004)	
Jp.	Shōji jissōgi (聲字實相義)	2429
Eng.	*The Meanings of Sound, Sign, and Reality* (in *Shingon Texts*, 2004)	
Jp.	Unjigi (吽字義)	2430
Eng.	*The Meanings of the Word Hūṃ* (in *Shingon Texts*, 2004)	
Jp.	Gorin kuji myōhimitsu shaku (五輪九字明秘密釋)	2514
Eng.	*The Illuminating Secret Commentary on the Five Cakras and the Nine Syllables* (in *Shingon Texts*, 2004)	
Jp.	Mitsugonin hotsuro sange mon (密嚴院發露懺悔文)	2527
Eng.	*The Mitsugonin Confession* (in *Shingon Texts,* 2004)	
Jp.	Kōzen gokoku ron (興禪護國論)	2543
Eng.	*A Treatise on Letting Zen Flourish to Protect the State* (in *Zen Texts,* 2005)	

Title		Taishō No.
Jp.	Fukan zazengi (普勧坐禪儀)	2580
Eng.	*A Universal Recommendation for True Zazen* (in *Zen Texts,* 2005)	
Jp.	Shōbōgenzō (正法眼藏)	2582
Eng.	*Shōbōgenzō: The True Dharma-eye Treasury* (Volume I, 2007) *Shōbōgenzō: The True Dharma-eye Treasury* (Volume II, 2008) *Shōbōgenzō: The True Dharma-eye Treasury* (Volume III, 2008) *Shōbōgenzō: The True Dharma-eye Treasury* (Volume IV, 2008)	
Jp.	Zazen yōjin ki (坐禪用心記)	2586
Eng.	*Advice on the Practice of Zazen* (in *Zen Texts,* 2005)	
Jp.	Senchaku hongan nembutsu shū (選擇本願念佛集)	2608
Eng.	*Senchaku Hongan Nembutsu Shū: A Collection of Passages on the Nembutsu Chosen in the Original Vow* (1997)	
Jp.	Kenjōdo shinjitsu kyōgyō shōmon rui (顯淨土眞實教行証文類)	2646
Eng.	*Kyōgyōshinshō: On Teaching, Practice, Faith, and Enlightenment* (2003)	
Jp.	Tannishō (歎異抄)	2661
Eng.	*Tannishō: Passages Deploring Deviations of Faith* (1996)	
Jp.	Rennyo shōnin ofumi (蓮如上人御文)	2668
Eng.	*Rennyo Shōnin Ofumi: The Letters of Rennyo* (1996)	
Jp.	Ōjōyōshū (往生要集)	2682
Jp.	Risshō ankoku ron (立正安國論)	2688
Eng.	*Risshōankokuron or The Treatise on the Establishment of the Orthodox Teaching and the Peace of the Nation* (in *Two Nichiren Texts,* 2003)	
Jp.	Kaimokushō (開目抄)	2689
Eng.	*Kaimokushō or Liberation from Blindness* (2000)	
Jp.	Kanjin honzon shō (觀心本尊抄)	2692
Eng.	*Kanjinhonzonshō or The Most Venerable One Revealed by Introspecting Our Minds for the First Time at the Beginning of the Fifth of the Five Five Hundred-year Ages* (in *Two Nichiren Texts,* 2003)	
Ch.	Fumu enzhong jing (父母恩重經)	2887
Eng.	*The Sutra on the Profundity of Filial Love* (in *Apocryphal Scriptures,* 2005)	

Jp.	Hasshūkōyō (八宗綱要)	extracanonical
Eng.	*The Essentials of the Eight Traditions* (1994)	
Jp.	Sangō shīki (三教指帰)	extracanonical
Jp.	Mappō tōmyō ki (末法燈明記)	extracanonical
Eng.	*The Candle of the Latter Dharma* (1994)	
Jp.	Jūshichijō kenpō (十七條憲法)	extracanonical